Socio-Economic and Education Factors Impacting American Political Systems:

Emerging Research and Opportunities

Pamela Hampton-Garland
University of the District of Columbia, USA

Lisa Sechrest-Ehrhardt
University of the District of Columbia, USA

Benson George Cooke
University of the District of Columbia, USA

A volume in the Advances in Electronic Government, Digital Divide, and Regional Development (AEGDDRD) Book Series

IGI Global
DISSEMINATOR OF KNOWLEDGE

Published in the United States of America by
IGI Global
Information Science Reference (an imprint of IGI Global)
701 E. Chocolate Avenue
Hershey PA, USA 17033
Tel: 717-533-8845
Fax: 717-533-8661
E-mail: cust@igi-global.com
Web site: http://www.igi-global.com

Library of Congress Cataloging-in-Publication Data

Names: Hampton-Garland, Pamela, 1970- author. | Sechrest-Ehrhardt, Lisa, 1960- author. | Cooke, Benson George, author.
Title: Socio-economic and education factors impacting American political systems : emerging research and opportunities / by Pamela Hampton-Garland, Lisa Sechrest-Ehrhardt, and Benson George Cooke.
Description: Hershey, PA : Information Science Reference, [2018]
Identifiers: LCCN 2017022540| ISBN 9781522538431 (h/c) | ISBN 9781522538448 (eISBN)
Subjects: LCSH: United States--Politics and government. | United States--Economic conditions. | United States--Social conditions.
Classification: LCC JK275 .H355 2018 | DDC 320.60973--dc23 LC record available at https://lccn.loc.gov/2017022540

This book is published in the IGI Global book series Advances in Electronic Government, Digital Divide, and Regional Development (AEGDDRD) (ISSN: 2326-9103; eISSN: 2326-9111)

British Cataloguing in Publication Data
A Cataloguing in Publication record for this book is available from the British Library.

All work contributed to this book is new, previously-unpublished material.
The views expressed in this book are those of the authors, but not necessarily of the publisher.

For electronic access to this publication, please contact: eresources@igi-global.com.

Advances in Electronic Government, Digital Divide, and Regional Development (AEGDDRD) Book Series

ISSN:2326-9103
EISSN:2326-9111

Editor-in-Chief: Zaigham Mahmood, University of Derby, UK & North West University, South Africa

MISSION

The successful use of digital technologies (including social media and mobile technologies) to provide public services and foster economic development has become an objective for governments around the world. The development towards electronic government (or e-government) not only affects the efficiency and effectiveness of public services, but also has the potential to transform the nature of government interactions with its citizens. Current research and practice on the adoption of electronic/digital government and the implementation in organizations around the world aims to emphasize the extensiveness of this growing field.

The Advances in Electronic Government, Digital Divide & Regional Development (AEGDDRD) book series aims to publish authored, edited and case books encompassing the current and innovative research and practice discussing all aspects of electronic government development, implementation and adoption as well the effective use of the emerging technologies (including social media and mobile technologies) for a more effective electronic governance (or e-governance).

COVERAGE

- Emerging Technologies within the Public Sector
- Case Studies and Practical Approaches to E-Government and E-Governance
- ICT within Government and Public Sectors
- ICT Infrastructure and Adoption for E-Government Provision
- Citizens Participation and Adoption of E-Government Provision
- E-Citizenship, Inclusive Government, Connected Government
- E-Government in Developing Countries and Technology Adoption
- Current Research and Emerging Trends in E-Government Development
- Electronic Government, Digital Democracy, Digital Government
- Online Government, E-Government, M-Government

IGI Global is currently accepting manuscripts for publication within this series. To submit a proposal for a volume in this series, please contact our Acquisition Editors at Acquisitions@igi-global.com or visit: http://www.igi-global.com/publish/.

The Advances in Electronic Government, Digital Divide, and Regional Development (AEGDDRD) Book Series (ISSN 2326-9103) is published by IGI Global, 701 E. Chocolate Avenue, Hershey, PA 17033-1240, USA, www.igi-global.com. This series is composed of titles available for purchase individually; each title is edited to be contextually exclusive from any other title within the series. For pricing and ordering information please visit http://www.igi-global.com/book-series/advances-electronic-government-digital-divide/37153. Postmaster: Send all address changes to above address.

Titles in this Series

For a list of additional titles in this series, please visit:
https://www.igi-global.com/book-series/advances-electronic-government-digital-divide/37153

Handbook of Research on Women's Issues and Rights in the Developing World
Nazmunnessa Mahtab (University of Dhaka, Bangladesh) Tania Haque (University of Dhaka, Bangladesh) Ishrat Khan (University of Dhaka, Bangladesh) Md. Mynul Islam (University of Dhaka, Bangladesh) and Ishret Binte Wahid (BRAC, Bangladesh)
Information Science Reference • ©2018 • 452pp • H/C (ISBN: 9781522530183) • US $245.00

Handbook of Research on Sociopolitical Factors Impacting Economi Growth...
Suleyman Ozdemir (Bandırma Onyedi Eylül University, Turkey) Seyfettin Erdogan (Istanbul Medeniyet University, Turkey) and Ayfer Gedikli (İstanbul Medeniyet University, Turkey)
Information Science Reference • ©2018 • 472pp • H/C (ISBN: 9781522529392) • US $275.00

Urbanization and Its Impact on Socio-Economic Growth in Developing Regions
Umar Benna (Benna Associates, Nigeria) and Indo Benna (Muhammad Al-Mana College of Health Sciences, Saudi Arabia)
Information Science Reference • ©2018 • 404pp • H/C (ISBN: 9781522526599) • US $195.00

Sustainable ICT Adoption and Integration for Socio-Economic Development
Charles K. Ayo (Covenant University, Nigeria) and Victor Mbarika (Southern University, USA, and ICT University, USA)
Information Science Reference • ©2017 • 264pp • H/C (ISBN: 9781522525653) • US $180.00

Digital Media Integration for Participatory Democracy
Rocci Luppicini (University of Ottawa, Canada) and Rachel Baarda (University of Ottawa, Canada)
Information Science Reference • ©2017 • 259pp • H/C (ISBN: 9781522524632) • US $200.00

Digital Governance and E-Government Principles Applied to Public Procurement
Rajesh Kumar Shakya (The World Bank, USA)
Information Science Reference • ©2017 • 323pp • H/C (ISBN: 9781522522034) • US $185.00

For an enitre list of titles in this series, please visit:
https://www.igi-global.com/book-series/advances-electronic-government-digital-divide/37153

IGI Global
DISSEMINATOR OF KNOWLEDGE

701 East Chocolate Avenue, Hershey, PA 17033, USA
Tel: 717-533-8845 x100 • Fax: 717-533-8661
E-Mail: cust@igi-global.com • www.igi-global.com

Table of Contents

Preface vii

Acknowledgment xviii

Chapter 1
Creating a Stereotype of a Race as Dangerous, Unintelligent, and Lazy: Examining Consequences of Cultural and Psychological Conditioning in America 1
Benson G. Cooke, University of the District of Columbia, USA

Chapter 2
An Overview of the Impact of Racial Hate and Its Manifestation of Homegrown Terrorism in America 29
Benson G. Cooke, University of the District of Columbia, USA

Chapter 3
Trade's Impact on the Profits and Losses for American Workers 57
Pamela Hampton-Garland, University of the District of Columbia, USA

Chapter 4
S.N.A.P. Today, Medicare Tomorrow: Save a Dollar, Sacrifice a Child or Grandmother 86
Pamela Hampton-Garland, University of the District of Columbia, USA

Chapter 5
What I Think I Heard You Say: Learning How to Improve Challenging Social and Political Interactions 109
Lisa Sechrest-Ehrhardt, University of the District of Columbia, USA

Chapter 6
Decoding Difference: How We Treat "Others" Examining the Effects of Marginalizing Those Viewed as Different 139
Lisa Sechrest-Ehrhardt, University of the District of Columbia, USA

Related Readings 166

About the Authors 187

Index 190

Preface

There's not a liberal America and a conservative America - there's the United States of America. – Barack Obama

In America, we have a Declaration of Independence, but our history, our advancements, our global strength all point to an American declaration of interdependence. – Cory Booker

America has the reputation of being one of the wealthiest and most powerful countries in the world, yet within its borders social problems stubbornly persist and negatively impact and plague Americans. Thousands of studies have been published on social differences, racial issues, human response to unjust treatment, seminal human and civil rights events. However, the authors suggest why, by all accepted standards of fairness, our society may remain unbalanced across some economic, political, racial and gender indicators. This may be a reality unless, within established constitutional processes, the state uses it power to move forward with corrective measures that would be viewed as profoundly unfair and, in the most odious way, involve the loss of privilege for the majority. *What is the optimal social condition or environment that we declare freedom for all Americans?*

Because this work is expected to be a resource for undergraduate and advance students and professionals as well as those experiencing their first introduction to the subject, the authors have collectively opted for inclusiveness in their respective topical coverage. In other words, the team of authors express their ideas, experience and research in layers of detail rather than present a cursory and illustrative format. This was accomplished with the idea that the text may be used selectively.

The readership will readily recognize that the writers are experts (as well as university professors) in their respective disciplines and perspectives. The team of intrepid authors and scholars represents over 100 years of academic, practical application, scholarly and social science research experience. Thus, the readership should be aware that this work is not a value-free, worldview-free, bias-free, milieu or *zeitgeist*-free, opinion-free or even color-free text (as in most social science treatises and as most educated researchers know "everything happens within a context"). Ergo, there is not a flood of neutrality articulated in or between the lines of the text. On the contrary, segments of each chapter present an unabashed and unapologetic articulation in recounting and critically reexamining historical issues and current facts from trade to race and racism to politic science to religion to history to psychology that are generally unknown to the United States populace. They go beyond their specialty by engaging and integrating academic topics that emphasize their perspective. No research lies beyond their observation and analysis as they integrate other disciplines relevant to the current treatise. The authors are emboldened to "telling it like it is" or simply "telling the truth".

Upon understanding the substantiated and adjudicated facts (as opposed to "alternative facts") of American history both past and contemporary, some of the chapter presentations are strategically formatted to stimulate memories curing historical-cultural amnesia while others show little known or even obscure empirical findings that should be committed to memory for future discourse and debate. Hence, more than learning about present issues and events, the intended readership of this treatise will feel as if they are engaging and identifying with it in ways rarely experienced with similar texts. In several chapters, the authors make appeals to the majority's mentality and directs their attention to people of color in terms of analysis and transformation of their social reality.

FEAR, TERROR, AND STEREOTYPE

Tyranny over the mind is the most complete and most brutal type of tyranny; every other tyranny begins and end with it! – Milovan Djilas, The New Class

Cooke discusses the psychology of stereotypes and cultural conditioning. He notes that the cultural conditioning and the incessant indoctrination of negative stereotypes about racial groups has a protracted, checked history in America. Throughout the history of America, the character of African Americans and other Americans have been scientifically attached and defamed. "During American history early every legislature, court of law, school, social club, business organization and church organizations has propagated the code of black contamination and disrepute" (Cross, 1984, pp. 155-156). Toys, games, various forms of visual entertainment (i.e., film, television and stage), mass media and popular literature, advertisements, other channels of communication, and public signage and statuary have depicted blacks as lazy, ignorant, and irresponsible as a class of persons requiring constant support and guidance from the majority population. Arguably since 1619, this defamation and stereotype of blacks and other minorities has severely undermined their hopes and dreams as well as adversely impacting all of America.

As James Baldwin, novelist, essayist, and social critic, stated, "Whoever debases others is debasing himself" (Baldwin, 1963, pp. 82-83). Few behaviors have debased white America like its own stubbornly entrenched racism. Cooke posits that this uninterrupted history continues to keep racial groups divided and miss opportunities to trust one another and grow closer socio-economically, educationally and politically. To this day, individual, institutional and structural racism has kept Americans socially and psychologically divided. *Is it easy for us to forget that in demeaning others we compromise not only their dignity but also our own?*

His insightful chapter calls for a candid discussion about the similarities of our human heritage before the destructive lies continue to sustain deep fractured divisions among one group against another. This chapter examines some of the issues that continue to support the stereotypes of racial differences juxtaposed to our cultural similarities. As a practitioner and professor of psychotherapy, Cooke concludes his chapter by calling for an understanding of the past and present history of these issues thereby facilitating a rejection of systematic prevarications and reversing stereotypical threats. This may lead to a realistic opportunity to begin healing multi-generational distortions and an awakening from a selective, self-induced cultural amnesia. *Are all of us stakeholders ready to hold our local academic, political leadership as well as ourselves accountable to the lofty American Dream, vision, and values? Can the truth and self-awareness set us free and finally allow us to exhale?*

Long before the founding of the United States, the contentious discourse of race and racism has been an uncomfortable exchange and oftentimes avoided by nearly all Americans apart from social scientists and social activists (Bonilla-Silva, 2010). In general, racism is a defense and adjustment mechanism employed by groups to deal with psychological and social insecurities like the way individuals employee psychic defenses and adjustment mechanism to deal with anxiety. It even takes the form of fear. For example, white racism in America is a part and parcel of fear and has its genesis of the social condition of the 16th century Europe and Africa and is molded by social forces and constructs – political, religious, geography and economics.

History is made and defined by landmark moments that irrevocably changed the human condition. However, in some cases, historical events are subject to incorrect interpretations. Moreover, historical misinformation is promulgated and intentionally designed to deceive, confuse, and control the public. Similarly, distortions are not new to American history (Shenkman, 1988). With recent technological advances in historical research, the facts we learned since elementary school are replaced with more detail and factual accounting/analysis. In his chapter, Cooke challenges the readership to react with a sense of respect for the validated historical facts that map out the perpetual struggle of African Americans against systematic inhuman abuse, fear of terrorism, ridicule and intimidation, targeting of vicious hatred, and the dissemination of untenable yet sophisticated myths and lies.

From contaminated water to pandemonium, hysteria and police brutality in American cities, to gun massacres and hate-mongering on the presidential campaign trail is a sign that America is at war with itself and the evidence is pervasive. These conditions are telling symptoms that Americans are potential causalities of this internal conflict. For example, blacks and whites are at war, rich and poor are at war, 2nd Amendment revelers are at war with America, real housewives are at odds with other real house wives, liberal and conservatives are at war, *Black Lives Matter* advocates are at odds with copycat sloganeers, straight and LGBTQ communities are at war, successful "American Dreamers" and the disenfranchised are at war, the Administration is at odds with the new media, "Baby Boomers" and subsequent generations are at war, Wall Street bankers at war with government regulators, and many others. *Is the obvious that difficult to see?*

Hate kills – figuratively and literally. Racial hatred undermines the survival of the country. As it is cried in closed debates, "You hate me because you ain't me" (Johnson, 2017) conjures a fear that the current social condition will never be resolved. This deep visceral sentiment deepens as news reports detail hate crimes committed too frequently across America. Cooke deconstructs the horrific tragedy within a Charleston, South Carolina church to illustrate what home-grown-terrorist-hatred, in general and racially motivated hate do to the spirit of a nation. *What must America do to mitigate these social scourges before national implosion?*

CONUNDRUM OF ENTITLEMENTS AND NATIONAL DEBT

The pundits' arguments are compelling when we hear the surreal fiscal numbers of the trillions of dollars surrounding our national debt. Even for disingenuous Washington-style math, the above claims are ludicrous. The faulty "fiscal cliff" deal that was recently approved hikes both taxes and spending and adds almost $4 trillion in red ink — requiring more borrowing. Yet that is what the administration is attempting to spin as a budget reduction. The total "cut," as noted by the Joint Committee on Taxation ("cut" being defined as an amount that increases slower than originally planned) is a meager $15 billion over a decade, which hardly counts as a dent in the skyrocketing totals of deficit spending. And the Congressional Budget Office sees spending rising every year over that period.

According to Tanner (2013), it is projected that the "federal government will spend $5.5 trillion in 2022, compared with $3.5 trillion this year. America will spend $2 trillion more per year and facing $1.5 trillion more in debt than if federal spending were to rise commensurate with population growth plus inflation over the next ten years. And this will only get worse after 2022, as entitlements, still unreformed after the cliff deal, explode. By 2050, our national debt will top $58 trillion in today's dollars." That is more than two times what it would be if increases in federal spending were limited to inflation and population growth (Tanner, 2013). While most Americans have enough common sense to know the government can't spend and tax the nation to prosperity, many are confused when presumptive leaders and experts make us believe it is possible.

What might be called an "entitlements precipice" is even more menacing than the condition that consumed Capitol Hill at the end of 2012. Consider the relative size of the entitlements (which, despite the implications of the name, are not immune to change). There are approximately 108 million Americans in households where there is at least one participant in a means-tested welfare program.[1] Using figures from the U.S. Census Bureau, they point out the nature of the increase during the Obama years – to the point where about 60 percent of total federal expenditures are currently being spent on entitlements. The U.S. Census Bureau reports 108 million Americans live in households where at least one person participates in a means tested program (U.S. Census Bureau, 2010). It is estimated that 52 million (or 21.3 percent) of the U.S. population were primary recipients in 2012 (Irving & Loveless, 2015).

If we add in the estimated 16 million new Medicaid beneficiaries because of the Patient Protection and Affordable Care Act (ACA), plus an estimated 18 million people who entered the health insurance exchanges beginning in 2014, where most will receive federal subsidies.

The budget implications of these programs produce "shock and awe" in the minds of Americans (Eskow, 2017).

With this brief overview of the national financial status, Americans are anxiously waiting to hear a viable solution and wondering if the issue will be relieved. The fiduciary responsibility of the federal government budgetary pundits and politicians are immense and require long-term due diligence, vigilance, and resolve. To that end, Hampton-Garland ushers/introduces the other side of the federal government with a description of entitlements – its history, evolution, its "moving parts" and those who depend on them. Her approach to the topic is direct, no nonsense, and absorbing. Her discussion ushers in a revealing examination of entitlement programs commenced by a Facebook repartee dialogue to entitlement addicts to a revealing personal account as a customer of entitlements – all intertwined with their intended purpose to ensure the survival of disenfranchised, disaffected and marginalized Americans.

She asks the readership to consider the definition, promise and context of the American Dream. Her discussion is guided by seven penetrating questions regarding the so-called 'forgotten Americans' (i.e., Donald Trump's forgotten men and women) and the multi-layered interpretation of the famous 'Make America Great Again' slogan.

Hampton-Garland examines the history and assumptions of international trade agreements or acts impact on job losses and campaign promises by candidate Trump to return those jobs back to American workers from other foreign countries. *But haven't Americans heard this before during the campaigns and administrations of Presidents Nixon and Reagan? Is this a Trumpian replay of how political culture triumphs over political economy in American politics?*

Her underlining and meta-discussions of the interdependency and intertwined nature of international trade, politics, jobs opportunity and personal economics are captivating and thought-provoking. Indeed, trade agreements are not delimited to one factor (e.g., job growth). More ostensibly, they impact virtually all Americans.

DA POOR

Historically, poverty in America has been regarded not as a social issue, but as a manifestation of individual weakness, moral deficiency, and self-induced-sloth-like helplessness. This reflects American religious, cultural and political traditions. Given the prevailing cultural perspective, it should not be surprising that government assistance to the poor and disenfranchised was deemed untenable. Aid to the poor was a local responsibility divided between charities and local municipal programs. State governments took a more active role in the late 19th century after industrialization, urbanization, and immigration created wide-spread conditions of congestion, overcrowding and squalor. Concomitantly, The Great Depression compounded those conditions with high rates of unemployment, poverty and welfare. Hampton-Garland breaks down and demystifies the other side of the headline news story of that era and details how the early evolution of entitlement programming (social safety nets, social insurance, public assistance) impacts all if us – today.

MIXTURE OR SUSPENSION OF THE "OTHERS"?

I just want to say, you know, can we all get along? Can we get along? Can we stop making it, making it horrible for the older people and the kids? – Rodney King (1992)

The United States' society is in a constant and dynamic shift from the original predominantly White, heteropatriarchal, hegemonic, Judeo-Christian, capitalist society to a robust global community characterized with diversity and multiculturalism presenting anticipated and unanticipated challenges to the emerging societal constructs and how the general populace can negotiate questions of citizenship and the daunting tasks of providing equal opportunity, social justice, and unfettered socio-political participation. The global forces of immigration, religious fanaticism, internecine warfare, police brutality, and unpredictable fluctuations in economic conditions have all contributed to the new challenges to the authority of the nation state and its institutions (Asumah, Nagel, & Rosengarten, 2016).

Before the founding of the United States, the construct of race has been a constant and prime factor in differentiating, separating and tribalizing Americans. The current racial situation in the United States has been contentious from the beginning. Specifically, while Eurocentrism is ubiquitous and much broader than the social concept of race, it is race and color(ism) that have been liberally used to determine and define the social order. The European race has been self-marketed, self-promoted and self-appointed as superior and its culture as normative. America retains a tainted history with respect to certain populations that were compromised and inhibited by discrimination, alienation, and marginalization before and since the nation's founding. Hence, recounting of historical events of American history must include a study of overt and covert racist practices levied at people of color (Bonilla-Silva, 2010). The oppression and forced relocations of Native American, the brutal wholesale kidnapping and enslavement of Africans, widespread segregation of Hispanic and Latino Americans, passage of exclusionary laws targeted at Chinese immigrants, and the forced internment of Japanese Americans during World War II are historical facts whose psychological baggage weighs heavy on the collective and contemporary American psyche (Sue & Sue, 2013).

Sehcrest-Ehrhardt provides an overview of the tensions of understanding diversity and inclusion training – a popular strategy to manage prejudice within organizations and educational settings. As a diversity consultant and trainer, she presents an unvarnished account of the racial tension between the majority and people of color that impacts virtually all Americans. Moreover, she posits that critical race theory facilitates the understanding of past and current racial tensions.

If you are a product of American public education, you may not know Native Americans are more than a short history lesson; that, in fact, they thrived before the United States was a concept. Since the 17th century, accounts for the First Civil War between Native Americas and Americans driven by the notion of *manifest destiny* that some argue continues today. By design, her discussion does not include quixotic notions regarding the outstretched arms of welcoming Native Americans of the first Thanksgiving. Certainly, there existed natural suspicions of European explorers and of the soldiers, settlers and clerics who followed them. *To what extent do Native Americans still harbor these thoughts given their ongoing history?*

She describes the history of the major so-called "other" groups. For example, Africans were torn from their native land and transported to the Americas under the "guise and lies" of a *full employment program* in the southern and northern American states (Warren, 2016). Quite the reverse, it was the American *hellocaust* (Amani, 2001). Thus, the romantic moonlight and magnolia plantation myths of southern culture are summarily dismissed in her chapter.

Sehcrest-Ehrhardt examines how the centuries of enslavement and the government's condoning of the invidious racial discrimination in all sectors of American life have had and continue to have, a negative impact on the development of people of color in America. Past inequalities perpetuate cycles that have been so pervasive that they were institutionalized and transferred from one generation to the other. *Could these be the memes our parents warned us about?*

Usually, one group is currently regarded as subject to discrimination, racism, derogative slurs, and micro-aggressions. In this case, there is a certain historical myopia at play here. Other groups have also suffered for discrimination and ridicule over long periods of American history and still are in some quarters. For example, the other Americans who began their American journey from Angel Island (i.e., the so-called West Coast Ellis Island) were offered their niche as railroad workers and coolies where they labored and lived in near-slave status. Chinese immigrants faced overt hostility in the form of legal obstacles such as the Chinese Exclusion Act (Lee, 2002).

Sehcrest-Ehrhardt enhances and refines our historical-cultural literacy with examples of "other" journeys to America; all struggled, yet all prevailed to tell their stories, their truth. Within this chapter, unknown, little known, or omitted historical facts are revealed and are sure to enlighten the readership and provide much to ponder regarding our national character. Only by learning about each other's American journeys, can we learn to communicate effectively and honestly with one another in our national community.

Without knowledge or the decoding of others background and history, how can we appreciate and respect each other? Can social change agents like diversity trainers save us from ourselves? It can be argued that human beings are change averse. To that end, Sehcrest-Ehrhardt extends the discussion in her second chapter of the racial and ethnic differences and appeals to our causal vacancy of rational thought, principle and respect for others.

CONCLUSION

Overall, the six chapters comprising this book represent the most current scholarship assessing the status of some of the most persistent and compelling American issues. The chapters reflect a plurality of theoretical and methodological orientations that together make an insistent case that the *American Dream* for all remains elusive. The authors recognize profound changes taking place in the social, economic, and cultural contexts of America. These changes are precipitating the stressed presence of an urgency for equal opportunity and social justice in business, government, and educational polities and the community environments in which they are embedded.

Schuyler "Sky" C. Webb
McCray Webb & Associates, LLC, USA

REFERENCES

Amani, K. (2001). *Ghetto religiosity II*. New York: Writer's Club Press.

Asumah, S. N., Nagel, M., & Rosengarten, L. (2016). Two: New trends in diversity leadership and inclusive excellence. *Wagadu: A Journal of Transnational Women's and Gender Studies, 15*, 139-161.

Baldwin, J. (1963). *The fire next time*. New York: Dial Press.

Bonilla-Silva, E. (2010). *Racism without racists: Color-blind racism and the persistence of racial inequality in the United States*. Lanham, MD: Rowman & Littlefield.

Cross, T. (1984). *The black power imperative*. New York: Faulkner.

Eskow, R. (2017). *A soul-sick, 'shock and awe' budget*. Retrieved from http://www.huffingtonpost.com/entry/a-soul-sick-shock-and-awe-budget_us_58cb3306e4b0537abd956f5c

Irving, S., & Loveless, T. (2015). *Dynamics of economic well-being: Participation in government programs, 2009-2012: Who gets assistance?* Washington, DC: U.S. Department of Commerce.

Johnson, J. (2017, May 5). *The Russ Parr morning show* [Radio broadcast]. Washington, DC: Radio One.

Lee, E. (2002). The Chinese exclusion example: Race, immigration, and American gatekeeping, 1882-1924. *Journal of American Ethnic History, 21*(3), 36–62.

Shenkman, R. (1988). *Legends, lies & cherished myths of American history*. New York: Morrow.

Sue, D., & Sue, D. (2013). *Counseling the culturally diverse: Theory and practice* (6th ed.). Hoboken, NJ: Wiley & Sons.

Tanner, M. (2013). The spending cliff. *National Review*. Retrieved from https://www.cato.org/publications/commentary/spending-cliff

U.S. Census Bureau. (2010). *U.S. population: 2010*. Washington, DC: U.S. Printing Office.

Warren, W. (2016). *New England bound: Slavery and colonization in early America*. New York: Norton/Liveright.

ENDNOTE

1 Means-tested programs are those that require the income and/or assets of an individual or family to fall below specified thresholds to qualify for benefits. There may be additional eligibility requirements to receive these programs, which provide cash and noncash assistance to eligible individuals and families.

Acknowledgment

I would like to thank my husband, Vernon Garland and my daughters Domonique and Gabrielle Garland for their patience and faith throughout this project. I would like to also thank my co-authors Dr, Lisa Sechrest-Ehrhardt and Dr. Benson G. Cooke along with our editor Dr. Schuyler Webb who all worked with me to make this project a great success. Finally, I would like to thank God for giving me the ability and passion for the issues facing marginalized people that made this book possible. -

Pamela Hampton-Garland, Ph.D.

I thank my spouse, David Ehrhardt, and my children, Nicole, Jessica, and Joshua, for their support throughout this project. I also thank my esteemed colleagues, Pamela Garland-Hampton and Benson Cooke, for their continued guidance and support.

Lisa Sehcrest-Ehrhardt, Ph.D.

I'm indebted to the many scholars who set our foundation in the discipline of the issues discussed. They continually challenged us to explore beyond the accepted and known standards of knowledge and scholarship. I'm proud to stand upon their shoulders of their seminal contributions. I pray that my use of their research raises the consciousness and increases the collective insight of current and future generations. I acknowledge and thank those whose foundational influence has been indispensable in the envisionment of this project. My beloved are Elfreda Foster, Benjamin Cooke, Carol Cooke, Floyd Foster, Samuel Hocker, Lynne Jones, Cassandra Cooke, Freida Taylor,

Angela Cooke-Jackson, Ayanna Cooke-Chen, Dawn Cunningham, Daa'iyah Cooke, Siddeeq Cooke, Zuri Cooke, Patrice Butler, Na'im Akbar, Schuyler Webb, Edwin Nichols, Rev. Willie Wilson, Wade Nobles, Asa Hilliard, Halford Fairchild, Thomas Parham, Cheryl Grills, Daryl Rowe, Robert L. Williams, Vivian Ota Wang, Derrick Humphries, Ayana Jackson, Lester Bentley, John Wright, Deborah Sims, Steven Jones, and Donnell Davis.

Benson G. Cooke, Ed.D.

Chapter 1
Creating a Stereotype of a Race as Dangerous, Unintelligent, and Lazy:
Examining Consequences of Cultural and Psychological Conditioning in America

Benson G. Cooke
University of the District of Columbia, USA

ABSTRACT

The cultural conditioning and the indoctrination of negative stereotypes about racial groups has a long-damaged history in America. Unfortunately, this history continues to keep racial groups divided and missed opportunities to trust one another and grow closer socio-economically, educationally and politically. Individual, institutional and structural racism has kept people in this nation torn and divided socially and psychologically. Understanding the root of this problem requires an honest and open historical and philosophical discussion about the similarities of our human origins before the destructive lies told continue to sustain deep divisions among one group against another. While America was created to support an idea that "all men are created equal", this has not been a social experience practiced by all men and all women. This chapter examines some of the issues that continue to support the stereotypes of racial differences juxtaposed to our cultural similarities.

DOI: 10.4018/978-1-5225-3843-1.ch001

Africa is in a profound sense the fount of human evolution.

- Ian Tattersall

For history, as nearly no one seems to know, is not merely something to be read. And it does not refer merely, or even principally, to the past. On the contrary, the great force of history comes from the fact that we carry it within us, are unconsciously controlled by it in many ways, and history is literally present in all that we do...And it is with great pain and terror that one begins to realize this. In great pain and terror, one begins to assess the history which has placed one where one is, and formed one's point of view. In great pain and terror, because, thereafter, one enters into battle with that historical creation, oneself.

- James Baldwin

The association between socioeconomic status and race in the United States has its origins in discrete historical events but persists because of contemporary structural factors that perpetuate those historical injustices.

- Camara Phyllis Jones

THE PROBLEM WITH BLACK[1] PEOPLE IS...

How is it that in the 21st century African American's are frequently and more often than not erroneously perceived by some law enforcement personnel, or right-wing media outlets, radio or news pundits, bloggers or right-wing extremists or even neighbors as dangerous, unintelligent or lazy? Mis-educated rhetoric that supports bigotry, prejudice and intolerance, which in turn espouses an ideology over fact only reinforces racism, sexism, misogyny, xenophobia, homophobia, and religism[2] (i.e., religious intolerance). These misconceptions have been propagated from family conversations, mis-educated oratory and written accounts reinforced by lies. Within each society, this dogma is exposed in racially divisive children's books, movies, or contemporary radio and television shows passed down from one generation to the next. The longevity of these falsehoods has been driven by ignorance and constructed to stoke fear of the unknown through irrational ideas and outrageous beliefs that become culturally conditioned into hatred without knowing the soul of the person. Subsequently, that person becomes the object of their hate. Accordingly, early American speeches, books, religious sermons, theatrical performances, songs and conversations would play a role in setting the foundation that would become a culture of falsehoods and misconceptions regarding race, ethnicity, gender, class and religious practice.

Probably the most poignant propaganda used by slave holders and Southern aristocrats to validate, culturally manipulate and maintain psychological control of enslaved Africans, as well as to justify their atrocities was their self-serving misinterpretations of biblical scripture. While the "biblical world predated any systematic notion of races and theories of racism" (Felder, 2002, p. 43), efforts to interpolate ideas for the purpose of authorizing and empowering human domination acts were not uncommon in America. One example of biblical interpolation of scripture used to mistreat and keep enslaved Africans docile and under the yoke of human bondage and trafficking were the so-called biblical references conveying the belief that Black people were cursed. Therefore, they owed a debt to their capturers for rescuing them as "the descendants of Ham" and from being "cursed by being Black and are sinful with a degenerate progeny" (Felder, 2002, p. 13-14). Ostensive, there is no scholarly or layperson reference that confirms this as a biblical fact. Felder posits that:

> *Proslavery jurists argued that in order for the slave to remain a slave, he or she must be convinced that the master's power is in no way usurped: "[Slavery] is conferred by the laws of man at least, if not by the law of God." Obedience and submission to the master—self-designated as "God overseer"—were synonymous with "exhibiting good Christian character." In short, blacks could be "saved by Christ," but never "free from their masters." (Felder, 1991, p. 215)*

Stigma Matters

Storytelling has been used since the beginning of time to convey ideas, to bring to light a message, to reveal knowledge and wisdom, and to communicate beliefs. Indeed, the power of storytelling can change the world. Human history has witnessed an evolution of innovative ways to share stories with various and diverse audiences. One innovation that had a profound impact on the art of storytelling was the invention of moving pictures during the mid-1830s.

This form of entertainment would result in motion pictures (later called movies). At the turn of the 20th century, one of the most provocative motion pictures would take center stage by skillfully manipulating and presenting racial stereotypes to a racist nation and the world. That film was The Birth of a Nation produced and directed by D.W. Griffith (1915) and was conceived and fashioned to articulate his extreme racial and stereotypical beliefs. Simply put, his intention was to promulgate "that things were in order only when whites were in control and when the American Negro was kept in his place" (Bogle, 1992, p. 10). Specifically, "Griffith propagated the myth of slave contentment and made it appear as if slavery had elevated the Negro from his bestial instincts" (Boggle, 1992, p. 13). Despite its misrepresentation and controversy, Griffith's film would become one of the first nationwide blockbusters. It was so popular that it received "a private White House screening by President Woodrow Wilson who would exclaim, "It was like writing history with lightening!" (Bogle, 1992, p. 10).

What forms the basis for this belief and more importantly, why does this stigma continue to permeate the judgements and justifications of others and some African Americans as principally the source of societal poverty, violence, crime, drugs, illiteracy, fatherless children, flashy and ostentatious dressers, overly-erotic, and highly emotional? Long before the trade and sale of enslaved Africans in America, false ideas began to take shape about Africa and Africans. What socio-cultural underpinnings can address this perception that affects the safety, dignity and overall quality of life for this group? To answer this question, it's important to examine the ideas of one of the key 18th century philosophers David Hume.

I am apt to suspect that Negroes and in general all the other species of men (for there are four or five different kinds) to be naturally inferior to the whites. There never was a civilized nation of any other complexion than white, nor even any individual eminent either in action or speculation. No ingenious manufactures amongst them, no arts, no sciences. (Davies, 1988, p. 13)

While history exposes this 18th century idea as unscientific and logically unsubstantiated, it was representative of the values, beliefs and attitudes of Hume's time. Additionally, what cultural foundations could induce the personal objectification that exist along racial lines as well as gender, ethnicity, class, language and religion lines? One answer explaining the cause of these perceptions is to understand the impact and the context of the stereotype.

Consequently, some researchers suggest that finding ways to inhibit the stereotype through cultural conditioning may focus on the source of the prevarication and work to reveal the damage it created. Thus, one resolution for this issue is to create an awareness of the impact of stereotyping.

Stereotype inhibition requires sufficiently powerful and plentiful contrary examples so that whites have enough anecdotes in their minds that problems such as welfare and crime do not immediately and automatically suggest the involvement of African-Americans. (Peffley, Hurwitz, & Sniderman, 1997, p. 55)

Unfortunately, African Americans, in particular, have been unfairly and negatively exaggerated and depicted in media as chronic welfare recipients, violent and petty criminals, sex-crazed, and lazy and boisterous uncommitted workers. Consequently, African Americans stigmatized in this manner actually distorts the facts regarding their individual and collective humanity, values, morals, dignity, and industrious character. Negative stereotypes have kept our society divided racially, socially, economically, educationally and politically since the colonial era. Therefore, increasing awareness about how stereotypes are formed can help reduce prejudices, bias and bigotry that damages interpersonal, institutional and societal relationships. As centuries of U.S. Supreme Court cases and Amendments to the Constitution have shaped the philosophical underpinnings of civil rights, constitutional privileges, legal guarantees to all people in spite of race, color, religion and gender. In addition, they have also helped to affect perceptions that influence the deterioration as well as the improvement of race relations. According to psychologists and other social scientists, creating social perceptions that help reduce the negative impact of stereotypes can be enhanced by utilizing the approach of perspective-taking[3]. Social advocates throughout American history have advocated for the oppressed by discussing and humanizing their struggles and their strengths in overcoming obstacles by tapping into their values, attitudes and beliefs. These efforts effectively contradict the negative stereotypical perceptions associated with their cultural, racial, ethnic, gender or religious group.

Perspective-taking, however, appears to diminish not just the expression of stereotypes but their accessibility. The constructive process of taking and realizing another person's perspective furthers the egalitarian principles themselves; perspective-taking is an effective reinforcement of contemporary admonitions to consider previously ignored or submerged perspectives as a routine part of social interchange and inquiry. (Galinsky & Moskowitz, 2000, p. 722)

As we share our life stories with one another in a manner that encourages perspective-taking, we may find that we will increase our understanding and empathy for human differences. At the same time, it may raise our sensitivity to and awareness of our own standards for rationale critical thinking and engagement.

DEEP BEGINNINGS

It is important to begin this section's conversation with the fact that all people past and present originated in Africa, the continental and cultural home of all civilizations (Shreeve, 2015; Diop, 1991; Ki-Zerbo, 1981). Propelling the rich history of African civilizations (Ajayi, 1989; Boahen, 1985; Mazuri, 1986; Samkange, 1971; Ogot, 1992; Ade 1989; and Adu Boahen, 1985), is a more than 200,000 yearlong historical legacy of African people being the center of humankind's first civilizations (Jackson, 1972; Diop, 1991; Mazrui, 1986). Additionally, Africa is the birthplace of the first spoken and written language (Browder, 1992), philosophy (Obenga, 2004), mathematics (Zaslavsky, 1999), engineering (Van Sertima, 1983), architecture (Eglash, 1999), science (Van Sertima, 1983), and technology (Van Sertima, 1992), medicine (Van Sertima, 1983; Finch, 1990), religious practice (Karenga, 2006), literature, art, music, and other cultural contributions (Mokhtar, 1981). It is from this rich heritage that other groups of people populated other continents resulting in the development of Asia, South Pacific Asian Countries, European continent, and the Americas (Owusu, 1994). Based upon the fossil, archeological, metallurgical, linguistic, oceanographic, navigational, epigraphic, pictorial, iconographic, botanical, cartographic, oral and documented evidence, African people contributed to subsequent societies and civilizations (Rashidi & Van Sertima 1985; Van Sertima, 1976; Van Sertima, 1983; Van Sertima, 1985; Van Sertima, 1986; Van Sertima, 1988; Van Sertima, 1989; Van Sertima, 1992; Van Sertima, 1994; Van Sertima, 1998; Ki-Zerbo, 1981; Mokhtar, 1981; Elfasi, 1988; Niane, 1984). Additional data of the out of African hypothesis includes DNA evidence that supports the anthropological and cognitive roots of the human family having beginnings in Africa (Bräuer, 1984; Stringer & Andrews, 1988; Wolpoff, Wu, & Thorne, 1984).

The single African origin notion received an enormous boost from molecular systematics when DNA comparisons (Cann, Stoneking, and Wilson, 1987); (Stoneking, Sherry, Redd, and Vigilant, 1993) began strongly supporting earlier conclusions based on proteins (Neil and Roychoudhury, 1974) that Africa had been the ultimate source of modern human populations worldwide. Over the last quarter-century, evidence on both the molecular and the fossil fronts has accumulated to the point where there can be little doubt that humankind ultimately originated in Africa. (Tattersall, 2009, p. 16019)

The significance of these scientific findings is that they refute the myth that Europeans represent the first group of people to seed civilizations and that Africans by virtue of a darker, melanin-rich skin color are totally devoid of making significant contributions to civilizations past or present. In many ways, the distinctive differences that represents the diversity of our species in skin-color, hair texture, eye color, height, and facial features, culture and language has nothing to do with one group of humans being superior to another. However, the differences are a consequence of the process of evolutionary adaptation over tens of thousands of years of migration into wide-ranging varieties of geographical landscapes, inhospitable environments and temperate locations. As a result, early humans experienced extreme variations in climate, topography, food and water sources, and other environmental challenges.

Unfortunately, some groups armed with "alterative facts" have totally dismissed the fact that we have more in common as human beings than we have differences despite our linguistic, physical, and cultural differences. However, the root of stereotypes is not limited to racial, gender, class or religious insults. Stereotypes are supported by a lack of engagement and interaction as well as a consequence of a lack of historic literacy and perspective. The lack of engagement and interaction has a profound impact on how we perpetuate stigma through what we are taught to believe, how we demonize human difference via socio-economic policies, or how we sustain discrimination practices through political systems is a part of our worldview.

Worldviews always imply a coherent set of values—(these values center around the following questions)—What is the meaning of life? What purpose does our existence serve? How do we best live our lives? Why do suffering, injustice and misery persist? (Kalberg, 2004)

Worldviews are sets of beliefs and assumptions that describe reality. A given worldview encompasses assumptions about heterogeneous variety of topics, including human nature, the meaning and nature of life, and the composition of the universe itself, to name a few issues. The term *worldview* comes from the German word, *'weltanschauung*, meaning a view or perspective on the world or the universe "used to scribe one's total outlook on life, society and its institutions" (Wolman, 1973, p. 406). In a broad sense, a worldview is the interpretive lens one uses to understand reality and one's existence within it (West & Miller, 1993). Moreover, worldviews are shaped by the acquisition of culturally learned axiology, epistemology, and logic (Jones & Nichols, 2013). The shaping of a worldview is through evolutionary adaptation. *Axiology* is the study of values; *epistemology* is ways of knowing, and logic is ways of reasoning to an answer. (NB: In this context, epistemology is not knowledge, rather it is the way in which one knows knowledge.) For example, in order for slaveholders involved with human trafficking in the U.S. to maintain control over those enslaved, was to create whiteness.

All women, people ineligible to become citizens (Native Americans and Asians), the enslaved, and free people of African descent outside New England continued to be excluded, as well as paupers, felons, and transients such as canal workers and sailors. . . . In this situation, "universal suffrage" meant adult white male suffrage, though from time to time the definition of "white" came into question. Were men with one black and one white parent or three white and one black grandparent "white"? Did "white" mean only Anglo-Saxons, or all men considered Caucasian, including those classed as Celts[4] ? The abolition of economic barriers to voting by white men made the United States, in the then common parlance, "a white man's country," a polity defined by race and limited to white men . . . the first enlargement of American whiteness. (Painter, 2010, p. 107)

The purpose of whiteness was to divide the former white (i.e., English debtor prisoners) and African indentured servants. These two groups were of the same class and therefore intermarriage and interaction was normal for them. Together they represented an economic threat to the plantation owners. Virginia Slavery Laws and the conditions under which Africans would suffer chattel slavery offers a clear progression of this process.

Under Virginia and Maryland law, the slave had been chattel since the seventeenth century. Slaves could be sold by their owners, moved by their owners, and separated from others by their owners. Georgia and Carolina cut-and-pasted many aspects of the Virginia Slave Code into their laws. But in practice, the laws were implemented differently. Almost all of the slaves down here were new to the whites who owned them, and they used them without constraint. (Baptist, 2014, p. 32)

Efforts were made throughout early American history to give a higher human value, authority, independence and power to those people who represented whiteness as a way of endorsing the belief and logic that one race and one gender was superior to others. This became evident when examining the negative stereotypes and subsequent acts of discrimination exhibited during the arrival of other immigrants coming into the U.S. during the mid-nineteenth century, which included the Irish, Slavic from the Austro-Hungarian Empire, Jews from Russia and Poland, and Italians, who were not initially designated as having whiteness (Painter, 2010, p. 206). When the philosophical aspects of cultural difference is defined by the axiological (i.e., things that are valuable), and epistemological (i.e., ways of knowing), framework that invents information to support racial supremacy through a justification of racial whiteness this projects a worldview with no logically factual foundation.

As a result of using the dominant *logic* system for European culture, which is dichotomous logic (i.e., either/or) that results in illogical conclusions concerning racial differences. Through its misuse one develops "*isms*", and isms give the perception of privilege to one group over others. The diagram below illustrates the misuse of isms regarding the justification of reasoning that White Men are more positive because of their Male gender and racial whiteness over other groups, especially African American women. According to Dr. Edwin J. Nichols (2017), within the European worldview, (Diagram 1), examines race (i.e., White and Black), juxtaposed to gender (i.e., Male and Female). This diagram also includes Positive versus Negative qualities/characteristics, as a dichotomous (i.e., a division into two parts), of positive and or negative gender and race. Thus, the column to the left represents White people seen as Positive and the column to the right represents Black people seen as negative. The far left top row represents gender for Male as a positive characteristic, while row below represents gender for Female as a negative characteristic. Nichols (2017) concludes that by ascribing value (axiology) to one column over the other that the outcome would result in the good column placing Male and over the bad column place Female. Thus he concludes that this matrix forms what amounts to a value of sexism, listing the attributes of maleness over femaleness. He further indicates that by having over the good column white and over the bad column black, which results in having ascribed to white good and to black bad. If we take these two columns and we ask what the characteristics are of white males, they are all positive. We would also see that the characteristics of black females are all negative (Nichols, 2017). This negative outcome is also referred to as the 'double whammy effect' (Hughes, 2014). The general picture from this worldview is that privilege should be afforded to Males who are White over Males who are Black. However, by virtue of being White, Females should be afforded privilege over Females who are Black. This racial and gender bias can be seen across the American landscape, but no better place can it be seen as in government. For example, White males have dominated the Presidency of American until 2008 when Barack Obama was elected. To date there has not been a White Female elected, but one did recently win the Democratic primary to participate in a run-off for the Presidency. However, no Black Female has reached the status of winning a primary to participate in a run-off presidential election. The same can be said for the Supreme Court. Here again, for centuries it was the domain of White Males until Thurgood Marshall (a Black Male) served as an Associate Justice from 1967-1991. Following his term, Clarence Thomas (a Black Male) is currently serving as an Associate Justice. As is the case with the majority gender to serve as our nation's presidency, dichotomous logic shaped by American cultural conditioning may help to explain why White Males and Black Males have served with White Females and even Latino Females, but not Black Females. This is just one example of the power of the dominant worldview shaping the philosophical construct of logic, which is illustrated in Table 1.

Epistemology in European context is to count and to measure. The pedagogy of European Epistemology is to have a series of parts that become the whole. The methodology is to place things in a linear and sequential pattern. For example, the product line of the Ford Motor Company's invention. Car frames

Table 1. Illustrating dichotomous logic

	Race White People seen as Positive (+)	**Race Black People seen as Negative (-)**
Gender for Male Positive (+)	**White Male** (+ +)	**Black Male** (+ -)
Gender for Female Negative (-)	**White Female** (- +)	**Black Female** (- -)

are placed on a moving assembly or production line, where workers or robots insert each part until the car is becomes a complete unit. The manufacturing process to assemble a completed (whole) car is accomplished in a linear and sequential pattern. Juxtaposed to this would be the approach of other cultures approximating a holistic conceptual framework. The holistic framework would incorporate a methodological fuse of a critical path analysis, which in a common vernacular, would take an approach of "getting the big picture" and "cutting to the chase".

Epistemologically, Europeans believe that you must look at the little pieces in order to formulate and visualize the big picture, whereas other cultures are able to view the whole picture. A relatively new concept helps to explain part of the problem that continues to perpetuate the belief in lies. This concept is called agnotology, which refers to the study of willful acts to spread confusion and deceit (Proctor & Schiebinger, 2008). Agnotology contributes to the ignorance that keeps some individuals unaware about the facts of difference in regard to race, ethnicity, gender, language, religion and socio-economic level. White ignorance has been able to flourish uninterrupted because a white epistemology of ignorance has safeguarded it against the dangers of an illuminating blackness or redness, protecting those who for "racial" reasons have needed not to know. Only by starting to break these rules and meta-rules can we begin the process that will lead to the eventual overcoming of this imposed white darkness and the achievement of an enlightenment that is genuinely multiracial (Mills, 2008, p. 247).

Humanizing Diversity by Uncovering Lies and Revealing Facts

What we believe, practice and ritualize is based upon the happenings of our past and how we learn to culturally contextualize those experiences into ways of being. When we uncover the lies that marginalize our humanity towards one another, it magnifies the facts. Consequently, when some people suggests that they are born superior to others because of their race, gender or religion, we allow that lie to dehumanize the rich diversity of humanity. This intensifies acts of destructive cultural conditioning, which suggest that racism, sexism and all other forms of hate are justifiable. Accordingly, when we are not corrupted by hate, bigotry, prejudice, bias and racism, we are more open to accepting the diversity of humanity. Subsequently, this becomes foundational and transformational to our willingness to establish constructive interpersonal connections with people. When facts of our human existence are turned upside-down concerning the issues that are foundational to how we value the humanity of one another, it becomes easier to engage in the objectification of self and others to the degree that perceptions of humanity are minimized, devalued and disregarded. It is at this point that invalidating a life or denigrating groups based upon race, ethnicity, gender, class and religious beliefs becomes a common explicit and implicit practice in spite of humane policies designed to protect civil or human rights. Instead, it is at this point that cultural conditioning undermines civility and rational engagement between people who embody differences. One outcome of preconceived opinions that are not based on actual experience or facts is the perception that African Americans are the primary benefactors of Food Stamp programs (i.e., Supplemental Nutrition Assistance Program or SNAP) (Delaney & Scheller, 2015). This perception has been the battle cry of political pundits who support an ideological and biased perspective designed to provoke the majority population into thinking that African Americans abuse social programs and deprive the general public of the same resources. A social program that was a precursor to SNAP was created during The Great Depression (1929-1939) when efforts to incentivize farmers to destroy their surpluses of crops, as a way of raising farm profits in the market place. Unfortunately, nationwide hunger protests resulted in the government purchasing the extra crops previously destroyed in order to create the first pilot food stamp program in 1939. The success of this program instituted by President Franklin D. Roosevelt was a consequence of nationwide approval without aspersions cast to the recipients, who were mostly white. With a more robust economy following World War II, the pilot program was ended. It would be reconstituted in the 1960s as part of the war on poverty programs instituted by President Lyndon B. Johnson. As of 2013, the food stamp program supports approximately 9.1 million white Americans; 5.9 million African Americans; 2.4 million Hispanics; 486,000 Asian Americans; 265,000 Native Americans; 2.9 million multiple races; and 1.5 million Unknown (Delaney & Scheller, 2015). Figures 1 and 2 below provide an overview of the percentage and numbers of people who use food stamps based upon 2013 data from the Department of Agriculture. This data reveals that images can convey ideas that effect behavior, even when devoid of factual information. In this case, the cultural conditioning leans more toward scapegoating one population segment for overuse of a social program when in fact this is not the case.

Figure 1. 2013 percentage of SNAP recipients based on race in the U.S
(Source: http://www.huffingtonpost.com/2015/02/28/food-stamp-demographics_n_6771938.html)

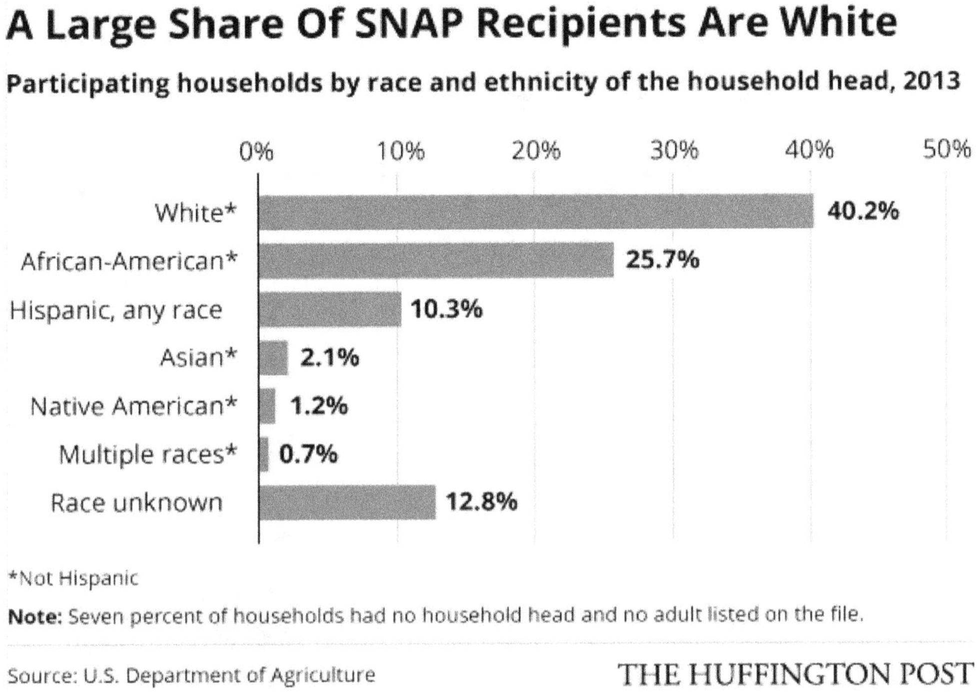

We are often unaware of the scope and structure of our ignorance. Ignorance is not just a blank space on a person's mental map. It has contours and coherence, and for all I know rules of operation as well. So as a corollary to writing about what we know, maybe we should add getting familiar with our ignorance.

- Thomas Pynchon

THE TRANSFORMING TOPOGRAPHY OF MESSAGING A LIE

This section examines some of the personal factors that have contributed to a societal falsehood becoming more accepted, and in some cases more believable than facts. This section is concerned with exploring the impact of a lie on a national level, which psychologically denigrates a group of people as well as

Figure 2. 2013 Population number of SNAP recipients based on race in the U.S (Source: https://www.google.com/search?q=welfare+statistics+by+race+2016&sa=X&tbm=isch&tbo=u&source=univ&ved=0ahUKEwj05OrYlOPSAhXm3YMKHclqAccQsAQIOw&biw=1680&bih=955#imgrc=a2eiMx5WoeJ34M:&spf=242)

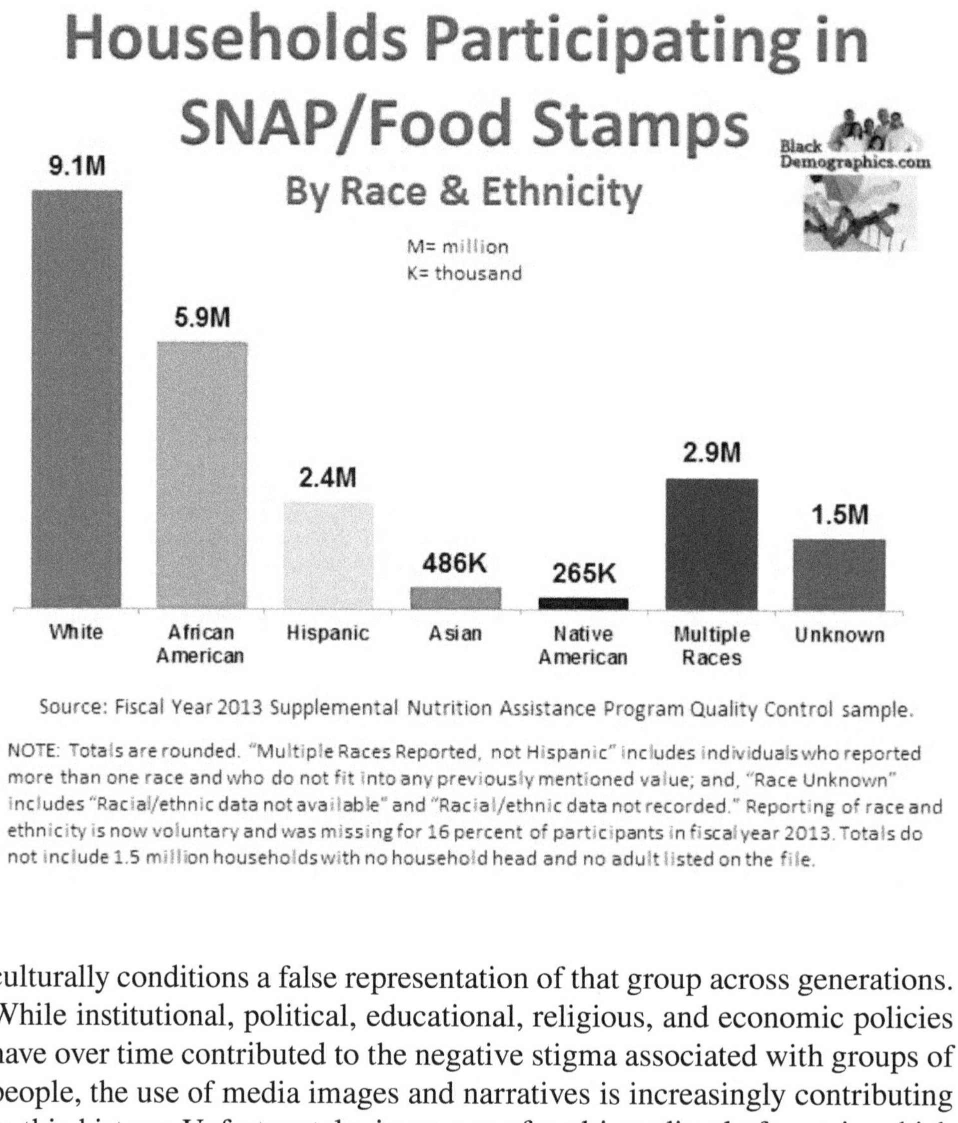

culturally conditions a false representation of that group across generations. While institutional, political, educational, religious, and economic policies have over time contributed to the negative stigma associated with groups of people, the use of media images and narratives is increasingly contributing to this history. Unfortunately, in an age of multi-media platforms in which news sources are a key-stroke away on a smartphone device, electronic tablet, computer or flat-screen TV, which is streaming continuous data from the cloud, cable or satellite feed; information is instantaneously available. This raises even greater concerns when unreliable media sources are just as accessible as reliable media sources. The days of conventional journalistic-run media programs has now been almost overtaken by multi-media programs where journalists have been coupled with or simply replaced by political pundits, community activists, bloggers, and conspiracy advocates. This 21st century forum has moved to replace most investigative journalistic reporting of the facts with sensationalistic stories slanted to entertain or to provide a dogmatic perspective. Ostensibly, it is becoming more difficult to authenticate and validate facts that inform a myriad of truths versus stereotypes, which influence not only how we see our self and others, but also our knowledge and understanding of the consequences of cultural and psychological conditioning in America. This is especially true if the untruth gives value, importance, and control over to the storyteller and their historical or societal revisionist perspective. More frequently we are likely to hear the stories benefitting or justifying the invention of a stereotypical untruth. Whether driven by fear, insecurity, hatred, greed, privilege, injustice, cruelty, intolerance, or self-importance, the lie being conveyed is used to rationalize ones beliefs while disparaging those who collectively share different racial, cultural, religious, gender or class identity.

"Alternative Facts": The New Language and the Rationale for Revising American History

On January 22, 2017, during an NBC *Meet the Press* interview, Kellyanne Conway, Advisor to President Trump, told Chuck Todd the moderator of the program that Press Secretary Sean Spicer used the term "*alternative facts*" in his first statement to the Press Corps. After a fact check, it was determined that he actually departed from the truth. Immediately, the major news outlets along with countless other national and international news media outlets began paraphrasing the new lexicon of how to lie in public without repercussions and coined a phase that was difficult to ignore.

In his dystopian novel, *1984,* George Orwell used the novel genre to explore social as well as political issues resulting from an oppressive world where leadership's lies were mixed with the truth to create double-speak or double-messages. For example, the themes expressed throughout the novel conveyed messages like that "*War is peace. Freedom is slavery. Ignorance is strength*" (Orwell, 2003, p. 91). This new language for sustaining a revisionist historical perspective in the novel spoke to the rationale of revising history in a manner that sustained the cultural conditioning of a lie. The language was used to exploit influence resulting in achieving total control over human nature with the understanding that "*Who controls the past controls the future. Who controls the present controls the past*" (Orwell, 2003, p. 119). Since January 2017, American politics has reflected this Orwellian-like dystopian stance in the use of words that are strategically articulated by people in positions of political power to whitewash the facts in an effort to revise or even create a new history. The example below emphasizes this point.

On March 13, 2017, *New York Times* reporter, Jennifer Steinhauer, wrote a story on a series of twitter messages sent by Iowa State congressional representative Steve King. According to the *New York Times*, he wrote a message that was against the backdrop of an emboldened white nationalist movement in the United States. He wrote, "We can't restore our civilization with somebody else's babies." Indeed, Mr. King was sliding from his typical messages to something far darker. Predictably, his comments were praised by both the white supremacist, David Duke, and *The Daily Stormer*, a neo-Nazi website. (Steinhauer, 2017). This message was not the first time that Congressman King espoused a position that raised concerns about his white supremacy leanings. During a panel discussion on MSNBC on July 18, 2017, King stated,

What have non-whites contributed to civilization... ? This whole 'old white people' business does get a little tired. . . . I'd ask you to go back through history and figure out where are these contributions that have been made by these other categories of people that you are talking about? Where did any other subgroup of people contribute more to civilization . . . than Western civilization itself that's rooted in Western Europe, Eastern Europe and the United States of America, and every place where the footprint of Christianity settled the world? That's all of Western civilization. (Victor, 2016, on-line publication)

The recent presidential elections of 2016 has not so much revealed an ongoing debate concerning the longstanding national divide within the U.S., which is based upon race, gender, class, and religious practices as much as it has resuscitated the mythology of the White Christian Male as the entitled and dominate group ordained to control the direction of socio-economic development within government, education and culture. Since the founding of America, issues of European or white hegemony has influenced the leadership, control and cultural direction of American society leading to the antebellum period, Civil War and Reconstruction Period. One critical problem that has exacerbated this divide has been the lie of racial and gender superiority ordained by European White Males in America.

A lie has many variations, the truth none.

- African Proverb

An Op-Ed contributor of *The Washington Post* was asked by her child why we celebrate President George Washington in American history if he actually owned Black slaves. This question became a catalyst for an editorial where she examined the challenges of white Americans in engaging in truth telling about racism in America. Below is a portion of her article:

The consequences are serious. When we don't talk honestly with white children about racism, they become more likely to disbelieve or discount their peers when they report experiencing racism. "But we're all equal" becomes a rote response that actually blocks white children from recognizing or taking seriously racism when they see it or hear about it...Parents of black and Latino children have long made thoughtful choices about when and how to engage in difficult and nuanced discussions about difference. Studies show that such parents are two to five times more likely than whites to teach their children explicitly about race from very young ages to counter negative social messages and build a strong sense of identity.

Those of us who are not immigrants or Muslim and who are raising white children stand to learn much from parents like these, even as we apply the teachings differently for our particular families.

For example, I've tried to go beyond the abstract "be kind to everyone" to encourage my children to recognize racial meanness and understand that white kids have a particular responsibility to challenge racism. These are necessary skills when the racism emboldened by this administration shows up in the world. (Harvey, 2017, on-line article)

Understanding racism requires that we also recognize that beyond cultural conditioning, new insights from neuroscience and positive psychology have now added to our awareness of its psychological impact. In the book, *Are We Born Racist?* (Marsh, Mendoza-Denton, & Smith, 2010), researched that:

Years before these neuroscience findings, social psychologists had documented the instant (and unfortunate) associations people make toward "out-groups"—those groups they don't consider to be their own. Whether they differ by age, ethnicity, religion, or political party, people favor their own groups over others, and they do so automatically. (Marsh, Mendoza-Denton, & Smith, 2010, pp. 10-11)

What's more, we all have to contend with our culture's influential role in shaping prejudice. Years, even generations, of explicit and implicit cultural messages—gleaned from parents, the media, firsthand experiences, and countless other sources—link particular physical appearances with a host of traits, positive or negative. The roots of these messages can stretch back centuries, as is the case with racism toward people of African descent in the United States and its origins in the age of slavery. Such messages are absorbed, accepted, and perpetuated, often unconsciously, by our culture's members and institutions. That's how prejudices become so widespread and autonomic. (Marsh, Mendoza-Denton, & Smith, 2010, pp. 11-12)

Another example of racism explained from a white perspective occurred during the 1960s when Bill Moyers was a young staffer in the President Lyndon B. Johnson administration. During this engagement, President Johnson shared a candid view of what happens when truth is misused in an effort to sustain the *status quo* of racism.

Yet by the time Johnson became president after the assassination of John F. Kennedy in 1963, he was ready to plow all of his political capital to the passage of the civil rights legislation initiated by his predecessor. By most accounts, the Civil Rights Act of 1964 couldn't have become law when it did had not LBJ personally wheedled, cajoled, and shamed his former colleagues in the House and Senate into voting for it. One of the secrets of his success was the ability to speak the racially insensitive language of his fellow Southerners. He understood them. He understood their reluctance and in some cases downright refusal to tear down the walls of racial segregation. He knew racism from the inside, and he knew well the role the rich and powerful played in promulgating it.

That's the context of one of the most famous statements on race ever attributed to President Johnson, an off-the-cuff observation he made to a young staffer, Bill Moyers, after encountering a display of blatant racism during a political visit to the South. Moyers tells it in the first person: We were in Tennessee. During the motorcade, he spotted some ugly racial epithets scrawled on signs. Late that night in the hotel, when the local dignitaries had finished the last bottles of bourbon and branch water and departed, he started talking about those signs. "I'll tell you what's at the bottom of it," he said. "If you can convince the lowest white man he's better than the best colored man, he won't notice you're picking his pocket. Hell, give him somebody to look down on, and he'll empty his pockets for you." (Moyers, 1988, on-line publication)

The Implications of Racism

Miller and Garran (2008) argued that "race is a social construction, and racism is a very real, multifaceted, historical, and contemporary force" (p. 16). This position is important as the conversation about what race is, and how racism impacts those who are affected by it continues to be an ongoing debate shaped by subjective viewpoints and worldviews. However, a close examination of American history reveals that skin color, physical features, geographical birthplace, and even culture have contributed to how people are not only seen, but educated to see self. Therefore, within this context, racism refers to a distinctive doctrine of hate based upon racial (i.e., color, physical features, hair texture, body build, and ethnicity) differences. White and Cones (1999) provided a definition of racism as it is constructed and operating at three levels. The three levels are Structural Racism, Institutional Racism, and Individual Racism. Table 2 explains some of the ideas operationalized in defining racism.

While attending the 2007 Annual International Convention of the Association of Black Psychologists (ABPsi), I was engaged in a lengthy conversation with the late Dr. Asa Hilliard about my having been invited to present in a panel discussion. The question we were discussing was "Could Black people be reverse racists as a counter argument to communication concerning white supremacy?" This was an important conversation as it was common to hear arguments that Blacks could be just as racist as Whites. As we deliberated on this issue, we both agreed about the distinction of what constitutes individual racism, systemic racism, and institutional racism. From this discussion, we both agreed that the rubric Table 3 below served as guide for my presentation.

The significance of Table 4 is that it provides clarity concerning the impact of racism on the historical cultural, collective identity, socialization process,

Table 2. Defining racism

Racism operates at three levels:	• Structural, • Institutional, and • Individual level
Structural Racism	Structural racism stems from the fact that White people, especially White males, control the political, economic, and legal power bases of society. White power ultimately decides where low-income and moderate-income housing project will be built, where jobs will be located, where urban transportation will be routed, and what policies the federal government will advocate in terms of job training, urban renewal, social services, medical care, and criminal justice.
Institutional Racism	Institutional racism exists where Whites restrict equal access to jobs and promotions, to business and housing loans, and the like. White bankers and mortgage companies can secretly collaborate to redline a neighborhood so that such loans are nearly impossible to obtain. White senior faculty members in predominately White universities (public and private) determine who gets promoted to tenured faculty positions. A young African American teacher in an all-White psychology department places himself at risk if his research area is in African American psychology. His senior colleagues may not consider his area legitimate and may not understand what he is writing about. Indeed, they may consider African American psychology as not the "real study of psychology." Good-old-boys' clubs in the corporate structure determine who will be mentored and guided through the promotional mine fields; Black males are often excluded from such informal insider networks.
Individual Acts	Individual acts of racism, prejudice, and discrimination range along a continuum from mildly annoying frustrations (i.e., microaggressions) to acts of physical violence, maiming and murder directed at Blacks by Whites.

(Source: Adapted from White, J.L. & Cones III, J.H. (1999). *Black man emerging: Facing the past and seizing a future in America.*, pp. 134-139.)

Table 3.

Can Blacks Be Reverse Racists?
African Americans as individuals or as a collective group could exhibit reverse racism, only if they can exhibit all of the actions below. Otherwise, their actions are representative of bias, bigotry and prejudice.
8. A history/record of Behavior/Actions intentionally designed and implemented with success to systematically destroy another's history.
9. A history/record of Behavior/Actions intentionally designed and implement with success to systematically destroy another's culture.
10. A history/record of Behavior/Actions intentionally designed and implemented with success to systematically destroy another's collective identity.
11. A history/record of Behavior/Actions intentionally designed and implemented with success to control the socialization process of another.
12. A history/record of Behavior/Actions intentionally designed and implemented with success to control teaching forms of racial supremacy supporting their intellectual, cultural, ethnic and racial dominance in society.
13. A history/record of Behavior/Actions intentionally designed and implemented with success to maintain power and control over political, economic, and legal actions that lead to the enforced segregation of society.
14. A history/record of Behavior/Actions intentionally designed and implemented with success to maintain power and control over political, economic and legal avenues designed to prevent the accumulation of wealth among other groups in society.

(Source: Dr. Benson George Cooke)

and educational, political, and socio-economic level. Additionally, it helps to remove ambiguity about the power differential between racism and its affects compared to the practice of prejudice, bigotry, and bias.

CONCLUSION

The Need for Generational Healing From the Lies

Psychologically supportive cultural conditioning is necessary to begin to create cure for the impact of generational lies. This approach can provide the necessary healing to provide support for those who are victims of this tragedy or similar ones, or people who see themselves as less than due to the negative stereotype about their race, ethnicity, gender or beliefs need to be especially aware of the psychological impact of both direct and generational trauma as well as the lies concerning these issues. This is especially true for those impacted by lies that they are inferior racially, ethnically or with regards to gender in America. This later issue is one that requires emotional healing strategies that are contextualized with culturally salient interventions that support community, family and individual healing. With regards to African American's who share a historical legacy of institutional victimization to sustain dominance, the deep psychological scar requires first an awareness as a key to establishing mental health (Cooke et al., 2007). Additionally, it is important that emotional healing occurs with the expressed purpose of revealing the lies of black inferiority and white superiority, which perpetuate fear and prompt post-traumatic emotional response to the horrors experienced by black families, neighborhoods or communities and generational trauma.

The Community Healing Network (CHN) in collaboration with The Association of Black Psychologists (ABPsi, 2011)[5], formed a professional partnership designed to help African American's work through the emotional pain and trauma experienced by people of African ancestry in America. The ultimate goal is to free ourselves, our children, and the world from the lies (and myths) of Black inferiority that is the root cause of the devaluation lives of Black people. It is imperative that we examine the lies that have resulted in individual, institutional and structural forms of racism. The broadcast of lies born out of white supremacy support levels of oppression which perpetuate generational trauma and result in lifelong psychological problems (Patterson, 1998; Eyerman, 2001; Leary, 2005; Horton & Horton, 2006; Akbar, 2003;

Nobles, 2006). Most importantly, we must identify the onslaught of the calculated lies in order that we can effectively engage in developing and implementing healing strategies that will serve to empower our mind and body and increase our capacity to repair multigenerational psychological damage caused by centuries of oppression resulting in the suppression of our optimal self. By accomplishing this important directive, we will be able to create and sustain improved educational systems that support our collective socio-economic growth and to safeguard political governance.

REFERENCES

Ade Ajayi, J. F. (Ed.). (1989). General history of Africa—VI: Africa in the nineteenth century until the 1880s. Berkeley, CA: Heinemann Educational Books and UNESCO University of California Press.

Adu Boahen, A. (Ed.). (1985). General history of Africa—VII: Africa under colonial domination 1880-1935. Berkeley, CA: Heinemann Educational Books and UNESCO University of California Press.

Ajayi, J. F. A. (Ed.). (1989). *General history of Africa VI. Africa in the nineteenth century until the 1880s*. London: UNESCO, Heinemann Educational Books, Ltd.

Akbar, N. (2003). *Akbar papers in African psychology*. Tallahassee, FL: Mind Productions and Associates, Inc.

Baptist, E. E. (2014). *The half has never been told: Slavery and the making of American capitalism*. New York: Basic Books.

Boahen, A. A. (Ed.). (1985). *General history of Africa VII. Africa under colonial domination 1880-1935*. London: UNESCO, Heinemann Educational Books, Ltd.

Bogle, D. (1992). *New expanded edition of toms, coons, mulattoes, mammies, & bucks: An interpretive history of blacks in American films*. New York: A Frederick Ungar Book.

Bräuer, G. (1984). Chapter. In F. Smith & F. Spencer (Eds.), In the origins of modern humans: A world survey of the fossil evidence (pp. 327–410). New York: Alan R. Liss.

Browder, A. T. (1992). *Nile valley contributions to civilization*. Washington, DC: The Institute of Karmic Guidance.

Cann, R. L., Stoneking, M., & Wilson, A. C. (1987). Mitochondrial DNA and human evolution. *Nature*, *325*(6099), 31–36. doi:10.1038/325031a0 PMID:3025745

Cooke, B., Cokley, K., Moon, L., & Webb, S. (2007). spring/summer). Therapeutic cultural competence in theory and practice following hurricane Katrina: Culturally appropriate therapeutic responses to disaster relief. *The Journal of Race and Policy*, *3*(1), 141–165.

Davies, A. (1988). *Infected Christianity: A study of modern racism*. Kingston, Canada: McGill Queens University Press.

Delaney, A., & Scheller, A. (2015). Who gets food stamps? White people, mostly. *Huffington Post—Politics Section*. Retrieved from http://www.huffingtonpost.com/2015/02/28/food-stamp-demographics_n_6771938.html

Diop, C. A. (1991). *Civilization or barbarism: An authentic anthropology*. New York: Lawrence Hill Books.

Eglash, R. (1999). *African fractals: Modern computing and indigenous design*. New Brunswick, NJ: Rutgers University Press.

Elfasi, M. (Ed.). (1988). General history of Africa—III: Africa from the seventh to the eleventh century. Berkeley, CA: Heinemann Educational Books and UNESCO University of California Press.

Eyerman, R. (2001). *Cultural trauma: Slavery and the formation of African American identity*. New York: Cambridge University Press. doi:10.1017/CBO9780511488788

Felder, C. H. (2002). *Race, racism, and the biblical narratives*. Minneapolis, MN: Fortress Press.

Finch, C. S. (1990). *The African background to medical science: Essays on African history, science & civilizations*. London: Karnak House Publishing.

Flynn, A., Holmberg, S., Warren, D., & Wong, F. (Eds.). (2006). Rewrite the racial rules: Building an inclusive American economy. New York: A Roosevelt Institute Report.

Galinsky, A. D., & Moskowitz, G. B. (2000). Perspective-taking: Decreasing stereotype expression, stereotype accessibility, and in-group favoritism. *Journal of Personality and Social Psychology*, *78*(4), 708–724. doi:10.1037/0022-3514.78.4.708 PMID:10794375

Harvey, J. (2017). Are we raising racists? Opinion pages. *New York Times*. Retrieved from https://www.nytimes.com/2017/03/14/opinion/are-we-raising-racists.html?_r=0

Horton, J. O., & Horton, L. E. (2005). *Slavery and the making of America*. New York: Oxford University Press.

Hughes, C. (2014). Implications for future American black women leaders and mentors. In *American Black Women and Interpersonal Leadership Styles*. Boston: SensePublishers. doi:10.1007/978-94-6209-878-7_7

Jackson, J. G. (1972). *Man, god, and civilization*. New York: Kensington Publishing Company.

Jones, B. A., & Nichols, E. J. (2013). *Cultural competence in America's schools: Leadership, engagement and understanding. In Educational policy in the 21st century: Opportunities, challenges and solutions*. Charlotte, NC: Information Age Publishing, Inc.

Kalberg, S. (2004). The past and present influence of world views: Max Weber on a neglected sociological concept. *Journal of Classical Sociology*, *4*(139), 139–163. doi:10.1177/1468795X04043931

Karenga, M. (2006). *MAAT: The moral ideal in ancient Egypt*. Los Angeles, CA: University of Sankore Press.

Ki-Zerbo, J. (Ed.). (1981). General history of Africa—I: Methodology and African prehistory. Berkeley, CA: Heinemann Educational Books and UNESCO University of California Press.

Leary, J. D. (2005). *Post traumatic slave syndrome: America's legacy of enduring injury and healing*. Milwaukie, OR: Uptone Press.

Malcomson, S. L. (2000). *One drop of blood: The American misadventure of race*. New York: Farrar, Straus, and Giroux.

Marsh, J., Mendoza-Denton, R., & Smith, J. A. (Eds.). (2010). *Are we born racist? New insights from neuroscience and positive psychology*. Boston: Beacon Press.

Mazrui, A. A., & Wondji, C. (Eds.). (1993). General history of Africa—VIII: Africa since 1935. Berkeley, CA: Heinemann Educational Books and UNESCO University of California Press.

Mazuri, A. A. (1986). *The Africans: A triple heritage*. Boston: Little, Brown and Company.

Miller, J., & Garran, A. M. (2008). *Racism in the United States: Implications for the helping professions*. Belmont, CA: Thompson Brooks Cole.

Mills, C. W. (2008). Chapter. In Agnotology: The making & unmaking of ignorance. Stanford, CA: Stanford University Press.

Mokhtar, G. (Ed.). (1981). General history of Africa—II: Ancient civilizations of Africa. Berkeley, CA: Heinemann Educational Books and UNESCO University of California Press.

Moyers, B. (1988, November 13). What a real president was like. *The Washington Post*. Retrieved from http://www.snopes.com/lbj-convince-the-lowest-white-man/

Neil, M., & Roychoudhury, A. K. (1974). Genic variation within and between the three major races of man, caucasoids, negroids and mongoloids. *American Journal of Human Genetics*, *26*, 421–443. PMID:4841634

Niane, D. T. (Ed.). (1984). General history of Africa—IV: Africa from the twelfth to the sixteenth Century. Berkeley, CA: Heinemann Educational Books and UNESCO University of California Press.

Nobles, W. W. (2006). *Seeking the sakhu: Foundational writings for an African psychology*. Chicago: Third World Press.

Obenga, T. (2004). *African philosophy: The pharaonic period: 2780-330 BC*. Paris: Per Ankh.

Ogot, B. A. (Ed.). (1992). General history of Africa—V: Africa from the sixteenth to the eighteenth century. Berkeley, CA: Heinemann Educational Books and UNESCO University of California Press.

Orwell, G. (2003). 1984. New York, NY: Houghton Mifflin Harcourt.

Owusu, O. K. (1994). *Origins: Time chart of world civilizations a wholistic worldview of cultures and civilizations*. Baltimore, MD: Cultural Eye Productions.

Painter, N. I. (2010). *The history of white people*. New York, NY: W.W. Norton & Company.

Patterson, O. (1998). *Rituals of blood: Consequences of slavery in two American centuries*. Washington, DC: Civitas Counterpoint.

Peffley, M., Hurwitz, J., & Sniderman, P. M. (1997). Racial stereotypes and whites' political views of blacks in the context of welfare and crime. *American Journal of Political Science, 41*(1), 30-60. Retrieved from http://users.clas.ufl.edu/dcothran/politicalscience/Examples/RacialStereotypes.pdf

Proctor, R. N., & Schiebinger, L. (Eds.). (2008). Agnotology: The making & unmaking of ignorance. Stanford, CA: Stanford University Press.

Rashidi, R., & Van Sertima, I. (Eds.). (1985). African presence in early Asia. New Brunswick, NJ: Transaction Publishers.

Samkange, S. (1971). *African saga: A brief introduction to African history*. New York: Abingdon Press.

Shreeve, J. (2015, October). Mystery man. *National Geographic*, *228*(4), 30–57.

Steinhauer, J. (2017). Steve King, hurling insults at immigrants, is rebuked by his own party. *New York Times—Politics Section*. Retrieved from https://www.nytimes.com/2017/03/13/us/politics/steve-king-babies-civilization.html

Stoneking, M., Sherry, S. T., Redd, A. J., & Vigilant, L. (1993). New approaches to dating suggest a recent age for the human mtDNA ancestor. *Philosophical Transactions of the Royal Society B. Biological Sciences London Series B.*, *337*, 167–175.

Stringer, C. B., & Andrews, P. (1988). Genetic and fossil evidence for the origin of modern humans. *Science*, *239*(4845), 1263–1268. doi:10.1126/science.3125610 PMID:3125610

Tattersall, I. (Ed.). (2009). Human origins: Out of Africa. *Proceedings of the National Academy of Sciences, 106*(38), 16018-16021. http://www.pnas.org/content/106/38/16018.full.pdf

Van Sertima, I. (1976). *The African presence in ancient America: They came before Columbus*. New York: Random House.

Van Sertima, I. (Ed.). (1983). Blacks in science: Ancient and modern. New Brunswick, NJ: Transaction Publishers.

Van Sertima, I. (Ed.). (1988). Black women in antiquity. New Brunswick, NJ: Transaction Publishers.

Van Sertima, I. (Ed.). (1988). Great black leaders: Ancient and Modern. New Brunswick, NJ: Transaction Publishers.

Van Sertima, I. (Ed.). (1989). Egypt revisited. New Brunswick, NJ: Transaction Publishers.

Van Sertima, I. (Ed.). (1992). *Blacks in science: Ancient and modern*. New Brunswick, NJ: Transaction Books.

Van Sertima, I. (Ed.). (1992). The golden age of the Moor. New Brunswick, NJ: Transaction Publishers.

Van Sertima, I. (Ed.). (1992). African presence in early America. New Brunswick, NJ: Transaction Publishers.

Van Sertima, I. (Ed.). (1994). Egypt: Child of Africa. New Brunswick, NJ: Transaction Publishers.

Van Sertima, I. (Ed.). (1998). Early America revisited. New Brunswick, NJ: Transaction Publishers.

Van Sertima, I., & Williams, L. O. (Eds.). (1986). Great African thinkers. New Brunswick, NJ: Transaction Publishers.

Van Sertima, I. (Ed.). (1985). African presence in early Europe. New Brunswick, NJ: Transaction Publications.

Victor, D. (2016). What, congressman Steve King asks, what have nonwhites done for civilization? *New York Times—Politics*. Retrieved from https://www.nytimes.com/2016/07/19/us/politics/steve-king-nonwhite-subgroups.html

West, M., & Miller, A. (1993). Influence of world view on personality, epistemology and choice of profession. In J. Demick & P. Miller (Eds.), *Development in the work place* (pp. 3–19). Malden, MA: Blackwell.

White, J. L., & Cones, J. H. III. (1999). *Black man emerging: Facing the past and seizing a future in America*. New York: W.H. Freeman and Company.

Wolman, B. (Ed.). (1973). Dictionary of behavioral science. New York: Van Nostrand Reinhold.

Wolpoff, M. H., Wu, X., & Thorne, A. G. (1984). Chapter. In F. Smith & F. Spencer (Eds.), In the origins of modern humans: A world survey of the fossil evidence (pp. 411–483). New York: Alan R. Liss.

Zaslavsky, C. (1999). Africa counts: Number and pattern in African cultures (3rd ed.). Chicago: Lawrence Hill Press.

ENDNOTES

1 Black and African American people will be used interchangeably throughout this chapter as representing the same racial/ethnic group.

2 Religism: "the expression of fear towards, hatred towards, or discrimination against, persons of a specific religion affiliation, usually a minority faith." This is a word that is not currently found in printed dictionaries, because they tend to lag public usage of new words by about a generation. Retrieved from http://www.religioustolerance.org/religism.htm

3 Perspective-taking—viewing the world from something other than one's habitual vantage point—covers a broad range from the literal to metaphorical. For example, one can literally take a visual perspective by physically positioning oneself and gazing in a particular direction, often replicating another person's physical position and directional gaze in an attempt to see what that person sees. Alternatively, one can imagine a particular visual perspective or mentally construct a visual or psychological perspective. However, perspective-taking often goes beyond the visual, referring to attempts to adopt an overall mindset that differs from one's default mindset or worldview.

4 Rhode Island delayed ratification of the Fifteenth Amendment to the Constitution until 1870, because legislators feared it might enfranchise members of the Celtic race. Black men had been able to vote there since 1840 (Painter, 2010, p. 107).

5 The Association of Black Psychologists (ABPsi-website: www.abpsi.org). < http://communityhealingnet.com/globalsummit/>.

Chapter 2
An Overview of the Impact of Racial Hate and Its Manifestation of Homegrown Terrorism in America

Benson G. Cooke
University of the District of Columbia, USA

ABSTRACT

Since the 2008 election of the first African American President of the United States, Barack Obama, racial hatred has been on the rise. During the 2016 presidential election, right-wing extremist groups like the Ku Klux Klan and Ultra-Right groups have become more vocal resulting in civil rights organizations like the Southern Poverty Law Center reporting a significant rise in hate crimes and threats. Unfortunately, President Donald Trump helped to stoke the fears of these hate groups with his incendiary campaign rhetoric of hate mostly against immigrants. This chapter provides a historical overview of racial hate and its manifestation of homegrown terrorism in America. Additionally, this chapter examines how hatred and fear became the source of lynching and race riots in America from the 18th to the 21st century. Understanding the past and present history of hatred directed at racial, ethnic and gender groups can help to bring a factual and more truthful point of view that can help reduce the recurrence of homegrown terrorism.

DOI: 10.4018/978-1-5225-3843-1.ch002

I imagine one of the reasons people cling to their hates so stubbornly is because they sense, once hate is gone, they will be forced to deal with pain.

Darkness cannot drive out darkness: only light can do that. Hate cannot drive out hate: only love can do that.

- Dr. Martin Luther King, Jr.

Strange Fruit

Southern trees bear a strange fruit,
Blood on the leaves and blood at the root,
Black body swinging in the Southern breeze,
Strange fruit hanging from the poplar trees.
Pastoral scene of the gallant South,
The bulging eyes and the twisted mouth,
Scent of magnolia sweet and fresh,
And the sudden smell of burning flesh!
Here is a fruit for the crows to pluck,
For the rain to gather, for the wind to suck
For the sun to rot, for the tree to drop,
Here is a strange and bitter crop.

- Lewis Allan

THE LEGACY OF HATE, RACISM, AND HOMEGROWN TERRORISM IN AMERICA

It can be argued that America's greatest sin (Wallis, 2016) was not simply the enslavement of African abductees who became victims of international human trafficking to America as early as 1619, but the very act of racism itself, which existed before kidnapping became a catalyst for the capture, bondage and oppression of African male and female children, youth (King, 2011), and adults brought to America (Horton & Horton, 2005; Horton &

Horton, 2006; Bennett, 1998). Racism allowed for untrue beliefs to become a significant part of an effort by those who subjugated other people to establish hegemony, which demonstrated a need to convey supremacy in domination and authority of power and control. The legacy of racism, hate and homegrown terrorism in America calls for an in-depth examination of the fact that racism preceded and inspired almost four centuries of intense personal and institutional cruelty and brutality throughout both the slave trade, as well as the eradication of Native American Indian populations in pursuit of a European manifest destiny in America.

Before, during and following the Civil War (1861-1865), racism would continue to be the driving psychological and social force used by those invested in sustaining and maintaining systems of oppression and domination through practices designed to confine, and inhibit in particular people of African ancestry. This was accomplished by creating slavery by another moniker – Jim Crow[1]. Jim Crow[2] was an era in American history in which legal and civil rights were denied to African Americans. The price for challenging either local practices/rules/statutes, societal values, states' rights (especially in the South), was to become a victim of assault, personal property destruction, unwarranted incarceration and even death. Historians often refer to the Jim Crow era (Chafe et al., 2001; Packard, 2002) as being worse than slavery (Oshinsky, 1996). During this era, only Constitutional laws and statutes would begin to spell out the protection of specific civil rights of all American citizens. The laws governing the rights of all citizens regardless of race or color to vote was ratified by the U.S. Congress in the 15th Amendment in 1870 (Heffner, 1991, p. 38). The rights of women to vote was approved by the U.S. Congress in the 19th Amendment in 1920 (Heffner, 1991, p. 39). The 24th Amendment to the Constitution in 1964 addressed the ongoing discrimination of rights of African Americans –especially those living in the Southern states– who continued to be denied the right to vote by majority whites during national, state or local elections. Many Southern whites in official positions used of illegal, deceptive, and unfair practices like poll taxes (Heffner, 1991, p. 41) to prevent African Americans from voting. Again, it is important to know that while African Americans were the target of these acts of hate, other groups suffered from similar indignities as well.

During the 19th and 20th centuries, the Supreme Court heard important court cases that would further validate hate and shape the fate of citizenship rights and the moral question of fairness concerning the idea that a nation could impose pseudo-equality by sustaining racial separate but equal laws. Regrettably, the inconvenient truth was that at the heart of fierce legal debates coexisted a racial bias, prejudice, bigotry and structural and institutional racism supporting proslavery. These debates also revealed an economic institution that devalued African Americans and considered them sub-human (Carroll, 2015). For example, one of the first Supreme Court rulings that supported the institution of enslavement is referred to as the Dred Scott Case. In 1857, the *Dred Scott vs. Stanford* case involved an enslaved man born with the name Sam Blow was sold to an Army officer stationed in Illinois, "a state where slavery was prohibited by the Northwest Ordinance of 1787" (Appiah & Gates, 2003, p. 208). When the officer died, he left his property including enslaved Africans to his wife. Mr. Blow (subsequently renamed Dred Scott), sued for his freedom as he resided at that time in a free state. However, the widow of his former slave owner appealed to the Missouri Supreme Court restoring him back as her enslaved servant. The case would eventually reach the U.S. Supreme Court with the argument that "Scott was still a slave and even if he were free, a black descendant of slaves was not entitled to bring suit" (Appiah & Gates, 2003, p. 209). Eventually, on March 6, 1857, "a mostly Southern 7-to-2 majority found that Scott was still a slave" (Appiah & Gates, 2003, p. 209). A major interpretation of this decision rendered by the then Chief Justice Roger Taney was that "…The Constitution never intended blacks—even free blacks in free states—to be citizens" (Appiah & Gates, 2003, p. 209).

Less than 40 years later another Supreme Court case would further buttress the emotion of hate and reinforce the idea of minimizing equal protection under the law for non-dominant races, especially affecting African Americans. This case, 1896 *Plessy vs. Ferguson*, was in direct contradiction of the 14th Amendment, which was established to guarantee equal protection under the law for all citizens. This case allowed for state-imposed racial segregation under the phrase "separate but equal" (Appiah & Gates, 2003, p. 755). In this case, a man named Homer Plessy refused to leave his seat on a New Orleans train in 1892, thereby initiating a legal argument that would become a major Supreme Court challenge to the 14th Amendment.

The court ruled seven to one (one justice did not participate) that Plessy's constitutional rights had not been violated. In a lone but strong dissent, Justice John Marshall Harlan, a Southerner, cited cases in which segregated juries had been found unconstitutional and went on to say in plain language what Plessy's opponents would not admit: that the separate car law not only separated the races but did so to accommodate white racial prejudice. Harlan's words provided prophetic. The "separate but equal" doctrine relegated

African American children to inadequate, unsafe schools, while the South's Jim Crow laws forbade black citizens from exercising their rights as citizens on an equal footing with white citizens. (Appiah & Gates, 2003, p. 756)

Another 60 years would pass before another major Supreme Court ruling impacting attitudes toward hatred that embodied statutory inequalities and the need for the U.S. Constitutional right to equal protection under the law to become true. This case occurred on May 17, 1954 and is known as *Brown vs. The Board of Education*. There were numerous court cases leading up to the Brown vs. Board of Education that would not be hampered by hate, prejudice, bias and bigotry. However, this case is historic because it helped to move the nation closer to establishing justice in civil and human rights struggle for equality. Throughout the Jim Crow era, segregation was an institutional practice and was state sanctioned by earlier Supreme Court rulings like the Dred Scott Case and *Plessy vs. Ferguson*. During the 1950s, a burgeoning civil rights movement began in the South and impacted the educational, economic and political institutions in America. In particular, majority Americans found it increasingly problematic to deny the humanity of a people who continued to make collective sacrifices to the nation's defense in both world wars and other armed conflicts, as well as their significant contributions to national economic, educational and political growth of this nation. This era was also a time when key alliances of faith groups, civil rights organizations, educational institutions, and concerned citizens would unite to support overturning the harsh inequities of 'separate but equal'. For example, through the efforts of the National Association for the Advancement of Colored People (NAACP) lawyers were focused to make a stand against 'separate but equal' policies and practices that denied constitutional rights and equal protection under the law.

One critical argument that helped overturn past Supreme Court rulings would come from an expert educational witness – the noted psychologist, Dr. Kenneth B. Clark. He explained the harmful and negative psychological impact of the nation's imposed racial segregation policies and practices that deprived educational resources to African American students and schools. He helped expose the psychological message of hate that was interwoven within the educational lessons. He revealed a subliminal propaganda with racist overtones that conveyed a negative self-concept concerning black appearance (i.e., racial-colorism). Clark's method for validating the impact of bias, bigotry, prejudice and racism on damaging the self-esteem of African American children was by using a doll study. Simply put, this doll study allowed children (boys and girls), ages 3 through 7 to assign positive or negative characteristics to either a black or white doll. Unfortunately, the African American children overwhelmingly preferred the white doll as more desirable and the black doll as less desirable. This action helped to convey to the Supreme Court the devastating and traumatic impact of racism on self-concept and psyche of African American children, who for centuries had been exposed to unwarranted negative stigmas about their race. This was especially deleterious as it often validated a view of Black Americans as being inferior just because they were Black. Consequently, his doll studies demonstrated that an adverse outcome of hate, prejudice, bias, and bigotry was that Black children more often would display dislike or even hatred toward the doll that looked like them while valuing and liking a doll that looked white.

The opinion, written by Justice Warren and read on May 17, 1954, was short and straightforward. It echoed Marshall's expert witnesses, stating that for African American schoolchildren, segregation "generates a feeling of inferiority as to their status in the community that may affect their hearts and minds in a way unlikely to ever be undone. (Appiah & Gates, 2003, p. 97)

It is important to remember that while the Founding Fathers drafted the Declaration of Independence in 1776, many of them owned enslaved Africans that were transported to America after their capture and kidnapping (Wiencek, 2003; Wilkins, 2001). This recognized fact highlights the hypocrisy of their signature achievement in declaring freedom for some, but not for all. It underscores how our government's identity would continue to be troubled by principles that did not live up to the creed that all men were created equal. Instead, the fact of this nation's beginnings would see enslaved Africans (men, women and children), assigned to a wide range of responsibilities (e.g., toiling on plantations, managing farms, maintaining homes and raising the children), of the founding fathers. While some enslaved African Americans resisted, others willingly gave of themselves in the belief that the promise of freedom to some would one day apply to all. Consequently, being forced to comply as enslaved property, some secretly hoped that their denial of freedom as human beings and citizens would one day be realized. As a result, many willingly fought for the freedom of America to become an independent nation (Berlin, 1998; Bennett, 1998).

Psychologically, public contradictions and political and social incongruences created generations of cognitive dissonance in the mind and soul of both the oppressor and of those oppressed. One of the most glaring contradictions conveyed was the inconsistent rhetorical language expressed in the writing of the Declaration of Independence "...We hold these truths to be self-evident, that all men are created equal, that they are endowed by their Creator with certain unalienable rights, that among these are life, liberty and the pursuit of happiness" (Heffner, 1991, p. 15). Ironically, the document would continue to be both an emotionally depressive reality for victims of oppression as well as a glimmer of hope that one day the noble idea of equality and freedom would extend beyond the concocted barriers of color, gender, and religious practice. However, hate would continue to cloud the guarantee of civil rights and freedom to those held captive to build, feed and clothe the citizens of their newly founded nation. Instead, it would require more than a century of struggle, a Civil War and numerous state and federal legal debates to address the inequities that sustained discrimination and injustice for groups devalued by color, gender or religious practice. It would take more than three hundred years of nationwide protests, marches and legal interventions, hate crimes and homegrown terrorism before socio-economic, educational and political systems would address the influence of hate. Racism driven by a hate directed at African Americans would become the cornerstone of personal and institutional practices of hatred carried out throughout American culture. Hatred that became reflected in the greater societies acquiesce to both hate and white supremacy would continue to sustain America's greatest sin. Thus, hate would become the arbiter of terrorism against people perceived as less than human. Hate would fuel the century's long period of lynching, race riots, and discrimination. This, in turn, would fuel political, educational and economic oppression, the internalization of beliefs supporting the psychological objectification, dehumanization, marginalization, humiliation, disrespect, rejection, nullification, degradation, and stereotype of people. In addition to hate, fear clouded the prospects for lifting the scourge of oppression. Fear and hate may have influenced Thomas Jefferson in his correspondence to George Washington. He stated, "We have the wolf by the ear: and we can neither hold him, nor safely let him go. Justice is in one scale, and self-preservation in the other" (Wiencek, 2003, p. 358). Like many other slave owners, it is likely that their expressed hatred of their enslaved captive was driven by an unconscious fear that emancipation of enslaved Africans would ensure the wrath of freed Africans who suffered immensely throughout their captivity in America. Thomas Jefferson would go on to write:

It will probably be asked, Why not retain and incorporate the blacks into the state, and thus save the expense of supplying, by importation of white settlers, the vacancies they will leave? Deep rooted prejudices entertained by the whites; ten thousand recollections, by the blacks, of the injuries they have sustained; new provocations; the real distinctions which nature has made; and many other circumstances, will divide us into parties, and produce convulsions, which will probably never end but in the extermination of the one or the other race.—To these objections, which are political, may be added others, which are physical and moral. (Wiencek, 2003, p. 359)

In other words, Jefferson is explaining that the object of hate – enslaved Africans – must be controlled and restricted by exerting educational, political and economic prejudice and bigotry or else the fear is that the person who is hated will one day take over and destroy the one who hates. This reasoning might help explain why homegrown terrorism became an extension of the personal hatred, racial prejudice, and bigotry stoked by the fear of reprisals.

THE SEEDS OF HOMEGROWN TERRORISM IN AMERICA

In order to maintain dominance, whites needed more than the statutes and signs that specified "whites" and "blacks" only; they had to assert and reiterate black inferiority with every word and gesture, in every aspect of both public and private life. Noted theologian Howard Thurman dissected the "anatomy" of segregation with chilling precision in his classic 1965 book, The Luminous Darkness. A white supremacist society must not only "array all the forces of legislation and law enforcement," he wrote; "it must falsify the facts of history, tamper with the insights of religion and religious doctrine, editorialize and slant news and the printed word. On top of that it must keep separate schools, separate churches, separate graveyards, and separate public accommodations—all this in order to freeze the place of the Negro in society and guarantee his basic immobility." Yet this was "but a partial indication of the high estimate" that the white South placed upon African Americans. "Once again, to state it categorically," Thurman concludes, "the measure of a man's estimate of your strength is the kind of weapons he feels that he must use in order to hold you fast in a prescribed place." (Chafe, Gavins, & Korstad, 2001, p. 1)

From 1619 through the Civil War (1861-1865), the changes that were taking place through Reconstruction (1865-1877), and Jim Crow (1870s-1960s) produced a fear that some whites felt warranted an application of more extreme measures to sustain power, control and authority, while upholding white privilege steeped in hatred. As indicated above, one outcome of this combination of feelings, beliefs and values would be homegrown terrorism in America.

The concept of terrorism is has more than one definition. In fact there are hundreds of definitions of terrorism (Schmid, 2011). According to Webster's 11th Edition Dictionary *Terrorism* is defined as:

The systematic use of terror esp. as a means of coercion (Webster, 2007, p. 1290). According to the 11th Edition Revised of the Concise Oxford English Dictionary *Terrorism* is defined as: The unofficial or unauthorized use of violence and intimidation in the pursuit of political aims (Oxford, 2008, p. 1489).

Milestones for homegrown terrorism in America appear to be outgrowths of bigotry, prejudice and bias against a people who were deemed less than human because of their ethnic, cultural, and racial designation. This resultant racism would, in turn, become foundational to the reign of terror symbolized by groups like the Ku Klux Klan (KKK) formed in 1865. The psychological and social impact of homegrown terrorism as well as other racial hate groups in America has engendered a foundation of fear, anger, mistrust, suspicion, uncertainty about the future, and an idea that opportunities for economic and educational advancement will somehow be suppressed for one group over another. Often without evidence to support attitudes and viewpoints, people have been intimidated, beaten, and killed, while whole communities destroyed. While racial differences were more often easy to identify dissimilarities on a personal level, in time differences in worship, language, customs, traditions, and beliefs would add to the rise of homegrown terrorism and racial hate groups.

Homegrown Terrorism Milestones: The Thoughts and Symbols of the Confederacy

The justification of States Rights was just one of the reasons used by the advocates of the Southern states' decision to cede from the Union resulting in America's Civil War. Another more accurate justification was the idea of sustaining the enslavement of Africans to maintain the economic and political viability of the southern economy. Consequently, it is not uncommon to hear politicians and TV/Radio pundits support the idea of the Civil War having been a justifiable struggle to sustain States Rights. An iconic symbol of South's secession from the United States of America to form the Confederate States of America is the Confederate Flag. For some it represents the heritage of the South prior and during the Civil War. For others, it represents the rebellion of 13 southern states in an effort to sustain their states' rights that included the enslavement of African Americans. As an iconic symbol of rebellion and states rights' some southerners use this iconic symbol to validate their belief in pre-civil war values that include white supremacy. Consequently, for many the debate against displaying this iconic symbol of the old confederacy (i.e., the Confederate (battle) flag[3], statues and historic landmarks associated with the confederacy, is considered just being politically correct and ignoring southern heritage. The idea of Southern heritage goes hand-in-hand with this nostalgic symbol as it is an important place to begin this conversation by examining what the term heritage means. According to Webster's Dictionary (2010), *heritage* means:

1: property that descends to an heir; 2. a: *something transmitted by or acquired from a predecessor* : legacy, inheritance *b* : tradition *3*: *something possessed as a result of one's natural situation or birth* : birthright *<the nation's heritage of tolerance>. (Webster, 2010, p. 582)*

Within this context, we might understand heritage as valued cultural traditions, historic landmarks and man-made creations which are passed down from previous generations to the next. This notion of establishing the Confederate's heritage is best analyzed by reviewing its bedrock document, the *Constitution of the Confederate States*, which was signed on March 11, 1861. This document provides clarity about the goals and objectives of those states who decided to succeed from the Union. It clarifies their view and values of each other and those of the enslaved populations they owned. It is a reality which cannot be separated by romantic Hollywood productions (e.g., *Gone with the Wind, North and South*), reenactments of Civil War battles, statutes of Confederate soldiers or numerous military installations named after Confederate generals who enslaved Africans To understand why some hold onto this symbol, one must understand what elements transferred power and meaning to the symbol. There is no better place to start than the *Constitution*. Highlighted below are sentences which provide some clarification about issues of race and (legalized) white privilege.

CONSTITUTION OF THE CONFEDERATE STATES: MARCH 11, 1861*

Article IV

Section I. (I) Full faith and credit shall be given in each State to the public acts, records, and judicial proceedings of every other State; and the Congress may, by general laws, prescribe the manner in which such acts, records, and proceedings shall be proved, and the effect thereof.

Section. 2. (I) The citizens of each State shall be entitled to all the privileges and immunities of citizens in the several States; and shall have the right of transit and sojourn in any State of this Confederacy, with their slaves and other property; and the right of property in said slaves shall not be thereby impaired.

(3) No slave or other person held to service or labor in any State or Territory of the Confederate States, under the laws thereof, escaping or lawfully carried into another, shall, in consequence of any law or regulation therein, be discharged from such service or labor; but shall be delivered up on claim of the party to whom such slave belongs, or to whom such service or labor may be due to the Constitution of the Confederate States (1861).

While contemporary conversations suggest that the southern values of the Civil War heritage and related southern traditions are linked to "States Rights"; in reality economic pressures imposed by a mostly northern Congress created an economic challenge to the continued enslavement of African people in America. Unwilling to forge another path for economic prosperity that did not consider ending African enslavement, the Southern state governments decided that it was in their best interest to succeed from the Union and eventually triggering the Civil War.

It is important to remember that the South's perspective of the enslaved African people was a view which justified their personal beliefs and values as well as their religious interpretation on the nature of white citizens juxtaposed to those of African descent. This can be best summed up by Alexander H. Stephens, the Vice President of the Confederacy who in Savannah, Georgia on March 21, 1861 shared the South's values and ideas which would be the foundational to Southern traditions and heritage. Below are selected excerpts from his speech:

Corner Stone Speech

... The new constitution has put at rest, forever, all the agitating questions relating to our peculiar institution African slavery as it exists amongst us the proper status of the Negro in our form of civilization.

...Our new government is founded upon exactly the opposite idea; its foundations are laid, its cornerstone rests, upon the great truth that the negro is not equal to the white man; that slavery subordination to the superior race is his natural and normal condition. .... They were attempting to make things equal which the Creator had made unequal.

... Our system commits no such violation of nature's laws. With us, all of the white race, however high or low, rich or poor, are equal in the eye of the law. Not so with the negro. Subordination is his place. He, by nature, or by the curse against Canaan, is fitted for that condition which he occupies in our system.

... The substratum of our society is made of the material fitted by nature for it, and by experience we know that it is best, not only for the superior, but for the inferior race, that it should be so. It is, indeed, in conformity with the ordinance of the Creator. (Stephens, 1861)

This speech and the Confederate Constitution it refers to clearly cements the notion supported by political and military symbols glorifying the Confederate South as being, "...in conformity with the ordinance of the Creator", based as Vice-President Stephens stated, "...upon the great truth that the negro is not equal to the white man; that slavery subordination to the superior race is his natural and normal condition."

Given this historical fact about the value and heritage of the South during the period of the Confederate States, it is clear that it is impossible to separate the sediment from the belief's that became foundational to their views, practices and institutional practices supporting slavery. Therefore, when:

Many contemporary Southern whites state that they reject the notion that the flag is inherently racist. Rather it is a long-cherished symbol of their heritage and an expression of a distinctive Southern identity. They either are completely unaware, ill-informed or just do not care to be honest about the Constitution, or the symbols which reinforced the ideas transmitted by the founding fathers of the Confederacy.

The senior South Carolina Senator and 2016 presidential candidate, stated that…"This is part of who we are," and "the flag is simply a symbol of one of the sides that fought bravely in the Civil War,… and little more, even though some people may have used it in a racist way in the past. He too does not fully embrace the fact that if the Confederacy had won the Civil War, it was their clearly stated intention that enslaved Africans would continue to be perceived as nothing more than "soul-less" property with an inferior status to the white population.

Furthermore, the U.S. Supreme Court recently weighed in on the subject of the offensive nature of the symbol of the Confederate Flag by supporting the State of Texas.

On June 18, 2015, The U.S. Supreme Court case Walker v. Texas Division, Sons of Confederate Veterans, Inc. decided that the State of Texas had a right to refuse to print a specialty license plate bearing the much-loved and hated Confederate battle flag (Epps, 2015).

Opinion of the Supreme Court. The relevant statute says that the Board "may refuse to create a new specialty license plate" for a number of reasons, for example "if the design might be offensive to any member of the public . . . or for any other reason established by rule" October 2014—The Supreme Court Decision. No. 14–144Tex. Transp. Code Ann. §504.801(c), Section B (2014, p. 3).

In 2010 . . . The Board explained that it had found "it necessary to deny th[e] plate design application, specifically the confederate flag portion of the design, because public comments ha[d] shown that many members of the general public find the design offensive, and because such comments are reasonable." App. 64. The Board added "that a significant portion of the public associate the confederate flag with organizations advocating expressions of hate directed toward people or groups that is demeaning to those people or groups." Id., at 65 (p. 4). (Supreme Court Decision, 2014)

Both the State of Texas and The Supreme Court agreed that the Confederate Battle Flag is offensive and that "a significant portion of the public associate the Confederate flag with organizations advocating expressions of hate."

Supported by feelings of racial hate that would become combined with interpolations of religious views and socio-historical concepts all contributed to an idea of hegemony supported by manifest destiny to terrorize as a way to control the lives of those seen as inferior to whites (Carroll, 2015).

HOMEGROWN TERRORISM MILESTONES: THE ABBREVIATED HISTORY OF RACE RIOTS AND LYNCHING'S[4] IN AMERICA

The imposition of individual, city and state sanctioned vigilante justice created an era of terror for enslaved African Americans. Fear and punishment became the main instruments used to subdue and control those enslaved in the South. Since the beginning of enslavement in America, there were a few instances of rebellion (called slave rebellions), against slave owners because of their cruelty and inhumanity. The slave rebellions led by Gabriel Processor in Richmond, Virginia in 1800; the plot by Denmark Vesey in Charleston, South Carolina in 1822; and the uprising by Nat Turner in Southampton County, Virginia in 1831 all indicated that enslaved African Americans were willing to overcome the brutality and cruelty of slavery by any means necessary, even if it meant sacrificing their lives. Prior to the American Civil War, an emergent group of Northerners gathered to form organizations that were focused on supporting antislavery. This provoked the inciting of anti-black riots, which began in Philadelphia between 1832 and 1849 (Bennett, 1998, p. 157-160). As the father of the protest movement, Frederick Douglas would help to define the protest for freedom within the Abolitionist Movement, Civil War, Reconstruction, and post-Reconstruction period (Bennett, 1998, p. 160). On August 4, 1857, he would make a speech in which the following was spoken:

The whole history of progress of human liberty, shows that all concessions yet made to her august claims, have been born of earnest struggle…If there is no struggle there is no progress. Those who profess to favor freedom and yet deprecate agitation, are men who want crops without plowing up the g round, they want rain without thunder and lightning. They want the ocean without the awful roar of its many waters. (Bennett, 1998, p. 160)

Unfortunately, the struggle would come from this point forward (i.e., from1863 to contemporary times), take a historical turn that consisted of acts of home grown terrorism designed to strike fear in the hearts of those engaged in the struggle for their Constitutional freedoms and those innocently hoping for progress without coercion, violence and intimidation. Below are some of the documented race riots in America that represent homegrown terrorism.

Hatred also continued to impact social beliefs and interpersonal tolerance as manifested by the establishment of segregated communities/neighborhoods. On December 19, 1910, the City Council of Baltimore approved the first city ordinance designating the boundaries of black and white neighborhoods. This ordinance was followed by similar ones in Dallas, Texas, Greensboro, North Carolina, Louisville, Kentucky, Norfolk, Virginia, Oklahoma City, Oklahoma, Richmond, Virginia, Roanoke, Virginia, and St. Louis, Missouri. The Supreme Court declared the Louisville ordinance to be unconstitutional in 1917. The same was true for many other parts of the country, but it would be after the 1954 Supreme Court decision of Brown vs. The Board of Education that Civil Rights acts would create laws that could overturn these segregation oriented ordinances.

SUMMARY OF LYNCHINGS OF AFRICAN AMERICANS

Historical records from 1882 through the 1960s reveal that thousands of African American men, women and children were unjustifiably lynched presumably and exclusively by white males. The reasons for this savage regularity perpetrated on African Americans were highly suspicious and grossly unwarranted e.g., acting suspiciously, race hatred,; race troubles, improper with white woman, arguing with white man, resisting mob, insulting a white man, testifying against a white man, demanding respect, trying to vote, mistaken identity, vagrancy, and/or voting for wrong party, just to name a few (Bennett, 1998, pp. 443-600).

TIMELINE OF TERRORISM AGAINST AFRICAN AMERICANS IN THE HOMELAND

- **1863: New York City Draft Riots:** Anti-conscription riots started on July 13 and lasted four days, during which hundreds of black Americans were killed or wounded (Bennett, 1998, p. 470).

- **1866 - Memphis Massacre:** On May 1-3, white civilians and police killed forty-six African-Americans and injured many more, burning ninety houses, twelve schools, and four churches in Memphis, Tennessee (Bennett, 1998, p. 478).
    - **Police Massacre:** On July 30th Police in New Orleans stormed a Republican meeting of blacks and whites on July 30, killing more than 40 and wounding more than 150 (Bennett, 1998, p. 478).
    - **Massacre in Louisiana:** The Opelousas Massacre occurred in Louisiana on September 28, in which an estimated 200 to 300 black Americans were killed (Bennett, 1998, p. 478).
    - **Clinton Massacre:** On September 4-6, more than 20 black Americans were killed in a massacre in Clinton, Mississippi (Oshinsky, 1996, pp. 38-39).
- **1873 - Colfax Massacre:** On April 13, 1873 following a Republican Louisiana state election victory, a white mob of Democrats disgruntled with their defeat at the ballot box, descended on the court house where Blacks had gathered and massacred approximately 150+ African Americans. Approximately 3 whites were killed during the massacre (Keith, 2008).
- **1876 - Race Riots and Terrorism:** A July summer of race riots and terrorism directed at blacks occurred in South Carolina. President Grant sent federal troops to restore order (Bennett, 1998, p. 499).
    - **Terrorism:** September 15th -20th, White Terrorist attached Republicans in Ellenton, South Carolina. Two whites and thirty-nine blacks were killed (Bennett, 1998, p. 499).
- **1883 - A Political Coup and a Race Riot:** On November 3, white conservatives in Danville, Virginia, seized control of the local government, racially integrated and popularly elected, killing four African-Americans in the process (Bennett, 1998, p. 503).
- **1886 - The Carrollton Massacre:** On March 17, 20 black Americans were massacred at Carrollton, Mississippi (Bennett, 1998, p. 504).
- **1895 - A Race Riot:** Whites attacked black workers in New Orleans on March 11-12. Six blacks were killed (Bennett, 1998, p. 508).
- **1898 - A Race Riot:** On November 10, in Wilmington, North Carolina, eight black Americans were killed during white rioting (Bennett, 1998, p. 511).

- **1906 - Soldier's Riot:** In Brownsville, Texas on August 13, black troops rioted against segregation. On November 6, President Theodore Roosevelt discharged three companies of black soldiers involved in the riot (Burns, 2009, pp. 136-137).
    - **A Race Riot:** On September 22-24, in a race riot in Atlanta, ten blacks and two whites were killed (Burns, 2009, pp. 7).
- **1908 - A Race Riot:** Many were killed and wounded in a race riot on August 14-19, in Abraham Lincoln's home town of Springfield, Illinois (Barnes, 2008, pp. 50-52).
- **1917 - A Race Riot:** One of the bloodiest race riots in the nation's history took place in East St. Louis, Illinois, on July 1-3. A Congressional committee reported that 40 to 200 people were killed, hundreds more injured, and 6,000 driven from their homes (Barnes, 2008, pp. 124-127).
    - **A Race Riot:** On August 23, a riot erupted in Houston between black soldiers and white citizens; 2 blacks and 11 whites were killed. 18 black soldiers were hanged for participation in the riot (Barnes, 2008, pp. 197-199).
- **1918 - A Race Riot:** On July 25-28, a race riot occurred in Chester, Pennsylvania. 3 blacks and 2 whites were killed (Barnes, 2008, p. 217).
    - **A Race Riot:** On July 26-29, a race riot occurred in Philadelphia, Pennsylvania. 3 blacks and 1 white were killed (Barnes, 2008, pp. 10-11).
- **1919 - Red Summer:** This was the year of the "Red Summer," with 26 race riots between the months of April and October. These included disturbances in the following areas (McWhirter, 2011):
    - May 10 Charleston, South Carolina.
    - July 13 Gregg and Longview counties, Texas.
    - July 19-23 Washington, D. C.
    - July 27 Chicago.
    - October 1-3 Elaine, Arkansas.
- **1921 - A Race Riot:** On May 31-June 1, in a race riot in Tulsa, Oklahoma, 21 whites and 60 blacks were killed. The violence destroyed a thriving African American neighborhood and business district (Ellsworth, 1982 pp. 45-70; Johnson, 1998, pp. 27-80).
- **1922 - An Anti-Lynching Effort:** On December 4, a federal anti-lynching bill was killed by a filibuster in the United States Senate (Packard, 2002, pp. 219-221).

- **1955:** Fourteen-year-old Emmett Till was visiting relatives in Money, Mississippi, on August 24, 1955, when he reportedly flirted with a white cashier at a grocery store. Four days later, two white men kidnapped Till, beat him and shot him in the head. The men were tried for murder, but an all-white, male jury acquitted them. Till's murder and open casket funeral galvanized the emerging Civil Rights Movement (Metress, 2002; Tyson, 2017).
- **1963:** At 10:22 a.m. on the morning of September 15, 1963, some 200 church members were in the building–many attending Sunday school classes before the start of the 11 am service–when the bomb detonated on the church's east side, spraying mortar and bricks from the front of the church and caving in its interior walls. Most parishioners were able to evacuate the building as it filled with smoke, but the bodies of four young girls (14-year-old Addie Mae Collins, Cynthia Wesley and Carole Robertson and 11-year-old Denise McNair) were found beneath the rubble in a basement restroom. Ten-year-old Sarah Collins, who was also in the restroom at the time of the explosion, lost her right eye, and more than 20 other people were injured in the blast (Bennett, 1998, p. 571)

June 17, 2015—21ST Century Homeland Terrorism: South Carolina Black Church Massacre

The South Carolina church massacre reawakened the deep divisions of racial hate in America. The chilling statements of the homeland terrorist Dylann Storm Roof, to the lone survivor spoke to how hate can distort perceptions and justify crimes against humanity. His statement that, "You all rape women and you're taking over our country…I have to do what I have to do.", exposed his intention, which the surviving grandmother revealed. Her survival along with her five year old granddaughter, occurred as they attempted to play dead while Roof unloaded and reloaded his automatic handgun five times while assassinating nine church members including the pastor. The pastor who welcomed Dylann Storm Roof into the weeknight prayer meeting on June 17, 2015 also served as the state representative in South Carolina.

In the wake of his act of terror, Roof discovered that an elderly women and her five year old granddaughter survived the ordeal as a result of "playing dead". He reportedly asked the elderly woman, *"Did I shoot you?"* When the elderly woman responded "No," Mr. Roof said, "Good, because I need someone to survive…," purportedly allowing her to tell the world what happened (Battiste, Shapiro, & Stone, 2015). The gravity of this terrorist act is that it was not committed by a radicalized or extremist foreign based entity. Instead, it represented an all too familiar domestic brand of terrorism built upon ideals of white supremacy, which many thought might be relegated to the distant American past. However, the fact that it occurred within a nation which considers itself a 21st century post-racial society, and the fact that it occurred within the sanctity of a historic Black church -- Mother Emanuel AME Church in Charleston, South Carolina -- qualifies it as a despicable atrocity of home grown terrorism.

According to information shared by Roof, his act was motivated by racial hatred. Race and the racial tensions born from the American enslavement era (Felder, 2002; Jones, 1971; Wilson, 2004; Ellerbe, 1995; Felder, 1991; Perryman, 1994; Price, 1982) continue to be one of the most sensitive and avoided subjects in this nation. Unfortunately, we, as a nation, have yet to establish a comprehensive national forum to examine these issues as well as offer substantive remedies. What is equally troubling is the fact that this terrorist act was committed by someone who chose not to act anonymously unlike the white supremacist church bombings and church burnings frequently perpetrated in the 19th and 20th centuries (Allen, Als, Lewis, & Litwack, 2000; Ginzburg, 1988; Cameron, 1982; Keith, 2008; McWhirter, 2011; Johnson, 1998; Fast, 1951; Ellsworth, 1982; Barnes, 2009; Burns, 2009). Instead, Mr. Roof executed this fanatical attack after being seated next to the pastor and deceptively seeking fellowship before convincing himself he had to murder every Black person in the church.

This latest act of terrorism acerbates the cumulative emotional trauma of African Americans. The psychological wound inflicted compounds the legacy of cultural mistrust among the African American community towards specific institutions and symbols. The deeply felt emotional responses to this recent tragedy represents the historical legacy of continuous acts of oppression born out of centuries old beliefs that are linked to an ideology of white supremacy and racism, which all too often are committed as acts of terrorism. Thereby, once again providing another reminder that every act of sustained freedom for African Americans was secured only after the sacrifice of life. Thus, while the Post-Civil Rights Era did move some parts of the African American community into increased opportunities and freedoms, homegrown terror has always been around the corner to remind the most successful that there is a cost of life and sense of security for sustained freedom.

Victims of terrorism and racial intimidation face many challenges arising from highly stressful experiences. White Supremacist organizations in the U.S. were established for this purpose and continue to add to their numbers using old and new technology to increase membership. While some organizaitons may choose to act collectively, the indoctrinated senseless acts are committed by one individual are alone like the accused. Mr. Roof appears to have been proselytized to act as a "lone wolf" in preying and murdering innocent African Americans (Lartey, 2015).

Historically, racial tensions in America has a long tradition built upon misinformed (Black, 2012), unscientific (Washington, 2006; Hornblum, 1998; Tucker, 1996; Wyhe, 2004), extremist ideas (Herrnstein & Murray, 1994), beliefs and feelings of intolerance, and racial hatred traditionally resulting in acts of terrorism directed at African American people and their culture (Eyerman, 2001).

The Removal of the Indigenous Native-American Indian Populations

Another chapter of American history that reveals the negative impact of hate is that of the removal of indigenous populations from their native soil. This coupled with the invalidation of treaties by the United States government with more than 500 nations native to the North America. This genocide and mass-removal and displacement of Native Americans through wars and breached treaties represents one of the most tragic episodes of American history. The process of removal included the wholesale eradication and obliteration of traditional culture (e.g., language, customs, dress, traditions, faith practices, and beliefs) were replaced with the indoctrination of white culture. From the Atlantic Ocean to the Gulf of Mexico to the Pacific Ocean, each nation was broken apart as were most of the way of life of the native inhabitants. Many nations were threatened or bribed and tricked into signing treaties to take their land. Countless populations from the 500 nations were victims of racial wars and acts of terrorism that included the 1838 Trail of Tears. This act involved the forced march removal of countless tens of thousands of men, women, and children from their birthplace in the South and along the Southeast to western desert reservations (Josephy, 1994).

The Women's Suffrage Movement in America

The Woman's right to vote in 1917 was not acquired by racial designation or religious affiliation. Instead, women had to protest, march and petition the federal courts and eventually Congress for their right to practice what is now considered as a privilege every citizen enjoys since is born into. However prior to 1917, this was far from the fact. In many ways, the hate that would be placed on the livelihood of people of different races and ethnicities was also exhibited towards any woman who sought their rights of equality and to vote as an American citizen.

As Woodrow Wilson took office in January, demonstrators took up positions outside the White House, holding round-the-clock vigils demanding the vote for women. In spite of the on-going world war, they refused to step aside or muffle their demands... the National Woman's Party aimed to humiliate the president and expose the hypocrisy of "making the world safe for democracy" when there was none at home... as the infamous "Night of Terror," November 14, 1917. Forty-four club-wielding men beat, kicked, dragged and choked their charges, which included at least one 73-year-old woman. Women were lifted into the air and flung to the ground. One was stabbed between the eyes with the broken staff of her banner... Women were dragged by guards twisting their arms and hurled into concrete "punishment cells. . . ." For all the pain, this brutal night may have turned the tide. Less than two weeks later, a court-ordered hearing exposed the beaten women to the world and the judge agreed they had been terrorized for nothing more than exercising their constitutional right to protest. It would take three more years to win the vote, but the courageous women of 1917 had won a new definition of female patriotism. (Bernikow, 2004)

Many women fought for their rights as American citizens, but it was not until Congress passed United States to vote shall not be denied or abridged by the United States or by any States on account of sex" (Heffner, 1991, p. 39). The impact of hatred, prejudice and bias impacted gender over the span of more than 100 years, and courageous women like Susan B. Anthony (1820-1906), Alice Paul (1885-1977), Elizabeth Cady Stanton (1815-1902), Lucy Stone (1818-1893), and Ida B. Wells (1862-1931), helped to make a difference in sustaining rights for women. Given the significant role of women sustaining families, communities and institutions nationwide, the road to equality in respect, equal pay for equal work and leadership is only a matter of time. The international history of women in greater roles of leadership suggests that equality will only grow for women in America.

CONCLUSION

The ultimate tragedy is not the oppression and cruelty by the bad people, but the silence over that by the good people.

- *Dr. Martin Luther King, Jr.*

The psychological impact of sustaining and exhibiting generations of hate, prejudice, bias and bigotry increases unsubstantiated suspicions, anxieties and fears about the cultured productivity of all members of the human family. Left unchecked, interpersonal hatred turned outward against others as anger or rage destroys the constitutional right to life of others; increases the resentment of another's humanity; and can lead to the objectification and annihilation of another's existence. Whereas, internalized hate turns into a suppressed type of anger and rage easily manifesting the unsettling psychological symptoms of a mental illness. As a mental illness, internalized depression can be manifested as depressive illness, or characteristic of symptoms that may include a deficit of moral self-awareness, heightened confusion, and a disorientation of thought, behavior and mood. Consequently, this chapter has demonstrated that the impact of hatred directed towards others is capable of weakening one's capacity to improve their socio-economic standing, their educational growth and their ability to engage in political systems of governance.

The historical legacy of hatred in America is manifest in the attitude, self-concept, self-image and health of those who hate and those who are hated. Throughout history, healthy and well developed societies have invested in building universities, libraries and museums to provide its citizenry with an educational investment of knowledge of one's history, which is designed to provoke a strong sense of belonging and identity. This, in turn, provides group unity that promotes both political and economic empowerment within that society. Therefore, emerging research and opportunities must be afforded to engaging across generations to inform and change the hearts and minds of future generations. As our society embraces factual information that honestly reports and explains the truth about all people, our society can increase respect for the fact that all people have made some significant contribution to civilization. This factual reporting has the potential to create a transformational experience to increase dialog between the racial and gender divide. This factual reporting can also support sustainable pathways for improving an acceptance of the characteristics associated with diversity, while helping eradicate hate crimes that are behaviorally conditioned. Without question, 21th century America is once again at a crossroad, similar to that experienced from the 17th to the 20th century. However, it is imperative that all people look within to find the solutions leading to empowerment and resolve issues to promote emotional emancipation from generational trauma resulting from racial terrorism. Racial equality won't come exclusively from white people condemning the actions of overt racists like Dylann Storm Roof. Nothing will change if we turn a blind eye to the more subtle and pervasive systems of hate, bias, prejudice and bigotry that perpetuate such inequality. A large part of healing involves overturning the lies and acquiring an accurate historical knowledge from which to contextualize the problem. This chapter has provided relevant history and information explaining some of the lies sustaining the ideas supporting white supremacy in creed and symbol. Each person must take responsibility for finding solutions, in order to achieve culturally salient solutions born from knowledge and understanding of fitting strategies, which can optimally sustain current and generational health from acts of oppression and terrorism.

REFERENCES

Allen, J., Als, H., Lewis, C. J., & Litwack, L. F. (2000). *Without sanctuary: Lynching photography in America*. Hong Kong: Twin Palms Publishers.

Appiah, K. A., & Gates, H. L. (Eds.). (2003). *Africana: The encyclopedia of the African and African American experience: The concise desk reference*. Philadelphia, PA: Running Press.

Baldwin, J. (1962). *The fire next time*. New York, NY: Vintage Books.

Barnes, H. (2009). *Never been a time: The 1917 race riot that sparked the civil rights movement*. New York: Walker and Company.

Battiste, N., Shapiro, E., & Stone, M. (2015, June 18). *Charleston shooting: What the gunman allegedly told churchgoers before the shooting*. ABC News.

Bennett, L. (1998). *Before the Mayflower: A history of black America* (6th ed.). New York: Penguin Books.

Berlin, I. (1998). *Many thousands gone: The first two centuries of slavery in North America*. Cambridge, MA: The Belknap Press of Harvard University Press.

Bernikow, L. (2004). Night of terror leads to women's vote in 1917. *We News Covering Women's Issues*. Retrieved from http://womensenews.org/2004/10/night-terror-leads-womens-vote-1917/

Black, E. (2012). *War against the weak: Eugenics and America's campaign to create a master race*. Washington, DC: Dialog Press.

Burns, R. (2009). *Rage in the gate city: The story of the 1906 Atlanta race riot*. Athens, GA: University of Georgia Press.

Cameron, J. (1982). *A time of terror: A survivor's story*. Baltimore, MD: Black Classic Press.

Carroll, C. (2015). *The negro a beast (1900)*. London: Forgotten Books Classic Reprint Series.

Carroll, J. C. (2004). *Slave insurrections in the United States 1800-1865*. Mineola, NY: Dover Publications, Inc.

Chafe, W. H., Gavins, R., & Korstad, R. (Eds.). (2001). *Remembering Jim Crow: African Americans tell about life in the segregated South*. New York, NY: The New Press in Association with Lyndhurst Books of the Center for Documentary Studies of Duke University.

Ellerbe, H. (1995). *The dark side of Christian history*. Orlando, FL: Morningstar and Lark Publishing.

Ellsworth, S. (1982). *Death in a promised land: The Tulsa race riot of 1921*. Baton Rouge: Louisiana State University Press.

Epps, G. (2015). Clarence Thomas takes on a symbol of white supremacy. *The Atlantic*. Retrieved June 18, 2015 from http://www.theatlantic.com/politics/archive/2015/06/ clarence-thomas-confederate-flag/396281/?utm_source=SFTwitter

Eyerman, R. (2001). *Cultural trauma: Slavery and the formation of African American identity*. New York: Cambridge University Press. doi:10.1017/CBO9780511488788

Fast, H. (1951). *Peekskill USA: Inside the infamous 1949 Riots*. Mineola, NY: Dover Publications.

Felder, C. H. (Ed.). (1991). *Stony the road we trod: African American biblical interpretation*. Minneapolis: Fortress Press.

Geldenhuys, O. (1995). Housing segregation: Apartheid in Baltimore. *The Baltimore Sun*. Retrieved from http://articles.baltimoresun.com/1995-03-17/news/1995076191_1_racial-segregation-zoning-ordinance-apartheid

Ginzburg, R. (1988). *100 Years of lynchings*. Baltimore, MD: Black Classic Press.

Heffner, R. D. (1991). *A documentary history of the United States* (5th ed.). New York: Penguin Books.

Herrnstein, R. J., & Murray, C. (1994). *The bell curve: Intelligence and class structure in American life*. New York: The Free Press.

Hornblum, A. M. (1998). *Acres of skin: Human experiments at Holmesburg Prison—A true story of abuse and exploitation in the name of medical science*. New York: Routledge Press.

Horton, J. O., & Horton, L. E. (2005). *Slavery and the making of America*. New York: Oxford University Press.

Horton, J. O., & Horton, L. E. (Eds.). (2006). *Slavery and public history: The tough stuff of American memory*. New York: Oxford University Press.

Johnson, H. B. (1998). *Black wall street: From riot to Renaissance in Tulsa's historic greenwood district*. Austin, TX: Eakin Press.

Jones, C. (1971). *The religious instruction of the negroes in the United States*. Freeport, NY: Books for Libraries Press.

Josephy, A. M. (1994). *500 nations: An illustrated history of North American indians*. New York: Alfred A. Knopf.

Keith, L. (2008). *The Colefax massacre: The untold story of black power, white terror, and the death of reconstruction*. New York: Oxford University Press.

King, W. (2011). *Stolen childhood: Slave youth in Nineteenth-Century America* (2nd ed.). Bloomington, IN: Indiana University Press.

Lartey, J. (2015). *We avoid the word terrorism when the victims are black—not just when the killer is white. The Online Guardian*. Retrieved from http://www.theguardian.com/commentisfree/2015/jun/19/terrorism-victims-black-killer-white

McWhirter, C. (2011). *Red summer: The summer of the 1919 and the awakening of black America*. New York: A John Macrae Book Henry Holt and Company.

Metress, C. (Ed.). (2002). *The lynching of Emmett Till*. Charlottesville, VA: University of Virginia Press.

Oshinsky, D. M. (1996). *Worse than slavery: Parchman farm and the ordeal of Jim Crow justice*. New York: Free Press Publishing.

Packard, J. M. (2002). *American nightmare: The history of Jim Crow*. New York: St. Martin's Press.

Perryman, W. (1992). *The 1993 trial on the curse of Ham: With liberty and justice for all*. Bakersfield, CA: Pneuma Life Publishing.

Price, F. K. C. (2001). *Race, religion & racism: Perverting the gospel to subjugate a people* (Vol. 2). Los Angeles, CA: Faith One Publishing.

Schmid, A. P. (Ed.). (2003). *The Routledge handbook of terrorism research*. London, UK: Routledge.

Southern Historical Society Papers. Vol. XVI. Richmond, VA. January–December 1888.

Stephens, A. (1861, March 21). *Corner stone*. Retrieved from http://teachingamericanhistory.org/library/document/ cornerstone-speech/

Strausbaugh, J. (2006). *Black like you: Blackface, whiteface, insult & imitation in American popular culture*. New York: Penguin Group.

The Supreme Court Decision. No. 14–144. October, 2014. John Walker, III, Chairman, Texas Department of Motor Vehicles Board, et al., Petitioners v. Texas Division, Sons of Confederate Veterans, Inc., et al. On Writ of Certiorari to the United States Court of Appeals for the Fifth Circuit. Justice Breyer Delivered the Opinion of the Court. Retrieved from http://www.supremecourt.gov/opinions/14pdf/14-144_758b.pdf>

Tucker, W. H. (1996). *The science and politics of racial research*. Chicago, IL: University of Illinois Press.

Tyson, T. B. (2017). *The blood of Emmett Till*. New York: Simon & Schuster.

Wallis, J. (2016). *America's original sin: Racism, white privilege, and the bridge to a new America*. Grand Rapids, MI: Brazos Press.

Washington, H. A. (2006). *Medical apartheid: The dark history of medical experimentation on black Americans from colonial times to the present*. New York: Doubleday Press.

Washington, J. M. (Ed.). (1986). *A testament of hope: The essential writings and speeches. Where do we go from here?* San Francisco, CA: Harper Collins Publishers.

Wiencek, H. (2003). *An imperfect God: George Washington, his slaves, and the creation of America*. New York, NY: Farrar, Straus and Giroux Books.

Wilkins, R. (2001). *Jefferson's pillow: The founding fathers and the dilemma of black patriotism*. Boston, MA: Beacon Press.

Wilson, W. F. (2004). *How African religion changed the American church*. Washington, DC: UTBC.

Wyhe, J. V. (2004). *Phrenology and the origins of Victorian scientific naturalism*. Burlington, VT: Ashgate.

Young, K. (Ed.). (2006). *Jazz poems: Everyman's library pocket poets*. New York, NY: Alfred A. Knopf.

ENDNOTES

1 According to Webster's Dictionary 8th Edition, Jim Crow refers to the stereotypical depiction of a Black Male in the 19th century, related mostly to a song and dance act. It later became associated with ethnic discrimination especially against Blacks by legal enforcement or traditional sanctions (Webster, 2007, p. 673). A precursor to the minstrel show by white actors that involved imitating and over-exaggerating Black mannerisms, Jim Crow was a song and dance number done by a white actor in blackface. The goal of White actors in blackface performing song and dance acts in the 19th and 20th century was to overly-exaggerate Black mannerisms in song, speech and dance. According to T.D. Rice, the white man who put on black face to masquerade as a real-life black

man he reportedly watched in Louisville "*...he enjoyed the old man's unself-conscious song-and-dance routine that he just had to adapt it for the stage. The old man's name was Jim Crow*" (Strausbaugh, 2006, p. 58). Consequently, Jim Crow was referred to as a Black man who was a trickster and depicted as a derogatory African American character. Additionally, Jim Crow also drew reference to the black American bird called a crow. The goal was to suggest that darker skin color was an equivalency to stereotyping all Blacks as ignorant, dishonest and slothful. Thus, the Jim Crow era is known for subjugating, objectifying, stereotyping and controlling African Americans (Strausbaugh, 2006).

2 American history is replete of the discriminatory laws that segregated people by race in the American South from the end of the Civil War through passage of the 1965 Civil Rights Act. These were known as the Jim Crow laws. Tischauser, L. V. (2012). See Tischauser, L. V. (2012). *Jim Crow Laws.* Santa Barbara, CA: Greenwood.

3 Savannah newspaperman William T. Thompson, had a different name for it altogether: the "White Man's Flag." Thompson, an outspoken racist, was quoted in his own paper as saying: "As a people we are fighting to maintain the Heaven-ordained supremacy of the white man over the inferior or colored race; a white flag would thus be emblematical of our cause." (Daily Morning News, April 23, 1863) (http://www.rd.com/culture/confederate-flag-facts/)

4 Lynching refers to: "to put to death (as by hanging) by mob action without legal sanction (Webster, 2010, p. 743). Throughout the 18th to 20th century in America lynching became associated with an unauthorized mob gathering intent on punishing the guilty and more often the innocent of alleged crimes without a trial by jury. Lynching also became a method of intimidating African Americans, in particular, to not question white authority in the South (Bennett, 1988).

Chapter 3
Trade's Impact on the Profits and Losses for American Workers

Pamela Hampton-Garland
University of the District of Columbia, USA

ABSTRACT

Trade was a unifying topic for the Republican elected U.S. President Donald Trump in the 2016 election. Many of his supporters believed trade deals like NAFTA had destroyed the quality of life they lived before their manufacturing jobs were sent to Mexico, China and other countries where the jobs could be performed for much lower wages. This chapter will uncover misinformation about trade and the Trump revolutionaries who voted for him. In addition to challenging the assumptions of trades impact on job losses and the campaign promise by candidate Trump to bring those jobs back, this chapter will explore who the voters were, why they voted for Trump and what can be done now to create skilled workers for viable jobs.

INTRODUCTION

The American dream, what is it and is it really in every American's reach? The 2016 election campaign season revealed that many Americans lost faith that the American dream would ever be realized by maintaining the status quo and thusly revolted. Is the American Dream of today as it was when James Truslow Adams coined the phrase in 1931 in his book "The Epic of America"?

DOI: 10.4018/978-1-5225-3843-1.ch003

But there has also been the American dream, a dream of a land in which life should be better and richer and fuller for everyone, with opportunity for each according to ability or achievement. It is a difficult dream for the European upper classes to interpret adequately, and too many of us ourselves have grown weary and mistrustful of it. It is not a dream of motor cars and high wages merely, but a dream of social order in which each man and each woman shall be able to attain to the fullest stature of which they are innately capable, and be recognized by others for what they are, regardless of the fortuitous circumstances of birth or position (Adams, 1931, Pg. 404).

The impact of globalization on America's margins reached its boiling point more than a decade ago. However, hopelessness gave way to hopefulness when among a sea of blue suits, red ties and plausible deniability rhetoric presidential candidates stood a brash and unfiltered candidate who l may have appeared like the others, but unlike the others gave voice to the "forgotten" electorate. Those "forgotten Americans" (Nixon, 1969) started to emerge and become vocal when North America Free Trade Agreement (NAFTA)[1] was signed into law by former President Bill Clinton on December 8, 1993. In just over 10 years the Central America Free Trade Agreement (CAFTA) which is an expansion of NAFTA to five Central American nations (Guatemala, El Salvador, Honduras, Costa Rica and Nicaragua), and the Dominican Republic was signed by President George W. Bush on August 2, 2005. However, President Donald Trump as his first executive order scrapped the most recent trade deal, the Trans Pacific Partnership Agreement (TTPA) the day he entered office on January 23, 2017. His decision was in response to his constituents screams that their jobs were being performed by low wageworkers in foreign countries, or automated machines that made workers obsolete. They believed that something had gone terribly wrong and millions of forgotten Americans (Nixon, 1969) believed the America they knew and loved was slipping away. They worry about their children's future in an America where there are fewer opportunities for hardworking American men and women. Out of the traditions of Republican values Donald Trump emerged as an unlikely candidate who vowed to address their needs. The forgotten Americans were stunned that Donald Trump didn't create multiple innovative excuses and believed his offensive, not politically correct, and non-politicized language was a breath of fresh air. The forgotten Americans' rally cry started out quietly and many political leaders discounted the growing mass of people who were labeled as "uneducated", backwoods, or as "deplorables" (Murdock, 2016).

On September 9, 2016, Secretary Clinton addressed donors and stated "You know, to just be grossly generalistic, you could put half of Trump's supporters into what I call the 'basket of deplorables.' Right?" She went on to say "They're racist, sexist, homophobic, xenophobic, Islamophobic — you name it" (Murdock, 2016). Slowly and with ever increasing momentum their mass protests could no longer be ignored by the global community. The forgotten Americans remained involved in the process and voted in record numbers in the rural parts of the Rust Belt states[2] and the Sun Belt[3]. The forgotten Americans really are not traditionally active participants in the political process, but in 2016, their involvement in the political process was unprecedented (Malone, 2016). Many Trump supporters appeared to believe that a vote for the republican candidate was the best opportunity to return to the America they once knew.

In an effort to understand how this grassroots effort elected what appeared to be a most unorthodox candidate, the world community began to ask questions such as:

1. Who are these forgotten Americans?
2. Why did they rally with and elect a president with zero foreign intelligence, zero understanding of national security, and zero experience in politics and with twitter as his preferred mode of communication?
3. What should America do to respond to their protests?
4. What can those seeking to be heard do to help themselves?
5. Is it too late to "Make America Great Again" from their perspective?
6. If it is possible to "Make America Great Again," what does that mean for the hurdles that many have already jumped over with the goal of equality and making America greater?
7. Finally, is it possible for everyone to reach their perceived level of greatness?

These questions and others are explored in this chapter. This chapter moves fluidly from historical understanding of how international trade became a primary factor in the growth of profits and in the loss of human resources in the United States. It will discuss what industries were impacted most and were the Americans working in these industries blindsided or did they choose to close their eyes to the imminent changes. Why did it take them so long to find their voices and exercise their civic rights? Did the slogan "Make America Great Again" speak to their common dream of regaining their "rightful" place in the America that had slowly chipped away their superiority since Jim Crow? What did they hear in candidate Trump that said this is our guy, he had heard our cries and he will be our candidate. This chapter explores the realities of those who believed they lost their position and power in a nation where thriving was possible if you worked hard. Finally, I address the real question, "Did they really cast a vote for jobs or was it to retrieve the cherished power and privilege that slipped out of their hands in the dark of night?

BRIEF HISTORY OF TRADE IN NORTH AMERICA

Similar to many nations who experienced a significant break from the *status quo*, the U.S. revolt of 2016 started decades before the election of an unconventional president. This era of change in the approach to trade began in 1984, when the Canada-U.S. Free Trade Agreement (CUSFTA) was signed in 1988 ("Canada-U.S. Free Trade Agreement," 2017). Prior to this first Free Trade Agreement (FTA), the U.S. Congress voted and approved the Reciprocal Trade Agreements Act of 1934 ("Reciprocal Trade Agreement Act of 1934 | US House of Representatives: History, Art & Archives," n.d.) that allowed tariffs to be negotiated and approved by the President without intervention from Congress. At this time, trade consists of bilateral agreements with foreign nations. After the Second World War, the need for economic renewal sparked the first multilateral trade negotiation, which led to the General Agreement on Tariffs and Trade (GATT) (General Agreement on Tariffs and Trade, 1986). The result of these negotiations was reduced tariffs on eligible imports. Under GATT, tariffs were reduced from the 60% on imports implemented under the Smoot-Hawley Tariff Act of 1930[4] to a tender 5.7% in 1980. This was very significant when presidential candidate Donald Trump ran on a platform that included taxing Chinese imports (Applebaum, 2016). Understanding the move from the tariff based trade agreements to the FTA's will bring clarity to the decision to lift the taxes.

In the early 1980s, trade expansion was central to broader U.S. foreign policy during the Cold War[5]. The trade alliances provided all participants with unified militaries, improved economic benefits, in addition to binding together the major free-market democracies. The improved prosperity of the trade partners served as an effective counter to the centrally planned economies of the People's Republic of China and the Communist Bloc (i.e., Czechoslovakia, Soviet Union, Bulgaria, Romania, East Germany, Poland, Hungary and Albania) during the Cold War.

In 1984, Congress approved the negotiation of free trade agreement with Canada, which would make it the U.S. largest trading partner. The agreement was completed in 1988. At that time, Mexico requested an opportunity to become a trade partner with the U.S. Therefore, rather than drafting a new agreement, the Canada/United States agreement became the infamous North America Free Trade Agreement. NAFTA has been one of the most controversial trade agreements and is blamed for many blue collar job losses in the U.S. This agreement was controversial from its signing, particularly with the addition of Mexico. Forbes magazine contributor Robert Bowman (2014) wrote an article titled "A Growing Hostility toward Free Trade has put NAFTA on Life Support"; the article points out the ever increasing hatred of the agreement by many Americans. Many believed that because Mexico's labor cost was significantly cheaper than that of U.S. workers, companies rapidly began to relocate their manufacturing plants to Mexico to benefit from the lower cost of production.

ADVOCATES AND PUNDITS

The argument from the political and economic lens was that the U.S. would significantly benefit from lower priced goods that would keep more money in American workers' pockets (i.e., disposable income). Additionally, economists, politicians and employers who were in favor of NAFTA boasted about increased opportunities afforded to American workers in the forms of technology and services (Faux, 2016). The newly created jobs would pay higher wages as well as position the U.S. in an advantageous position to negotiate in other international agreements. The final rationale from the government was the value of creating additional allies that would support each other during international crises. These promises were realized in the form of goods that cost much less, new jobs in the technology and service sectors, increased pay for the technology and service jobs based on the position and certainly leverage with future trade negotiations (Worstall, 2016).

However, the stance of the people remained job security, as they realized that the benefits of the trade agreements were not available to everyone, and their concerns were realized throughout the 1990s with millions of low skilled jobs leaving the U.S. and jobs requiring higher education taking their place. *The Big Squeeze: Tough Times for the American Worker* by Steven Greenhouse (2008) uncovered many experiences of American workers in the manufacturing sectors across the nation who woke up on any given day, drove to their plant or factory to begin their day only to see the doors locked or to be informed that their jobs have been outsourced. For example he writes about one such worker at the Maytag plant in Galesburg, Illinois who along with 1600 of his coworkers, were shocked October 19, 2002 when they arrived at work and during their morning meeting were informed that they could go home, the plant was closed as of that moment (Greenhouse, 2008, p. 201). They were informed that their jobs had been farmed to Daewoo, South Korea and Reynosa, Mexico (Greenhouse, 2008, p.201). From the 2000 to 2014 more than 5 million American manufacturing workers went to bed with jobs that allowed them to enjoy a decent quality of life and woke the next day hoping the unemployment benefits would last until they found another job (Scott, 2015, p. 2).

AN ELECTION OF RECKONING

The Iron Law of Oligarchy, a political theory developed by Robert Michel stated, "In any organization or society, elite will eventually and inevitably emerge independently of democratic election. The theory holds that as businesses grow, so does power, and as power grows, so does corruption" (1911, p 253). Many of America's elites believed that President Trump has initiated an oligarchical state. From the perspective of his supporters, the U.S. had become an oligarchy where the elite ruled in favor of themselves and with zero consideration for others (e.g., forgotten Americans). Robert Michels (1911) based his socio-political theory on the supposed abuse by trade unions and socialist political parties of the early 20th century. He noted that European political parties of the time began to increase the complexity of the organization over time requiring a specialized elite (or bureaucracy). This bureaucracy was charged with curtailing ordinary member participation in decision-making. This may mirror the first few months of the Trump Administration and his family involvement in the day-to-day business of the country. It is important to note that Michels (1911) was a fervent supporter of Mussolini's fascist regime[6] in Italy. It is critical to understand the relevance of this theory as it relates to the United States in the 21st century and the election of Donald Trump as the 45th president of the United States of America, the most progressive, revered and hated country in the world. Moreover, The Iron Law of Oligarchy (Michels, 1911) expresses a deeply pessimistic viewpoint that progressive social movements inevitably become less democratic and dominated by a conservative élite. The theory has had its most influence on the analysis of trade unions and is associated with the view that unions are controlled by an unaccountable bureaucracy.

In some ways, the new world we have entered is not as novel as it looks. In reducing its global role, the U.S. is returning to the more historical position it held in the 19th century as one of several super powers. Donald Trump's domestic agenda may also result to be more familiar than most expect. The family-influenced transition group that is assembling the new regime suggests an attempt to found a new dynasty to replace the ones he has overthrown. An iron law of oligarchy may already have begun to operate, allowing a new ruling group to re-divide the spoils of office. Like most oligarchs, Trump was elected according to the laws of our democracy. However, what we must remain a part of the political process and fight against any decisions or executive orders that threaten our democracy. We must ask the important question, "Why did the *status quo* Washington Republicans and Democrats lose in favor of a man often referred to as narcissist; as defined by the DSM-IV "a disorder in which a person has an inflated sense of self-importance" (American Psychiatric Association, 2012). Before we self-righteously label this revolution as the rise of an oligarchy, let's determine how we arrived at this place in our history.

HURRICANE KATRINA A WHIRL WIND ANALOGY

The loss of low skilled and assembly line manufacturing jobs hit the U.S. like Hurricane Katrina hit New Orleans (NOLA) in 2005. It ravaged the city's most vulnerable citizens – poor, old, sick and black -- and the powers that could have minimized the losses helplessly watched. The loss was so great that the citizens could not recover; they swooped in and took the spoils (Cokley, Cooke, & Nobles, 2005). Like Katrina, there were warnings, notifications, news reports advisories, and an early warning of the impending storm, but without options of what to do and a lack of resources, exactly how could a warning help? Did NOLA residents really have time to vacate when the "early" warnings were broadcast that the storm was nearing the Bahamas Islands on August 23, 2005? Let's assume they heeded the warnings, where would the poorest of the poor go and how? With a 6 day notice the marginalized of NOLA lived life for the present day, not fully award of the impact that would befall them on August 29, 2005? But did the storm have to have such a grave impact? What about the years' prior when the U.S. Army Corp of Engineers were to build levees (Warrick & Whoriskey, 2006) in the event of such an event? Why weren't built? Was it because of cost savings that warranted top-of-the-line materials and no prior catastrophic events? Who lost and who won as a result of Katrina? More than 1,800 marginalized Americans loss their lives to a storm that was inevitable. But, did this tragedy have to happen? Many more citizens were forced to move out of their homes as well as their state with minimal options to return. On the other hand, the beneficiaries were business owners, and wealthy citizens who made NOLA one of the most expensive cities to visit and live.

The Awareness Divide

Let's think about this situation in a globalized world. Yes, we have had trade agreements since the 40s, but in the late 80s the U.S. enacted its first Free Trade Agreement (NAFTA). Consequently, we witnessed many jobs relocate to Mexico (Faux, 2016). At that time, we constantly heard that education was important for Americans in order to compete in a global world (Fleet & Winthrop, 2010). Access to information was limited to a few local television channels, unless you had money to pay for the newly emerging world of cable television. The "Digital Divide" or the limited access of some communities to the world wide web, hindered many rural and urban low income families from accessing and/or using the Internet, engaging with advances in technology, and recognizing the reach of technological innovation (West & Karsten, 2016).

Like Katrina, when outsourcing became evident to most workers it was too late to change the devastating effects. It was not until their plants, factories, distribution centers, and call centers closed their doors that these workers realized their lives could be forever changed. To reiterate, like those who lost their lives to Katrina what could they do when their factories were prospering, the work was rolling in, and when others factories closed it was because they were not as good, surely they did not imagine becoming displaced workers[7]. The boss man was smiling and friendly and the workers clocked in and out, until they came to clock in and chained fences prevented them from entering the parking lot or building. When should they have gotten other jobs? Where should they have gotten another job? What year should they have returned to school? What should they have majored in when they returned? These questions need to be answered with real tangible answers, not in abstract forms such as "they had been warned for years that changes were coming". That did not work for the experts responsible for the levies.

Billions of Americans had worked in these factories for decades and were happy with the feeling of providing daily bread to their loved ones. Therefore, in light of the fact that they had a good job, good pay and benefits. Surely tobacco, furniture manufacturing and fabric weaving, and agriculture would always be in demand.

TRUE AMERICAN VALUE

The U.S. has been a strong proponent of trade and through negotiations the United States has often emerged as the primary beneficiary of the agreements. It is important to understand that it has been the U.S. that has benefitted, not the American people. Oftentimes Americans are only aware of the impact of national trade agreements after the documents have been signed and their pocketbooks feel lighter. Again, it is first imperative that there is zero confusion about who the true beneficiaries are and what they value; it is not those of us who roll up our sleeves every day and earn a paycheck, it is indeed those who own the auto manufacturers, real estate moguls, oil refineries, Wall Street bankers, and others. If we have to work every day for a paycheck you and I have not "arrived", we are not "balling", and we are at the mercy of those who sign our paychecks. This is critical because politicians and groups like the American Legislative Exchange Council (ALEC)[8] are the puppeteers and their goals are simple to "continue to develop and create laws that benefit Americans. Really it does not matter who is in office, because America moves with money; not money given to workers but money that makes investors (i.e., true stockholders) and owners more money. So, what does that mean for the revolutionaries for Trump? What does it mean to the nearly 50% of the U.S. population that lives below the poverty line or those working in service industries, temporary or seasonal jobs and other low skill low wage positions (Bureau of Labor Statistics, 2016)? Where did the security of former decades go, where hard work opened the door to a home for the family, a cookout on Memorial Day, 4th of July and Labor Day and a nice Family Thanksgiving with a few presents at Christmas? Abraham Maslow's hierarchy of needs include as its lowest level of basic needs are physiological (food, rest, water, warmth, etc.) and safety needs (safety and security) and these Americans lost both of these critical needs which challenge their hope in the possibility of pursuit of self-actualization (McLeod, 2016), and many wonder why there was a revolt.

WHO ARE THE TRUMP REVOLUTIONARIES?

What is a revolution and why do I label this movement as such? Samuel Huntington defines revolution as "a rapid, fundamental, and violent domestic change in the dominant values and myths of a society, in its political institutions, social structure, leadership, and government activity and policies. Revolutions are thus to be distinguished from insurrections, rebellions, revolts, coups, and wars of independence (Huntington, 1968, p. 264). Moreover, revolutions are often presented as monumental, foundational political events that happen only rarely and historically e.g., the American Revolution (1776), French revolution (1789), Russian revolution (1917), Chinese revolution (1949), Cuban revolution (1959), Iranian revolution (1979), and others. How do revolutions occur? Most revolutions do not begin the day you witness the uprising. Usually, they have often been brewing for quite some time. Many revolutions or protests are instigated by a single event. Some notable examples are Trayvon Martin's[9] senseless murder, Rosa Park's refusal to give up her seat, four students from North Carolina A & T refusing to leave a store without service, and most recently, the acute policy changes of the Trump Administration. Often the leader has not aspired to lead the movement nor do they have experience, but the support and growing influence of the action propels them forward. Often as with most of the cited revolutions above, Donald Trump became the face of hope for the widespread conditions of poverty, oppression, and humiliation experienced by a majority of the population. His unfiltered, uncontrolled approach to communicating with Americans sparked a radicalization in people's sense of citizenship and power. In other words, they realized their internal feelings of individual dignity, rights, and freedom and their capacity to act on them. It was a moment in which, after living through decades of deplorable conditions, people suddenly recognized their own power and their own capacity to act.

Many Americans as well as members of the international community speculated on who these revolutionaries were, where did they come from, and why did they choose what seemed like a most unlikely candidate for President of the most powerful nation on earth? Let's dissect this American citizen while keeping in mind that we are not one race, ethnicity, gender or culture. This is not homogenous from those identifiers; they are only homogenous in their anger at the *status quo*. In this chapter the goal is to label that sums up this group and the best one so far has been the lamest "Trump supporters"! Seriously, haven't most Americans supported a president or politician since the Founding Fathers formalized the democracy? Of course we have, but now that's a "bad" thing… our judgment blinds our understanding and we seek to lash out rather than to study the true commonalities that led millions of Americans to go to the polls, fight for change, and threaten the very ideals of this nation's founding principles.

Let's look at one of the short sighted events that have marred this revolution and prevented the world from understanding the bigger issue, fake news, and alternative facts. It is not that both of the issues shouldn't be studied; however, I believe if the study is to dismiss the voters as an ignorant group of citizens than it is unproductive and shortsighted. Joining a "Trump Supporter" Group on Facebook many months prior to the elections offered insight into the thought process of some in this group. The Facebook group "Donald Trump President/ Trey Gowdy Intelligencei" provides some insight into the thinking and ideals of Trump supporters. One of the posts in this group comes from an article published on March 10, 2017 in the USA Politics Now (http://usapoliticsnow.com) titled *"Here Is The LIST of 20 REPUBLICAN SENATORS TRYING TO SABOTAGE TRUMP … HELP US EXPOSE THESE TRAITORS!"* The article goes on to condemn these "traitors" as follows:

Thirty-one Senators signed a letter asking the Department of Homeland Security to maximize the number of blue collar outsourcing visas that allow U.S. based corporations to import low-skilled workers instead of hiring Americans.

Lest you think these must be craven Democrats trying to make President Trump look callous and mean, think again. Twice as many Republicans (20) as Democrats (10) signed the letter, along with one Independent.

The number of H-2B visas issued had long been held to 66,000 visas but was wildly expanded by Obama in the last year of his presidency, to 264,000. Now, almost 40% of the Republican caucus wants to keep it at that level.

These are the turncoat Republican senators:

They go on to share the list of Republican "turncoats" and express their deplorable treasonous acts against President Trump:

This is a disingenuous attempt to undermine President Trump as anyone listening to Jorge Ramos try to sell his lies to Tucker Carlson last night will quickly realize.

Ramos insists that "overall, all immigrants contribute $2 billion to the United States' economy. Whoop-de-damn-doo!

That may be true on the surface, but that cheap labor comes at a steep price for many Americans who find themselves out of work and dependent on government because of it. It's just another form of corporate welfare but it comes at tremendous cost to the taxpayers.

This includes the incredible societal costs associated with the crime, in some cases surveillance, cost of incarceration, medical, educational, policing, welfare and other costs that dwarf the $2 Billion many times over.

Expect these same RINO's to support Senate Leader Mitch McConnell's slow walking of Trump's agenda in the Senate just as Speaker Paul Ryan is trying to do in the House.

When Trump ran for president no one knew just how little representation American workers really had in Congress (Dorothy, 2017).

The USApoliticsNOW.com, voxtribune.com and many other websites along with a number of Facebook groups like *"Donald Trump President/ Trey Gowdy Intelligencei"* and others that promote "alternative facts" are clearly delivering an effective form of propaganda that serves to promote the growth of the revolutionaries for Trump. Recently, fake news and the white nationalist "alt-right" movement have become two of the country's biggest problems in terms of fighting misinformation with the explicit purpose of gaining influence by pushing conspiracy theories and leading harassment campaigns (Kaplan, 2017). This is important as it continues to actively engage the group's members and prevents the wane in support that was the Tea Party[10] lost steam after the McCain/Palin ticket loss the election in 2008. In addition to Facebook and Twitter fringe "alt-right" forums also use sites like Reddit, 4chan, and 8chan to exercise influence and expand their reach by pushing conspiracy theories and leading harassment campaigns (Kaplan, 2017). It is no secret that these stories were received by millions who found their messages mirroring their long held beliefs about politicians i.e., the Clintons and Mr. Donald Trump at the time. According to Craig Silverman, a media editor for BuzzFeed, stated on NPR's Fresh Air that there's no question that these fake stories resonated with people (Silverman, 2016). He stated that there is no question people saw the fake stories and they shared them or they commented on them and they liked them, which created tremendous velocity on Facebook. Although Facebook was the dominant platform used by most Americans to push, confirm or validate a news story other social media sites, as previously mentioned were also commonly used. It is no secret that as a presidential candidate, Donald Trump, favored Twitter as his choice for communicating with his supporters, the media and the world but many of the popular social media platforms became sufficient marketing resources.

What was it about the individuals who created these sites that appeared to swing the political pendulum in the direction of Trump? Interestingly, Silverman (2016) stated that it was not Trump's supporters who created these sites and fabricated half or third truths, as a matter of fact, it was not fabricated in the U.S. (Silverman, 2016). Although many anti-Trump supporters believed after the elections that it was the "Russians or Wiki Leaks" both are far from the truth when it comes to fake news. After conducting very extensive research, Silverman (2016) found that a small town in central Macedonia was home to more than 140 pro-Trump sites. You might ask what Trump has to do with Macedonia and Vales, in particular. The answer is nothing. Interestingly enough Silverman (2016) and his research team found that all of the sites were owned and operated by individuals in their teens and early twenties who had zero interest in the U.S. elections but great interest in the money they made using Facebook as a vehicle to share partial truths that leaned to the audience who was hungriest for a win. When Silverman (2016) and his team asked how they made money creating so many pro-Trump websites in English and it was simply using the available electronic tools that allowed them to master and understand what received the most likes, clicks, and shares indicators. Silverman (2016) also noted that although the money was not generated from Facebook, their use of ad sites like Google Ad Sense, and other ad programs, they earn money as people visit their sites. After trying a variety of election sites, and realizing over time that their greatest profits resulted from pro-Trump propaganda, these non-American young adults capitalized on the strong appetite for the extreme anti-Obama rhetoric that fueled their beliefs about the first black president and all those connected with him. Through their research, Silverman (2016) found that the content that performed best fell into two categories. The first was sort of misleading information or completely false information. This type of information would receive high engagement, meaning high shares on Facebook, which were the main focus because shares lead to high traffic volume. Secondly, memes like a photo that expressed a very partisan opinion and although they were not factually based, they were effective at keeping the base constituency riled up and in the fight (Silverman, 2016).

A Few Voices

The fact that the fake information was received so favorably is interesting, in that so many Americans were eager to believe in the might of a man and his most recent tweet. Often they were characterized and debased as ignorant, uneducated, and "deplorable" white men and women (Murdock, 2016). There are human beings behind every vote and to learn more about the lived experiences that drew them to the orange faced, hair swooshing, uncensored, multi-billionaire. CNN published an article in that asked Americans in one Midwest town that overwhelmingly voted for Donald Trump how they felt about the election results and the stories were familiar to me (Long, 2017). Some of my brothers, sister's nephews and nieces in NC who work at "just-in-time" construction, manufacturing, day labor during farming season, Wal-Mart and in home healthcare positions felt that they would now have "someone in the White House that will help them get a good job". "I voted for Donald Trump because I feel like he understands me, he talks like me and he already has enough money and he is a business man so he can bring real jobs back" (I. Hampton, personal communication, December 19, 2016). In the CNN interview the individuals stated similar reasons "I voted for Trump 100%," says Barbara Puckett, a 55-year-old mom, who lives in the small and friendly town of Beattyville (Long, 2017). "It's the most hopeful I've been in a long time now that he's in there." Many others believe he will be the president that will think about their plight. One man in the CNN article stated "Trump will be a president for the common man." Statements like these are perceived and dismissed as ignorance or stupidity, however each of these people are coming from a very personal place of struggle, poverty, loss hope and helplessness to change their future. Let's examine and understand the voters a bit more clearly (Long, 2017).

White Women's Vote

White women overwhelmingly and successfully voted for Donald Trump and their reasons vary across the spectrum as much as their roles in life. These white women were highly educated, high school dropouts, stay at home moms, married, single and with a variety of reasons for their choice to elect Donald Trump as their president. One woman interviewed by *Guardian* reporters (Beckett, Carroll, Fishwick, Jamieson, & Thielman, 2016) after voting "I have worked so hard to get out of poverty. I was raised to earn my own success, and feel strongly that I deserve every dollar I will now earn as a surgeon. I see a lot of people who think they deserve a handout and aren't willing to do the work they are capable of. Trump is business-minded and not handout-minded, and I think this will instill a sense of effort and hard work in our country". Many others stated that they voted for common Republican views such as Roe vs. Wade legislation to be overturned and strong views on terrorism (Beckett, et. al., 2016). Others were confident that Trumps misogynistic views of women or his limited political experience would secure the women's vote for his contender. When asked about his views on women the overwhelming majority of white women who voted for Trump downplayed his behavior, they believed he fundamentally respected women or that his sexism would not undermine his ability to carry out the change they wanted (Beckett, et. al., 2016). Laurie Jones, a nutritionist who lives in downtown Manhattan stated, "He is an imperfect person, like all of us, but I do believe he does like women. He cares for his daughters and wife and female employees (Beckett, et. al., 2016). He does respect women."

National Election Pool Data (revealed that the majority of non-college educated white women (64%) voted for Trump, and less discussed, but just as important nearly half (45%) of all college educated white women also voted for Trump (Tyson & Maniam, 2016). Although the numbers are a glance at who voted for whom, there are faces and stories behind each number. Exploring the stories of the white woman voter would surely lead to a better understanding of what she wants in an elected leader. Because contrary to popular view white women are not seeking to be rescued; their collective voice of 64% showed that they are indeed strong and will choose in favor of their values and beliefs; not to break ceilings that they believed would not provide the cover they expect (Tyson & Maniam, 2016).

Black American's Vote

Black American voters were expected overwhelmingly support Hillary Clinton for president and we did, but not at the level that we did for President Obama during his two runs for the highest office in the land (2008 and 2012). One reason was because she was a democrat, yet just that alone meant that she had secured the Black vote, but is that security diminishing? There were other reasons just as insensitive as that one; because the Obama's spoke on her behalf, because she would be the first woman president; breaking another barrier, because her husband, former president Bill Clinton was popular with black Americans, and most insensitive of all because blacks were overwhelmingly democrats (Williams, 2016). Like many groups, there are common beliefs about their natural tendencies and when these beliefs go unchecked or become matter of fact they cause dissonance. This is common in marriages when one of the spouses feel taken for granted and it only becomes noticed when the divorce papers are issued. Well divorce papers were issued to presidential candidate Clinton in the form of minimal black voter turnout. Black Americans recognized that she did not come to their communities, that she did not court their vote, but expected it, and therefore they did not show up at the alter (polls) (Williams, 2016). Riding on the coat tails of President Obama, it was widely believed that Hillary Clinton assumed that black people would support her in becoming the first woman president with the same fervor they had supported the first black president. We know now that was a grave miscalculation. With the common issues above in addition to Trumps carefully orchestrated photo opportunities with important leaders in the black community and his almost sincere attention to the plight of many urban and rural black Americans Trump garnered favor and won nearly a half million black votes. He addressed the fact that poor, underserved black neighborhoods were a mess with lousy public schools, high crime and violence, and chronic joblessness and poverty. He bluntly blamed the Democrats who run and have led most of these cities for decades.

Trump also met with high-profile black preachers at black churches, and added rhetoric on "bread and butter" issues for many blacks such as abortion, gay marriage and school prayer as priority issues. He also commented on interest in small business, school choice, and family values as the best path to black advancement (Hutchinson, 2016). Trumps ability to recognize and blast the status quo for its lack of real change in the black community resonated with many Black Americans in their vote or refusal to vote. Although a mere

8% of the black vote went to President Trump (Tyson & Maniam, 2016), the thought that 1.2 million black Americans chose not to vote for the Democratic nominee suggested that it is time for candidates from all parties to begin to court a group that is searching to align with a candidate who acknowledges them rather than a candidate who takes them for granted.

Hispanic Vote

Hispanic voters were also expected to vote for the Democratic nominee in large numbers and many did, but to everyone's surprise 28% of eligible Hispanic voters voted for Trump. In an interview conducted by Haaretz journalist Taly Krupkin (2016) with Mayra Orozco stated "I'm very happy today. I tried to maintain a positive attitude because in my heart I knew that he has potential. He is a very smart guy," Orozco,a small business owner, believes like Jones that Trump will help those who are working hard to earn a quality living, "Trump will help small businesses, so that we'll all be able to help our families," says Orozco (Krupkin, 2016). Also, like the other outlier supporters of Donald Trump's Orozco and others in the Hispanic community stated that his comments about immigrants don't disturb her. "He is the best for us. Now we can expect more." In addition to Trumps admired business prowess like many of the Christian faith they voted for Trump for religious reasons. Jaime a man in Dallas, he and all his friends are evangelical Christians who voted for the Republican candidate. He says;

I wish there had been a different candidate, neither Clinton nor Trump, but Hillary is pro-abortion and pro-gay. I don't have anything against gays but God said marriage is between a man and a woman. Clinton thinks a fetus is just a cell even though in the New Testament it says that God knows us and is with us from the moment we are created, from the moment the fetus is in the woman's belly. I don't think Trump is really against abortions—it's not first place on his agenda, but Clinton and Obama took active measures for abortions. Trump will presumably work only on fixing the economy, and that's good for everyone. (Krupkin, 2016)

Morals, values and beliefs seemed to drive the votes in Trump's direction American's voted their faith, their prejudices, and their "pocket" and there is very little one can do to combat the personal perspectives of people. This is evident in each of these three groups previously discussed who voted with their values that include overturning abortion, repealing rights of the LGBTQ, school choice, and small business development. However, there is one group that does not quite fit this mold exactly.

Lesbian, Gay, Bi-Sexual, Transgender, and Queer (LGBTQ) Voters

Of those who identified themselves and a member of the LGBTQ community a surprising 14% voted for Trump and the reasons are truly "all" American, almost (Tyson & Maniam, 2016). Moral values were very strong for most of the unlikely groups that voted for Trump, but like many of the larger groups of republican voters, the LGBTQ voters voted their republican interest in the 2nd Amendment, national security and the economy. In an NBC OUT feature written by (O'Hara, 2016) on LGBTQ voters supporting Trump an interview with Trump supporter, Vincent Foster, 27, the president of the Miami chapter of gay conservative group Log Cabin Republicans. His chapter supported the Trump campaign and as a result Foster, a black gay man said he's been called everything from an "Uncle Tom" to a "self-hating f-g" for his support of Trump (O'Hara, 2016). However, undeterred Foster emphasized gun policy as a reason why he and his chapter decided that Trump was the best candidate for President. "Gay men, lesbians and the trans community are being targeted every single day," Foster said. "Gun rights are gay rights. The best way to protect yourself is your Second Amendment. Right (O'Hara, 2016)?" Foster also agreed that a stronger fight against the terrorist group ISIS is important. He stated "when you have a group that thinks I deserve to be thrown off a building because I'm gay, I want them eliminated." He believed Donald Trump was the best candidate to carry this out. Like the other groups the commercials that played over and over Trump's slanderous, racist, misogynist and chauvinistic views did not have an impact on these voters (O'Hara, 2016). This was the sign that Americans were less concerned about name calling and value attacks than they are with who they believe can do what they wanted done. In addition, this electorate seemed to want a non-politician who could easily say "You're fired!" and keep it moving.

WHAT DO THEY REALLY WANT?

It is important that we examine this from the top. Were Trump's views on trade the leading factor in his campaign? Was it the notion that America needed to return to a time where civil rights did not exist for people of color? Was it his stance on immigration and the proposed border (i.e., Mexico-United States barrier) or his forceful threats on what he would do to eliminate ISIS? Maybe in some part it is all of these, but what is missing from these high-level issues were the everyday concerns of all Americans who felt the greatest lack finding their voice and shouting with a vote so that everyone would know "they do exist". It was not just white men and women who voted for President Trump nor was it just faith, gender, race, lifestyles, poverty or wealth. President Trump won the election because of single mothers who wanted jobs that paid enough to afford childcare and their rent. Men regardless of their educational levels, wanted to work and earn a living by the sweat of their brow and the strength of their might. Trump had voters who wanted to be able to pay their student loans because their education paid them what society had promised it would. Retail workers who stood on hard floors wanted to rest on a soft bed that they owned. American workers voted for Trump because if he understood the tax codes well enough not to pay all of his hard earned money back to the federal government (Keith et al., 2016). It appears that many Americans believe that because Donald Trump used the existing tax codes to avoid paying taxes that he would rewrite the code so they too could benefit. Voters are not a large group of people that can be summed up into five categories based upon demographics, gender, race, socioeconomic status, and sexual orientation people who vote are significantly more complex than the polls indicate. This lack of acknowledgment will continue to compromise those who believe the *status quo* is the way to go.

Employment for All

Employment continues to be a top priority for many Americans. Many organizations are thriving today due to the billions of dollars in profits they earn annually on the backs of the American workforce. The challenge is that those profits have not dwindled down to the workers and minimum wage has not increased in decades. At the same time, insurance benefits have decreased to some of the lowest levels of coverage since it became part of an employer's compensation package. So, yes, jobs are a major concern but with the jobless rates being lower (4.7%) than they have been in more than 40 years (1975) the real issue it is the wage, the current federal minimum wage is $7.25 (some states have increased their minimum wage) and has not been increased since 2009. According to the cost of living index (Career Trends, n.d.), the average monthly cost of living in the United States for a married couple with two children is $5,466. This adds up to an average annual cost of living of $65,597. Additionally, for a given week, at the federal minimum wage of $7.25 and assuming a 1.5 times increase in hourly wage after 40 hours for overtime, a married couple with two children would need to work 130 hours in a week to be above the United States cost of living threshold of $1,261 per week. What this tells us that at the minimum required rate of pay a married family working fulltime would need to work 50 additional overtime hours just to meet the standard cost of living in the United States (Career Trends, n.d.). Therefore, I suggest jobs are not the issue, but wages. If a married couple with two children and both parents working full time earned minimally $15.75 per hour, that family of four working full-time would meet the current average cost of living in the United States (Career Trends, n.d.). A single mom with one child would need to earn $22.75 per hour to meet the standard cost of living. Although many Americans have jobs, those jobs like retail pay an average starting wage of $8.00 per hour. Very few retail employees clock 40 hours per week. After 12 years of employment at Kohl's in North Carolina and rising to the level of supervisor, the employee stated that she had finally made it to $12.00 an hour, jokingly adding that she earns $1.00 for every year of employment (D. Ross, personal communication, October 19, 2016). But it is no joking matter that her 36 maximum hours per week, and $22,464 per year falls short of the current cost of living standard for a single person without children of $28,458.

The wages paid by service employers, in the dominant areas of retail, fast food, or hotel and restaurant are paltry and unlike the manufacturing jobs where more than 7 billion jobs were lost since 1980, Americans cannot live a quality life in the richest nation on earth, without federal aid. Without raising the minimum wage substantially, providing training and apprenticeships in areas of work like welding, plumbing, mechanics, automation, and technology the only help for the unemployed and underemployed will be the dreaded entitlements that pro-Trump supporters want to cut. The question of implementation is purely a question of investment into adult education training that requires license and certifications by all facilitators, that is fully comprehensive including financial planning, budgeting, and the much needed soft skills required in business along with building bridges that will link training and apprenticeships that lead to small business development, long-term job security, and stipends to support participants. Former jobs will remain "former" they will not return, for very few businesses will diminish their profit margins to lift those unfamiliar to them, everyday paycheck earners. Therefore, the expectation that a thriving company whose investors are satisfied because every layoff yields a surge in the stock price is unrealistic. This is especially true in a government where every person including and most importantly President Trump is a "successful" business man. Although, you have just read that many who voted believed this is exactly what President Trump will do, as this presidential term continues their eyes may be opened to the truth that they were deceived by their candidate. I have no doubt that quality, high wage, skilled jobs are available and that anyone prepared for these jobs will be employed or become the employer. A skills gap, wage gap, or education gap, ultimately lead to the same end, unemployment and government dependency by those in the gap, how will America prepare for an ever disgruntled and defeated citizenry?

WHAT DOES THE DATA SAY?

Andrew Kelly (2015) conducted research with nearly 1,600 Americans within the age cohort of 25 and 44 years old who finished high school, but lacked a college degree. Specifically, he explored how adults without a college degree perceive the postsecondary system as a whole and the costs and benefits of their potential options. This is relevant when the skills gap is widening. Kelly (2015) found that 84% of the participants believed that education was important to get a good job; however, 60% of those surveyed believed it was cost prohibitive. They believed that the cost outweighed the benefits to the degree that they were better off the way they were. Kelly (2015) noted that the primary factor that many in the working age population of 2544 years old strongly stated that college, even with financial aid, was too expensive especially with a family. In addition, these adults believed that colleges did not provide enough flexibility for an adult with a family.

Most interesting in Kelly's (2015) findings were the notion that many Americans in this age cohort did not aspire to obtain more education; 43% reported that they were satisfied. Among those who wanted to earn a credential, the bachelor's degree was the primary choice (23%), and an additional 9% aspired to an advanced degree. However, only 10% aspired to an occupational certificate with 4% interested in an associate degree. Additionally, 51% of the high school graduates reported that they were satisfied with their current level of education, compared to just 33% of those who had attended some college. To expand these numbers Kelly (2015) found that 35% of African American and 36% of Hispanic respondents were less likely than white respondents to be satisfied with their current level of education and most likely to aim for a bachelor's degree or higher (35% and 40%, respectively). A 51% of white respondents reported that they were satisfied with their current level of education (Kelly, 2015). This speaks to the Trump electorate's plight regarding low skilled jobs but the belief that they have no need for additional education in the form of tactical skills in technology, math or science. According to a 2014 policy briefing by Emma Garcia, a recent survey of more than 400 employers in the U.S. revealed the four most important skills required by potential employees are oral communication, teamwork/collaboration, professionalism/work ethic, and critical thinking/problem solving. More than 90% of employers surveyed described these skills to be "very important." In contrast, writing, mathematics, science, and history/geography were ranked 6th, 15th, 16th, and 19th, respectively, out of 20 skills" (Garcia, 2014). This insight isn't meant to dismiss technology and related STEM training, but it should highlight the current and future workers needs of both strong job ability and strong soft skills. This sounds great but what does it look like for the revolutionaries' who are not interested in furthering their education? However, they seek satisfactory employment to take care of their families. This is the research question I close this chapter because it deserves more than a terse statement that is dismissive of this group's needs.

POSTULATING

Jobs are a bandage and will not be enough to put back in the box the isms that exploded when the civility that housed the racist views of the children, grandchildren and great grandchildren from the generations of slave owners and Jim Crow proponents. No, it will not be jobs and the idea of a Truth and Reconciliation Commission[11] is noble, however the systemic hatred of others that this nation was founded upon is its root and not until that root dies or is destroyed, will it be possible to rise from the ashes like the mythological phoenix and soar. For many Americans who do not have the opportunity to live in another country, there is a grim feeling of being in the day of Armageddon[12] and waiting for the bomb to be dropped. In light of President

Trumps Tweeting off the cuff remarks to enemies of the United States and his quick "shock and awe" bomb episodes, this election may take us into a war of biblical proportions.

CONCLUSION

The forgotten Americans of today have risen from the shadows to dominate the media platforms and screamed to be heard, unlike those addressed by President Richard Nixon in 1969, regarding their actions during the Vietnam War. Nixon (1969) admonished them for not participating in the large demonstrations and public discourse that opposed the war suggested that this silent majority was being overshadowed in the media by the more vocal minority (Nixon, 1969). Of course nearly 50 years ago many homes did not have a television, and if they wanted to scream often it was at the chagrin of their family members or neighbors. Now, we have tools that fit in our hand and reach the world, the former six degrees of separation, are likely down to two degrees, because of social media and our 21st century progressively expanding interest in optimizing our world with Artificial Intelligence. It is remarkable how advanced the world is and yet how poor its people are, wealth is a pursuit driving force for many, until the goal is a pack of crackers to prevent starvation for the night. Globalization has opened our planet up and for the most part it is exciting, but with advancements in technology and enlarged markets resulting from FTA's many people are experiencing the negative effects of "bigger and brighter".

For most U.S. citizens and me, I continue to believe that America is still the greatest place on earth to call home; but with caution I reflect on the mistakes of other great nations that caused their demise. Nearly, all resulted from greed from a few that resulted in division amongst the citizen's, and weakened faith that the system of government would provide a quality of life for all of its citizens. During those weakened national crisis, the enemy nations swooped in and destroyed the mighty nations. This mighty United States of America is on the brink of being overtaken, particularly with the President of the revolutionaries' who manages our national interest using 120 characters, unless there is an awakening by the mighty that focuses on unburdening the shoulders of the masses. It is my hope that this chapter provides an opportunity for its readers to consider the needs of all Americans; and not limit our decisions to our differences (race, gender, faith, sexual orientation or socioeconomic status) when we elect leaders to make decisions on our behalf. With the wrong choice, we can lose access to education, health care, right to work and earn a quality living, opportunity to marry the one we love, and the joy of debate. Our civil rights are non-negotiable and when one oligarch, dictator or president chooses to decide what freedoms are nullified, this nation will fall.

REFERENCES

Adams, J. T. (1931). *The epic of America*. Simon Publications.

ALEC - American Legislative Exchange Council. (2017, April 14). Retrieved from https://www.alec.org/

American Psychiatric Association. (2012). *DSM-IV and DSM-5 criteria for the personality disorders*. Retrieved from http://www.psi.uba.ar/academica/carrerasdegrado/psicologia/sitios_catedras/practicas_profesionales/820_clinica_tr_personalidad_psicosis/material/dsm.pdf

Applebaum, B. (2016, May 2). Experts warn backlash in Donald Trump's China trade policies. *New York Times*. Retrieved from https://www.nytimes.com/2016/05/03/us/politics/donald-trump-trade-policy-china.html?_r=0

Beckett, L., Carroll, R., Fishwick, C., Jamieson, A., & Thielman, S. (2016, November 10). *The real 'shy Trump' vote - how 53% of white women pushed him to victory*. Retrieved from https://www.theguardian.com/us-news/2016/nov/10/white-women-donald-trump-victory

Bowman, R. (2014, July 2). A growing hostility to free trade has put NAFTA on life support. *Forbes*. Retrieved from https://www.forbes.com/sites/robertbowman/2014/07/02/a-growing-hostility-to-free-trade-has-put-nafta-on-life-support/#1650e9011ba0

Bureau of Labor Statistics. (2016). *A profile of the working poor, 2014: BLS reports: U.S. Bureau of Labor Statistics* (Report 1060). Retrieved from Bureau of Labor Statistics website: https://www.bls.gov/opub/reports/working-poor/2014/home.htm

Canada-U.S. Free Trade Agreement. (2017, February 10). Retrieved from http://international.gc.ca/trade-commerce/trade-agreements-accords-commerciaux/agr-acc/united_states-etats_unis/fta-ale/background-contexte.aspx?lang=eng

Career Trends. (n.d.). *Cost of living: Career trends*. Retrieved from http://cost-of-living.careertrends.com/l/615/The-United-States

Cokley, K., Cooke, B., & Nobles, W. (2005). Guidelines for Providing Culturally Appropriate Services for People of African Ancestry Exposed to the Trauma of Hurricane Katrina. *The Psych Discourse*. Retrieved from http://cretscmhd.psych.ucla.edu/nola/Video/PTSD/materials/abpsi_article1.pdf

Fact check: Donald Trump unveils his economic plan in major Detroit speech [Television broadcast]. (2016, August 8). NPR.

Faux, J. (2016, November 30). *U.S. trade policy—time to start over | Economic Policy Institute*. Retrieved from http://www.epi.org/publication/u-s-trade-policy-time-to-start-over/

Fleet, J. V., & Winthrop, R. (2010, September 29). *To be Globally Competitive, We Must be Globally Competent | Brookings Institution*. Retrieved from https://www.brookings.edu/blog/up-front/2010/09/29/to-be-globally-competitive-we-must-be-globally-competent/

Garcia, E. (2014). *The need to address noncognitive skills in the education policy agenda* (Briefing # 386). Retrieved from Economic Policy Institute website: http://www.epi.org/publication/the-need-to-address-noncognitive-skills-in-the-education-policy-agenda/

General Agreement on Tariffs and Trade. (1986). *Text of the general agreement*. Geneva: Author.

Halperin, S. W. (1964). *Mussolini and Italian fascism*. New York: Van Nostrand.

Hutchinson, O. (2016, November 14). Why so many blacks backed Trump. *The Huffington Post*. Retrieved from http://www.huffingtonpost.com/earl-ofari-hutchinson/why-so-many-blacks-backed_b_12913720.html

Kaplan, A. (2017, April 6). *The alt-right assault on Susan Rice: A perfect case study of the pro-Trump propaganda machine*. Retrieved from http://www.alternet.org/right-wing/susan-rice-and-pro-trump-propaganda-machine

Kelly, A. (2015, April 4). The neglected majority: What Americans without a college degree think about higher education. *Forbes*. Retrieved from https://www.forbes.com/sites/akelly/2015/04/28/the-neglected-majority-what-americans-without-a-college-degree-think-about-higher-education-part-1/#6c49602b72cf

Krupkin, T. (2016, November 14*). Most Latinos voted for Clinton, but why did the others go for Trump?* Retrieved from http://www.haaretz.com/world-news/u-s-election-2016/.premium-1.752911

Long, H. (2017, February 6). *Trump has made America's 'poorest white town' hopeful again.* Retrieved from http://money.cnn.com/2017/02/06/news/economy/donald-trump-beattyville-kentucky/

Malone, C. (2016, August 5). *Trump's Campaign Focused On Attracting Unlikely Voters, A Memo Shows | FiveThirtyEight.* Retrieved from http://fivethirtyeight.com/features/trump-campaign-memo-unlikely-voters/

McLeod, S. (2016). *Maslow's hierarchy of needs | Simply psychology.* Retrieved from https://www.simplypsychology.org/maslow.html

Meet the LGBTQ voters who backed Trump [Television broadcast]. (2016, November 15). NBC News.

Michels, R. (1911). *Political parties: A sociological study of the oligarchical tendencies of modern democracy.* New York, NY: Collier Books.

Pappas, A. (2017, February 2). Trump meets with several dozen leaders of historically black colleges. *Washington Examiner.* Retrieved from http://www.washingtonexaminer.com/trump-meets-with-several-dozen-leaders-of-historically-black-colleges/article/2615934

Scott, R. E. (2015). Manufacturing Job Loss: Trade, Not Productivity, Is the Culprit | Economic Policy Institute. Retrieved from Economic Policy Brief website: http://www.epi.org/publication/manufacturing-job-loss-trade-not-productivity-is-the-culprit/

Silverman, C. (2016, December 14). Fake news expert on how false stories spread and why people believe them [Television series episode]. Interview by D. Davies. In Fresh Air. NPR.

South African History Online. (1995). *Tutu and his role in the Truth & Reconciliation Commission.* Retrieved from http://www.sahistory.org.za/article/tutu-and-his-role-truth-reconciliation-commission

The Reciprocal Trade Agreement Act of 1934 | US House of Representatives: History, Art & Archives. (n.d.). Retrieved from http://history.house.gov/HistoricalHighlight/Detail/36918

Trueman, C. N. (2015, May 25). *Mussolini's Dictatorship - History Learning Site*. Retrieved from http://www.historylearningsite.co.uk/modern-world-history-1918-to-1980/italy-1900-to-1939/mussolinis-dictatorship/

Tyson, A., & Maniam, S. (2016, November 9). *Behind Trump's victory: Divisions by race, gender and education | Pew Research Center.* Retrieved from http://www.pewresearch.org/fact-tank/2016/11/09/behind-trumps-victory-divisions-by-race-gender-education/

Valverde, M. (2016, June 26). *How Trump plans to build, and pay for, a wall along U.S.-Mexico border | PolitiFact*. Retrieved from http://www.politifact.com/truth-o-meter/article/2016/jul/26/how-trump-plans-build-wall-along-us-mexico-border/

Warrick, J., & Whoriskey, P. (2006, March 25). Army corps is faulted on New Orleans levees. *Washington Post*. Retrieved from http://www.washingtonpost.com/wp-dyn/content/article/2006/03/24/AR2006032401819.html

West, D. M., & Karsten, J. (2016). *Rural and urban America divided by broadband access | Brookings Institution*. Retrieved from Brookings.edu website: https://www.brookings.edu/blog/techtank/2016/07/18/rural-and-urban-america-divided-by-broadband-access/

What was the Smoot-Hawley Tariff Act of 1930? | The Capitalism Site. (n.d.). Retrieved from http://capitalism.org/free-trade/what-was-the-smoot-hawley-tariff-act-of-1930/

Williams, J. (2016, November 9). *Clinton made her case to Black voters. Why didn't they hear her?* Retrieved from https://www.usnews.com/news/politics/articles/2016-11-09/clinton-made-her-case-to-black-voters-why-didnt-they-hear-her

Worstall, T. (2016, October 19). The U.S. lost 7 million manufacturing jobs--And added 33 million higher-paying service jobs. *Forbes*. Retrieved from https://www.forbes.com/sites/timworstall/2016/10/19/the-us-lost-7-million-manufacturing-jobs-and-added-33-million-higher-paying-service-jobs/#56c8b294a205

ENDNOTES

1 The North American Free Trade Agreement is a treaty between Canada, the United States and Mexico. These three countries have agreed to remove trade barriers between them. By eliminating tariffs, NAFTA increases investment opportunities. NAFTA is the world's largest free trade agreement. Its members contribute more than $20 trillion as measured by gross domestic product.

2 The region of the United States from the Great Lakes to the upper Midwest States, referring to economic decline, population loss, and urban decay due to the shrinking of its once-powerful industrial sector, also known as deindustrialization.

3 The Sun Belt consists of the warm climate states that make up the Southern third of the Continental United States. These states include California, Nevada, New Mexico, Arizona, Texas, Louisiana, Mississippi, Georgia, North and South Carolina, and Florida.

4 The Tariff Act of 1930 signed into law by U.S. President Herbert Hoover on 17 June 1930 was duties (taxes) placed on over 20,000 imported goods. Its political intent was to preserve American jobs, particularly in the agricultural sector, by discouraging foreign imports.

5 The Cold War is the name given to the relationship that developed primarily between the USA and the USSR after World War Two, http://www.history.com/topics/cold-war/cold-war-history

6 Mussolini introduced a Fascist Grand Council which would decide policy for Italy without consulting the non-fascists in the government first. In February 1923, Mussolini and the Fascist Grand Council introduced the Acerbo Law. This law changed election results. Now if one party got just 25% (or more) of the votes cast in an election, they would get 66%of the seats in parliament. Mussolini appointed members to the Fascist Grand Council and from 1928; the Grand Council had to be consulted on all constitutional issues. As Mussolini appointed people onto the Council, logic would dictate that those people would do what Mussolini wished them to do.

7 Who qualifies as a "displaced worker"? A worker is considered displaced if he or she loses a job held for at least three years because a company moves a plant closes, work slacks off, or a job is eliminated. Job loss caused by displacement reflects changes in the industrial make-up of the economy, rather than ordinary economic cycles or temporary unemployment. Workers who are displaced are not expected to regain

their previous jobs (Bureau of Labor Statistics US Department of Labor, 2016)).

8 ALEC is the "largest nonpartisan, voluntary membership organization of state legislators dedicated to the principles of limited government, free markets and federalism".

9 Trayvon Martin was an unarmed American 17-year-old killed by George Zimmerman on February 26, 2012, sparking national controversy.

10 The Tea Party is a grassroots movement that calls awareness to any issue, which challenges the security, sovereignty, or domestic tranquility of our beloved nation, the United States of America. From our founding, the Tea Party represents the voice of the true owners of the United States: WE THE PEOPLE. Teaparty.org

11 The Truth and Reconciliation Committee was based on the Promotion of National Unity and Reconciliation Act, No 34 of 1995. It resembled a legal body that was bestowed with the authority to hear and try cases, resolve disputes, or make certain legal decisions. The policy of reconciliation embodied in the inquiry was predicated on the fundamental principle that "To forgive is not just to be altruistic, [but] it is the best form of self-interest."

12 The battle of Armageddon refers to the final war between human governments and God. These governments and their supporters oppose God even now by refusing to submit to his rulership. (Psalm 2:2) The battle of Armageddon will bring human rulership to an end.—Daniel 2:44.

Chapter 4
S.N.A.P. Today, Medicare Tomorrow:
Save a Dollar, Sacrifice a Child or Grandmother

Pamela Hampton-Garland
University of the District of Columbia, USA

ABSTRACT

Entitlements, social safety nets, benefits and welfare are just a few of the terms used to describe benefits provided to American businesses and individuals by the federal government. For decades since the FDR laws issued post WWII, politicians have been crying reform, in a vain attempt to dismantle the social safety nets that many of the country's most vulnerable populations need to survive. This chapter provides historical and current information on America's safety net programs and provide a deeper understanding of their importance and their beneficiaries. Finally, the chapter provides clarity to the impact that social safety nets have had on poverty in the U.S. and embedded in this chapter is a personal narrative of how the entitlements helped change my life.

A FACEBOOK CONVERSATION

In a robust Facebook conversation regarding *The Washington Post's* article "Do Whites Benefit Disproportionately from Welfare" (Williamson, 2017) a debate raged on the concept of white Americans and welfare. The article asserted that based on a recent study:

DOI: 10.4018/978-1-5225-3843-1.ch004

Government assistance and tax credits lifted 6.2 million working-class whites out of poverty in 2014, more than any other racial or ethnic demographic. Half of all working-age adults without college degrees lifted out of poverty by safety-net programs are white; nearly a quarter are black and a fifth are Hispanic. (Williamson, 2017)

The author of the *National Review* article asserts that the article was a misrepresentation of the data and as interpreted by one of the Facebook posts "[*The*] *Washington Post* is purposely misleading to make the wrong argument that white people are voting against their self-interest" (Williamson, 2017). This conversation enraged readers who believed that *The Washington Post* writer was incompetent and her suggestion that white people benefitted from welfare programs more than any other race. According to the Facebook posts, Williams neglected to inform her readers that social security was more of an "investment" that they were entitled to and that they received more because they lived longer and often earned more, and paid more thus deserving social security benefits. The conversation escalated on Facebook including the following statements:

Dye · Captain (civil aviation) at Jet Airways India Ltd

Okay, let me take a pass at explaining. First, a wealthy white person will get more money in SS benefits than a poor black person, because he contributed more money into the program over time. So that is one way that a white person would make more money: pure income inequality.

Second: Age Disparity. The median age of death for a black male is around 65 years old. So one half of black men die before they can get a single penny of SS money. Since white men die at around 72, and white women die at 78, this makes the 'pay out' larger for the white demographic than for the African American.

So a black cardiologist who dies at 74 would be getting just as much 'help' as his white colleague, but there are few black cardiologists. This is manipulating the numbers to play the "white guilt" card on the part of the WPo (Washington Post) and I resent the hell out of it.

Mayfield · Tacoma Community College His basic point was that the story presents completely un-newsworthy information and presents it as though it were something. It describes welfare as helping white people disproportionately, when the actual number is one % different between white and black people (44% versus 43% going from below poverty to above poverty) and Hispanic people have perfectly clear explanation for the lower rate. They take thoughts numbers and then describe the help to white people as disproportionate, when it is entirely proportionate.

As far as the numbers of people on the programs, white people make up greater numbers, but lower numbers in context of population. Basically, the writer of the column is either incompetent in dealing with statistics, or dishonest, which seems more likely. Williamson allowed for both possibilities, by the way, not actually using the term dishonest, as you claim he did.

As to the point about "voting against their interest," who but me determines what my interests are?

Blatt - Social Security and Medicare are the biggest spending programs. You can't address the deficit without reforming it. Moreover, Medicare does function as a redistributive welfare program; many get much more back in benefits than they paid in.

Richard · Works at Willy Wonka Candy Company

We "benefit" from social security and Medicare, perhaps . . . But we also had no choice in contributing towards them. If I hacked your bank account and invested your retirement account however I wanted to then started sending you monthly checks when you turned 62, you would be a fool to not accept the check.

Gatti · Brooklyn, New York: "I think Social Security and Medicare are stupid and destructive programs." If only the right campaigned this honestly...lol

Pavelyev · Charlotte, North Carolina: They are in fact the biggest welfare programs. And yes, whites benefit from them disproportionally because

1) Whites make up a much bigger share of the elderly than of the whole population and

2) SS benefits are related to past earnings, which were significantly higher for whites.

Sandidge · Victoria, Texas: SS is NOT a welfare program. It is an annuity type program that like millions of others, I was forced to pay into with a guarantee that if I lived long enough I would be able to collect on it. If SS is a welfare program then so is any annuity you buy from a private company that says put in this much and at age 65 you can draw this amount for life. I paid into it by force for over 45 years, and Medicare. I tried to get out many years ago and could not by law. Now if someone comes into the country at age high age and then gets it for life, then yes you can say that.

Bodi · Treasurer at Westshore Republicans:

Andrew Pavelyev, the point is that whites do NOT benefit "disproportionately." The key here is the term "proportional". If whites make up a larger "proportion" of those in the brackets that get the services, then it is not "disproportionate" at all.

Brown · University of Missouri:

The gist of this is that they've figured things out, although belatedly, at the Trailer Park that the ghetto/barrio folks have been onto from day #1 (which is about 1995when genius Newt Gingrich ended Welfare As We Know it and substituted the concept Gov. $$$ for babies with the EITC tax refunds. These people are by and large "poor" only if you take away the $8-15,000 they claim across their family/boyfriend/ex-husband spectrum for the tax refund, their child support, their student "loans", food stamps, unemployment, and other benefits, about 50% of which constitute rampant fraud, etc. We are all being "snookered", but, am glad to see a post on the subject because it is causing a lot of the problems in the country, and badly needs conservative attention, hopefully in form of a safety net based on income instead of # of 75 IQ babies. (Williamson, 2017)

This sentiment is the back drop for this chapter. The notion that only children from black families with "welfare queen mothers"—a phrase coined by President Reagan[1]—benefit from welfare programs or entitlements is one that created an image of welfare recipients that caused many white Americans to believe that black women were taking their hard-earned money (Levin, 2013). In 1976, he erroneously claimed:

The Welfare Queen has eighty names, thirty addresses, twelve Social Security cards and is collecting veteran's benefits on four non-existing deceased husbands. Moreover, she is collecting Social Security on her cards. She has Medicaid, getting food stamps, and she is collecting welfare under each of her names. Her tax-free cash income is over $150,000. (Levin, 2013)

Understanding the image that plays in the mind of many Americans regarding what a "welfare recipient" looks like, how she abuses the welfare system, and hyperbolic claims that cause hardworking white Americans to have to pay for her laziness and waste, is critical to understanding the Facebook posts listed above. Although, the idea of the welfare program exclusively assisting black women who have multiple babies, was a belief prior to President Reagans diatribe, it was sealed in the minds of many Republican voters since 1976.

Many of today's disgruntled and displaced workers want to return to their former employment status and work environments where they feel proud to and earn a quality wage. Many displaced workers are not interested in pursuing additional education that promises better skilled jobs in the new America where technology is "King" and manufacturing has been dethroned and beheaded. Most of these former workers never imagined they would need a "handout" from anyone and especially, the federal government. The picture of the "welfare" recipient was the indolent black woman who had a number of children, uneducated, and who wanted "something for nothing" (Levin, 2013). This this may have imprinted and indelible image in many Americans minds. However, the fact is the largest number of "welfare recipients" has always been the group with the largest number of citizens -- white Americans. The conversation is problematic because it is comparing apples and oranges, number of people and percentage of people. The current argument is that white Americans are the largest racial group receiving welfare because they are the largest demographic, but a percentage analysis reveals that black Americans maintain the largest percentage of the population by race receiving welfare (41% of blacks to 13% of whites). To help clarify this point, the discussion below chapter explores the impact of abandonment for both the 41% and the 13% when biased reform is instituted. The push to reform welfare has been a Republican Party agenda item since its inception by the Roosevelt administration in 1935. This chapter deconstructs the controversial subject of what is now identified in media as "entitlements" other known titles include welfare the most common, social safety nets, benefits, and social security the original name given to the federal support provided to Americans in financial deprivation.

HISTORY OF SOCIAL SAFETY NETS IN AMERICA

The Social Security Act was enacted in 1935 as a means to relieve job losses and poverty suffered by white Americans during and after The Great Depression (1929-1939). However, the Act of 1935 was not the first social welfare program in American history. Social support programs were established long before the government welfare programs most Americans are familiar with. For example, there were several programs beginning in the 17th century such as the English Poor Laws that were later revised in the 1830s (Higginbotham, 2017). In the early days of the United States, the colonies imported the *British Poor Laws* (Higginbotham, 2017). These laws made a distinction between the sick and disabled, who were assisted with cash or alternative forms of assistance from the government. The involuntary unemployed were given public service employment in workhouses (Higginbotham, 2017). They became most recognizable from Charles Dickens' 1843 famous novella, *A Christmas Carol.*

Similar to America's ongoing political concerns about social welfare systems, there was a constant focus on reforming the poor laws, some social changes focused on helping the poor return to being productive citizens. Many approaches to reform the social welfare programs included implementing a social casework approach that consisted of caseworkers visiting the poor and training them in morals and work ethic (Higginbotham, 2017). Often social welfare reformers, past and present believe training would be the best approach to mobilizing the unemployed to a state of employment. These early social programs became the template for Franklin Delano Roosevelt's Social Security Act of 1935. The Act was amended in 1939 and included establishing programs designed to provide aid to various segments of the population.

From its initiation, the policy had two tiers that intended to protect families from the lack of income (Rector, 2012). On one level, they were the contributory social insurance programs that provided income support to the surviving dependents of workers in the event of their death or incapacitation and Social Security for retired and elderly Americans. The second tier was a means-tested public assistance programs that included "Aid to Dependent

Children". This program was subsequently renamed the "Aid to Families with Dependent Children" in the 1962 Public Welfare Amendments to the SSA, during the Kennedy administration (Bertram, 2011). The objective of the tier 2 programs was to phase out as jobs increased and more families returned to self-sufficiency. The challenge with this objective was its lack of consideration for black Americans (and other marginalized groups) who were systemically discriminated against during hiring practices. As a result, most black Americans worked "under the table" where they received cash payments thus making them ineligible for the social insurance program benefits.

In addition to the challenge of discrimination in hiring the state-operated mothers' pension programs (Hansan, 2011), where white widows were the primary beneficiaries because the eligibility was determined by the state, thus black Americans were prevented from full-access to state benefits. "Separate but equal" laws did not change access for blacks for many decades and when the opportunity to participate fully was enforced; other laws were ratified to prevent black Americans from becoming self-sufficient and further compromising the family unit. One of the primary laws that perpetuated poverty and broken homes, residency requirements were proposed which barred blacks migrating from the South to qualify for the program. In addition to the "man in the house rule", required welfare workers to make unannounced visits to determine if fathers were living in the home. If evidence of a male presence was found, cases were closed and welfare checks to the family would be discontinued (Jimenez, 2010).

These two programs, unemployment compensation and Aid to Dependent Children (AFDC), still exist today. The controversial AFDC program had its most recent reform under President William "Bill" Clinton in 1996 after he signed the *Personal Responsibility and Work Opportunity Reconciliation Act*. This act stopped the distribution of funds to individuals and directed funding to the state level by allocating annual lump sums to the states to distribute among the poor. Under this act, states were additionally required to ensure that those receiving aid were being encouraged to transition from welfare to work. This program revision, like others, was not without its controversy. However, the proponents and many business leaders and owners argued that the change was been successful (Rector, 1999; Blank & Schoeni, 2003; O'Neil, 2001). Others believed that success has yet to be determined (Piven & Cloward, 1979; Soss, 2002; DeParle, 2012).

The 21st century reforms included the continuation of the welfare to work program with a caveat, the new program required work to receive time limited financial assistance or Temporary Assistance to Needy Families (TANF).

In 2004, the Welfare-to-Work program ended and the TANF program was initiated. According to its signatory, President Clinton, when the program was active millions of Americans lives were significantly improved. However, success was measured in the form of dollars saved and recipients no longer receiving the benefits. On the surface, this appeared successful; however, when Welfare-to-Work changed to TANF with states limiting the time that one could receive benefits from 2 to 5 years, the number of homeless families increased exponentially. Although it is difficult to accurately estimate the number of homeless Americans due to the questionable survey methodology employed to count the number of homeless in shelters in large cities one night per year in mid-January[2]. At the start of the 2013–2014 academic years, the Child Trends Databank reported that there were approximately 1.4 million children in the United States who attended school and did not have a home address to report to school authorities. This is a substantial increase from 10 years earlier when TANF was implemented with approximately 590,000 youth unable to report a permanent home address in the school year 2004-05 (Child Trends, 2015). Because TANF benefits have declined, housing prices in many states have increased causing many more families to find themselves living in substandard conditions, doubled up with family or friends, or homeless (Center on Budget and Policy Priorities, 2016). Reform is needed, but what is missing from the reform bills are adjustments for national economic crises, job availability for low skilled workers, consideration for those with limited or no education, impact of minimum wage, changing industries, cost of living, and the salient other factors that contribute to individuals not being able to secure a sustainable job.

BENEFICIARIES OR ADDICTS

It is imperative that there is no misinterpretation take about what entitlements are, as the term is adjusted based upon the targeted audience. Entitlements are discussed using various terms such as social safety nets, social supports, entitlements, benefits, welfare, etc. which are all federal funds transferred to states to provide support to America's underprivileged and poor citizens. The kind of government program that provides individuals with personal financial benefits (or sometimes special government-provided goods or services) to which an indefinite number of potential beneficiaries have a legal right (enforceable in court, if necessary) whenever they meet eligibility conditions that are specified by the standing law that authorizes the program.

The beneficiaries of entitlement programs are normally individual citizens or residents, but sometimes organizations such as business corporations, local governments, or even political parties may have similar special "entitlements" under certain programs e.g., tax breaks and corporate bailouts). The most important examples of entitlement programs at the federal level in the United States would include Social Security, Medicare, and Medicaid, most Veterans' Administration programs, federal employee and military retirement plans, unemployment compensation, food stamps, and agricultural price support programs (Pfeiffer, 2017). The amount of money that will be required in the coming year to fund an entitlement program is often extremely difficult to predict because the number of people with an entitlement may depend upon the overall economic environment. For example, the total amount of unemployment benefits to be paid out will depend upon the changing level of unemployment in the economy as the year wears on (Pfeiffer, 2017). Some large entitlement programs including Social Security pensions and government employee retirement programs have been "indexed" to inflation; hence, the size of the benefit is periodically adjusted according to a fixed formula based on unpredictable changes in the Consumers' Price Index. Additionally, the amount of spending on entitlement programs is impossible for the Senate and House Appropriations committees to even attempt to adjust or to control because those committees do not have the jurisdiction to rewrite the laws that specify who receives a certain amount of funds and under what conditions (Johnson, 2005).

According to Prager (2017), individuals who are multi-generation welfare recipients are dependent or "addicted" to welfare. This idea of social safety nets being a drug suggests that welfare is a career goal for family business that requires poverty persistence, rather than the know systemic poverty created in a nation where inequality prevents many from escaping the poverty that plague their community. Prager (2017) states that one indication of the power of entitlements addiction is the fact that while great numbers of people who have given up smoking cigarettes (or other recreational pharmaceuticals), misuse or abuse alcohol and other addictions because of the need for improved health; however, very few see the need to give up entitlements. The biggest difference is "motivation" if one refuses to give up smoking cigarettes after a scare of lung cancer, they make a conscious choice to accept the fact that the cancer will return, and will likely kill them. According to Prager (2017) many recipients of public assistance fear that if they choose to work they will lose healthcare coverage and adequate housing and not qualify for vouchers to assist with utility payments or other benefits, thus the fear of losing what is stable prevents recipients of public assistance from seeking and accepting viable work.

Many able-bodied Americans who receive cash payments, believe that going to work will cause them to lose their benefits, the thought of giving up any one of those and beginning to pay for them with their own earned money does not enter the mind and if it does the welfare system is punitive. The benefits cliff is a paradox. For employees living in poverty, the real cost of higher minimum wage could be benefits lost and a few dollars gained. Even as the higher minimum was attempts to lift low wage workers out of poverty and assist them with becoming self-sufficient, it may actually leave them worse off than before. The reason? The few extra dollars taken out of their paychecks cause them to lose the federal benefit including food stamps or housing subsidies. Anyone who has ever been on public assistance or what has been termed the benefits "cliff" understands the fear of losing everything while trying to move ahead. The benefits "cliff" is when one is currently receiving a benefit and after one has earned $1 many believe that the benefit stops abruptly and entirely (Rampell, 2016). For most other benefit programs, there is a phase out program where you lose part of your benefit for every dollar earned; this loss oftentimes is throughout the recertification period even if the earning was from a temporary position (Rampell, 2016). With these types of punitive measures, many recipients of safety net programs elect not to work or if they work prefer to "work under the table" rather than to report income from working and risk breaking the law. The challenge for most individuals living in poverty and receiving benefits is that work ethic is developed over time and for someone who has not been in the workforce it is difficult to arrive on time, have a positive disposition, perform well, communicate effectively and a host of other job related soft-skills can cause them to quit their job or be terminated. Politicians understand these concerns, which is why it is nearly impossible to reduce entitlements particularly when their constituents are losing subsidies that provide them with basic needs, they understand that a reduction in benefits will impact their constituents voting decisions. Democrats are keenly aware of this, which is why the political Left (i.e., conservatives) usually win debates over entitlements (Prager, 2017). Every American who is the beneficiary of an entitlement supports them, and many who are not beneficiaries of entitlements such as single non-parents, men, and students who often suffer from hunger and homelessness. Aside from ideology, this underscores the reason political conservatives constantly seeks to increase entitlements. The more people receiving government benefits, the more people vote conservatively (Prager, 2017). This addiction ultimately ruins the character of many of its recipients, the economies of all the countries in which it exists, and the value system that created the prosperity that made so many entitlements possible in the first place. But other than American conservatives, virtually no one even recognizes it as a major problem or an addiction (Prager, 2017).

ENTITLEMENTS BY OTHER NAMES

In the run-up to the 2012 election, the Fox Business website devoted a week to "Entitlement Nation: Makers vs. Takers" (Fox Business, 2011). Governor Mitt Romney denounced President Obama as the avatar of a dystopian "Entitlement Society" (Hertzberg, 2013). In his most memorable speech, Mr. Romney accused the "47%" of Americans who supposedly "believe that they are victims" of also believing "that they are entitled to health care, to food, to housing, to you name it—that that's an entitlement, and the government should give it to them" (Moorhead, 2012). In contrast, President Obama, in his inaugural address, did not let the word "entitlements" pass his lips. Instead, he mentioned Medicare and Social Security, which, he said, "do not make us a nation of takers; they free us to take the risks that make our country great." Yet he, like many other Democrats, returned to discussing "entitlements" and the need for reform (Greenblatt, 2013).

The Center for Budget and Policy Priorities considers Social Security, Medicare, Medicaid, children's health insurance, food stamps, school lunch programs, welfare, unemployment insurance, the Child Tax Credit and the Earned Income Tax Credit as entitlements (Policy Basics, 2015). It does not include a few discretionary programs (like rental assistance or low-income energy subsidies) that are aimed directly at the poor. Those programs, however, are significantly scaled down in comparison to entitlement programs. Understanding the different social insurance programs and the populations served by them should be a guide to improving policy decisions related to America's vulnerable citizens. It is very well documented that people living in poverty are more likely to victimize or become victims of crime. In an interview with Richard Rosenfeld, a criminology professor at the University of Missouri-St. Louis, stated "having less wealth puts a strain on individuals and families, and the added stress of living in poverty can sometimes lead people to commit crimes to get cash" (Burdziak, 2017). Social insurance as most entitlements are; is to ensure that no recipient has to commit a crime to feed themselves or their families; however, the battle of reform that focuses on reduction of investment only, rather than maximizing the investment by ensuring that recipients are required to invest in themselves through education and work using a positive reinforcement approach from a strength based model rather than the current negative reinforcement that leads to abuse.

There is a spate of misinformation and propaganda that confuses both the recipients and the tax payers who feel taken advantage of every pay period as they peruse their deductions. This misinformation keeps the welfare issue in the political discussions. It is unlikely that the U.S. will completely annihilate welfare programs, however the form at which they are administered may impact the lives our most vulnerable populations. It is critical that we forget political alliances and consider policies that make sense for the 21st century America that exist today and is starkly different from Roosevelt's 1935 America, where significantly more people must be assisted, but the unrestrained frustrations of those pushed to the fringes. Many votes along party lines. For example, Republicans vote against entitlements and Democrats vote for them; however, it appears that many votes without a full understanding of how their vote for or against policies will mean to the welfare of American families. To help simplify what is an entitlement by its formal title I have listed with definitions per the federal government (USA.gov, 2017). U.S. Welfare Programs fit into the 13 categories listed below. The common base of all U.S. welfare programs is to provide benefits to low-income individuals and families. The programs represent entitlements to all Americans but benefits are only paid to individuals and families with low income.

1. **Medicaid Program:** This program provides free or low-cost medical benefits to millions of Americans including some low-income families and children, pregnant women, elderly, people with disabilities, and in some states, other adults.
2. **Negative Income Tax:** Two tax credit programs are administered by the Internal Revenue Service (IRS) to distribute money to low-income Americans. The tax credits include a "refundable" portion which is paid to individuals and families that owe no income tax for the year. Therefore, this portion of the tax credits act as "negative income tax". The two programs are the Earned Income Tax Credit (EITC), and the Child Tax Credit.
3. **Supplemental Nutrition Assistance Program (SNAP):** This food program is implemented for low-income individuals and families. SNAP, formerly the food stamp program and is managed by the United States

Department of Agriculture (USDA). Program participants receive a debit card that is accepted in most grocery stories for the purchase of food.

4. **Housing Assistance:** Various housing programs are administered by the Department of Housing and Urban Development (HUD) including rental assistance, public housing and various community development grants.
5. **Supplemental Security Income (SSI):** This is a program distributes cash payments to low-income individuals over 65 years of age and 64 years old or less if the individual is blind or disabled. SSI is administered by the Social Security Administration.
6. **Pell Grants:** This is a grant program administered by the Department of Education to distribute up to $5,550 to students from low-income households to promote and support postsecondary education (colleges and trade schools).
7. **Temporary Assistance for Needy Families (TANF):** This is a combined federal and state program that pays cash to low-income households with the goal of moving individuals from welfare status to employment. TANF is administered by the U.S. Department of Health and Human Services.
8. **Child Nutrition:** These are food programs administered by the USDA provide breakfast, school lunch, and after school programs. The programs support children from low-income households and provide free or reduced-price meals.
9. **Head Start:** This is a pre-school program available to kids from low-income families. It is administered by U.S. Department of Health and Human Services (HHS).
10. **Job Training Programs:** These are a myriad of training programs administered by the Department of Labor (DOL) that provide job training, displacement and employment services generally targeting low-income Americans.
11. **Women Infants and Children (WIC):** This is a program to provide healthy food to pregnant women and children up to five years of age and are available to low-income households.
12. **Child Care:** This is a block grant program to states and local public and private agencies who administer child care programs for low-income families. Child Care is administered by HHS.
13. **Low Income Home Energy Assistance Program (LIHEAP):** This program provides aid to low-income households by paying a high proportion of household income for home energy, either heating or cooling a residential dwelling. LIHEAP is administered by HHS.

14. **Lifeline (Obama Phone):** This program provides discounted phone service, landline and cell phones, to low-income individuals. The program is administered by the Federal Communications Commission (Federal Safety Net, n.d.).

THE GREAT AMERICAN SAFETY NETS

In the face of welfare reform under the new administration will those promises that were declared to these angry unemployed, willing to work supporters be honored? Or will they be given to those prepared to work in this age of technology. With 51% of white men believing that additional education will not help them become employed (Kelly, 2015), what will happen when they lack the skills required for the jobs that "Make America Great Again"? Research shows that safety nets, welfare or entitlements lifted 12.2 million working-age adults without a college degree out of poverty in 2014 and benefited another 11 million people who live in these adults' families. In contrast, the safety net lifted 1.8 million adults with a college degree out of poverty that year (Shapiro, Trisi, & Chaudhry, 2017). While adults lacking a college, degree constituted 57% of all adults, they constituted 87% of the adults whom safety net programs lifted above the poverty line. This is the group that includes the 51% of uneducated white males who believe that education is not necessary to improve their future job prospects (Kelly, 2015). The safety net lifted 6.2 million working-age white adults without a college degree out of poverty in 2014, reducing their poverty rate by more than two-fifths — from 24.3% (before considering the safety net's effects) to 13.6%. About half of all working-age adults without a college degree whom safety net programs lift out of poverty are white (Shapiro, Trisi, & Chaudhry, 2017). Additionally, poverty substantially was reduced among other groups, as well. In 2014, it reduced the poverty rate for working-age black adults who lack a college degree from 43.1% before government benefits and taxes to 24.4% after the benefits and taxes are taken into account; this represents the largest %age point reduction in poverty among the groups examined. Still, poverty rates are significantly higher among people of color than whites before and after government benefits and taxes are taken into account (Shapiro, Trisi, & Chaudhry, 2017).

What happens when welfare has been reformed and there is no utility assistance, housing assistance, or food assistance programs for the unemployed or underemployed and no Pell grants to obtain the adequate skills for the new job market? These questions take me back to the conversation on Facebook that focused on shaming, denying and justifying the benefits used by white people. The notion that white people will receive more Social Security than others because they pay more and live longer is true. However, that is a myopic view of the article by Tracy Jan of *The Washington Post* (2017). The article reported on the findings of the Center on Budget and Policy Priorities (Shapiro, Trisi, & Chaudhry, 2017) titled *Poverty Reduction Programs Help Adults Lacking College Degrees the Most: Nearly 9 in 10 Working-Age Adults Lifted above the Poverty Line Lack College Degrees*. This article focused on the positive impact that entitlement programs has on all groups. The report noted more white people without a college degree were lifted out of poverty due to entitlement programs.

People of all races and ethnic groups who lack a bachelor's degree receive significant help from the safety net, but on two significant metrics, the results for white working-age adults stand out. Among working-age adults without a college degree, 6.2 million whites are lifted above the poverty line by the safety net more than any other racial or ethnic group. In addition, the percentage of people who would otherwise be poor that safety net programs lift out of poverty is greater for white working-age adults without a college degree than for other adults without a college degree. Still, poverty rates among people without a college degree are substantially higher for blacks and Hispanics than for whites whether or not safety net assistance is considered. (Shapiro, Trisi, & Chaudhry, 2017)

This statement is the part of the article that drew rage because the readers felt the article misrepresented the data. The CBPP article noted that the data is accurate and that a portion of the information from the National Review author is also correct. However, the focus on Social Security dismisses the actual report from the CBPP article that states "Among working-age adults, Social Security, SNAP, two refundable tax credits (the Earned Income Tax Credit and the Child Tax Credit), and the Supplemental Security Income program for poor people who are elderly or have disabilities all have their largest effects in reducing poverty among those without a college degree (2017, p. 5)." The point of the article is not focused on the percentages, but the sheer number of white people 6.2 million versus the 2.8 millions of black Americans whose lives changed for the better as a result of government entitlements. Additionally, the programs included in this study were Social Security as well as SNAP/Food Stamps, Earned Income Tax Credits, Child

Tax Credit, and SSI. The Earned Income Tax Credit (EITC) and Child Tax Credit (CTC) are successful federal tax credits for low- and moderate-income working people. These programs encourage work, help offset the cost of raising children, and lift millions of people out of poverty status. Recent research suggests that income from these credits leads to benefits at virtually every stage of life, including improved school performance, higher college enrollment, and increased work effort and earnings in adulthood (Shapiro, Trisi, & Chaudhry, 2017).

While white people responding to the *National Review* article attempt to deny the use of government benefits by their race, they also ignore that the data provided is not representing seniors receiving social security benefits but for preretirement individuals in the 18–64 age group (Williamson, 2017). A deeper examination into social security benefits 2015 data for those retired individuals 65 and older offered deeper insight into the benefits afforded to more than 12 million white seniors and to significantly lower numbers of all other races.

The data provided by the Center on Budget and Policy Priorities (Shapiro, Trisi, & Chaudhry, 2017) revealed that white children and adults, not retirees, benefitted from many of social safety nets, in similar numbers as blacks and Hispanics (p. 5). This is where many researchers and reporters believe that the so-called Trump revolutionaries (perhaps unknowingly) voted against their own interest. Upwards of 18 million white Americans benefit from SNAP, TANF, SSI, EITC, CTC, ACA, Medicaid, Housing Assistance, LIHEAP, Child Nutrition, WIC, Head Start, Pell Grants, Social Security and other programs that take them from a healthy birth to a respectable death (Chaudry et al., 2016).

RISING FROM POVERTY VIA ENTITLEMENTS: A PERSONAL STORY

Now, let's make this discussion personal. Born in North Carolina in 1970, I'm the middle child of 14 brothers and sisters. My parents were not only partners in marriage, but also partners in the demanding business of sharecropping. At that time, my family was at the mercy of our boorish landowners and yet we did not miss a meal, we were relatively happy and did not concern ourselves with how we ate, just that we ate. We thought we had big rolls of bologna because they were for big families, and large square blocks of cheese that we could taste sometimes. In February 1982, my father died of lung cancer. At 11 years old, my world changed forever. My siblings and I were all sent to our relatives and various group homes. My mother lost the home because the breadwinner of our home was gone. We lost the 2.5 acres of land and our family home that my father purchased just two years earlier. I landed in Philadelphia with an older aunt as my guardian, and my 1/14th share of my father's WWII veterans benefits of approximately $46.00 per month. No one can debate that $46.00 is insufficient to provide the needs of an 11-year-old child. Therefore, food stamps and the welfare check my aunt received as she worked full-time in a factory, were the only benefits available, with free school lunches, access to free summer camps. Later, fee waivers for college applications and Pell Grants gave me the opportunity to be lifted from poverty.

Upon graduating from high school, I was accepted in several great colleges. However, no matter how "smart" I was, I lacked the sociocultural capital to belong and eventually, I dropped out. I followed a predictable path for an inner-city black girl and became pregnant. I went back to North Carolina at the age of nineteen pregnant and undereducated. I went to work full time at McDonalds and to Social Services to receive more benefits. I received a welfare check of $224.00, Medicaid, food stamps of $150.00, rental reduction to $227.00 per month and WIC. So, until I delivered my daughter, I was sustained by these social safety nets or entitlements. After my daughter was born I was eligible for a child care subsidy that allowed me to work and return to college. I met my husband when my daughter was 3 months old and we married 1 year and 5 months later. At this time, I became ineligible for all of the previous entitlements because of his meager Burlington Industries factory pay of $376.00 bi-weekly and my variable, unpredictable waitress wages. My husband and I enrolled in college with the help of the Pell Grant entitlement. After completing my general education courses at the local community college, I transferred to North Carolina A&T State University under my entitled Pell grant, and graduated *Suma Cum Laude*. Now, my two daughters are University of North Carolina graduates one MA from Teacher's College. My husband graduated with a degree in computer science and is a successful project manager with a computer science degree and has earned numerous professional certifications. I continued my education and have a masters and doctoral degree in education. Yes, this is a common story for Americans born in poverty, but using the support systems that were established in 1935 to change the lives of poor whites suffering after The Depression.

I am a product of entitlements/benefits that lifted me from poverty to prosperity. I am not ashamed or apologetic of using the laws and policies to elevate myself, just as President Trump was not ashamed to use the entitlement of bankruptcy to resolve his unfavorable business decisions. This debate is only an issue because there is confusion about how many Americans benefit from all types of entitlements including tax breaks for the wealthy, bankruptcy claims to erase their financial failures, and, more importantly, the legal decisions that allow privileged whites to avoid prison sentences because they lack melanin. To reiterate, I understand this debate from both sides, that of the poor and of the middle class. I am challenged when I see the deductions from my salary each pay cycle and the huge end of year tax bill that interferes with my summer vacation. However, I do not forget that these entitlements afforded me an opportunity to become a productive citizen in a nation where I was more likely to be a statistic than an "over achiever".

To be clear, I am not an over achiever or an anomaly, the entitlements provided me with opportunities that my brilliance alone would not have and like me there are millions of Americans who need help wading through the milieu of a life where "shit happens". The deficit model is often used to describe those who need a chance encourages even the neediest citizens to be shamed into fighting against their own interest. Why is it that we ignore resilience and the strengths of those Americans who survive on meager incomes and still complain and shame them for using the law and its benefits to provide for their families? Unemployment, Pell Grants, School Lunch, Job Training, Housing and many other needs should be the joy of the wealthiest nation to offer those who helped build that wealth. My black, Hispanic, white and other ethnic brothers and sisters who revolted against the *status quo* candidate in November of 2016 were not lazy, just angry. Their anger stemmed from a loss unfamiliar and unexplainable to those who worked in factories, lumber and brick yards, and coal mines for generations building the wealth of their employers only to be shut out because the owners increased their profits and found ways to enjoy higher profits in other countries. Yes, it is progress for the nations who received what many Americans believed they were entitled and promised, but it was a backward move that caused them to chant "Make America Great Again" in unison with a business man (turned politician) who benefitted from compromising their jobs.

CONCLUSION

Many people are in the dark about what entitlements are and who benefit from them, like the Facebook posters people opposed to welfare and food stamps will cherry pick through the list of federal programs and argue that they have not received federal aid. Thus, one of the primary goals of this chapter was to clarify the definition of "entitlement programs". Another goal was that many are confused about how social security is actually calculated. It is true that "entitlement programs" have become a pejorative phrase in with the insinuation that poor people are receiving something they didn't earn; however, the term is used for any government program guaranteeing certain benefits to a segment of the population. It has nothing to do with whether recipients deserve, nor is it linked to a cost-benefit analysis on taxes paid versus benefits received. Secondly, Social Security and Medicare are not just entitlement programs. They are also an examples of entitlement redistribution. It is true that every American worker pays into the Social Security program, however Americans are not saving there funds are absorbed by citizens who are no longer able to work or have retired – redistribution. However, when Medicare is considered most senior citizens end up receiving more in Social Security and Medicare benefits than they paid into the system during their working years (Mack, 2012). It is critically important that we understand the beneficiaries of "entitlement programs" prior to cutting, disbanding or reforming entitlements. Millions of "baby boomers" are currently senior citizens and the largest entitlement programs are Social Security and Medicare, which comprise two-thirds of expenditures on mandatory federal entitlement programs. It is equally important to recognize that the most significant income redistribution in the United States is not from the rich to the poor, but from younger taxpayers to retirees. To vote for reform may diminish the value these social safety nets afford our America is like playing Russian roulette and no one knows who will lose. Given the discussion above, the same question of who loses arises. Will it be our children, our grandparents, our mothers, or our veterans?

REFERENCES

Abad-Santos, A. (2013, January 4). It's official Romney got 47% of the vote. *The Atlantic's Politics & Policy Daily*. Retrieved from https://www.theatlantic.com/politics/archive/2013/01/mitt-romney-47-percent-vote-total/319864/

Batko, S. (2014, January 9). *It's January. You know what that means….* Retrieved April 18, 2017, from http://www.endhomelessness.org/blog/entry/its-january.-you-know-what-that-means#.WPWTotLyuM8

Blank, R. M., & Schoeni, R. F. (2003). Changes in the distribution of childrens family income over the 1990's. *The American Economic Review*, *93*(2), 304–308. doi:10.1257/000282803321947245

Burdziak, A. (2017, February 7). Experts say connection between crime and poverty is complex. *Columbia Daily Tribune* [Columbia]. Retrieved from http://www.columbiatribune.com/news/leftbehind/experts-say-connection-between-crime-and-poverty-is-complex/article_51c865d8-9d32-58b9-b691-a52dcf6dff48.html

Center on Budget and Policy Priorities. (2016, August 5). *TANF at 20*. Retrieved March 4, 2017, from http://www.cbpp.org/research/family-income-support/chart-book-tanf-at-20

Chaudry, A., Wimer, C., MaCartney, S., Frohlich, L., Campbell, C., Swenson, K., & Hauan, S. (2016). *Poverty in the United States: 50-year trends and safety net impacts*. Office of Human Services Policy Office of the Assistant Secretary for Planning and Evaluation U.S. Department of Health and Human Services.

Child Trends. (2015). *Homeless children and youth*. Retrieved April 18, 2017, from https://www.childtrends.org/indicators/homeless-children-and-youth/

DeParle, J. (2012, April 7). Welfare limits left poor adrift as recession hit. *New York Times*. Retrieved from http://www.nytimes.com/2012/04/08/us/welfare-limits-left-poor-adrift-as-recession-hit.html

Federal Safety Net. (n.d.). *U.S. welfare programs*. Retrieved from http://federalsafetynet.com/us-welfare-programs.html

Fox Business. (2011, May 20). *Entitlement nation: Makers vs. takers*. Retrieved from http://www.foxbusiness.com/features/2011/05/20/entitlement-nation-makers-vs-takers.html

Greenblatt, A. (Producer). (2013, January 21). *It's all politics* [Television broadcast]. Washington, DC: NPR.

Hansan, J. (2011). *Widows pensions: An introduction*. Retrieved April 3, 2017, from socialwelfare.library.vcu.edu/programs/widows-pensions-an-introduction/

Hansan, J. E. (2011). *English poor laws: Historical precedents of tax-supported relief for the poor*. Retrieved March 15, 2017, from http://socialwelfare.library.vcu.edu/programs/poor-laws/

Hertzberg, H. (2013, April 8). *Senses of entitlement*. Retrieved from http://www.newyorker.com/magazine/2013/04/08/senses-of-entitlement

Higginbotham, P. (2017). *The new poor law*. Retrieved from http://www.workhouses.org.uk/poorlaws/newpoorlaw.shtml

Jan, T. (2016, February). The biggest beneficiaries of the government safety net: Working-class whites. *Washington Post*. Retrieved from https://www.washingtonpost.com/news/wonk/wp/2017/02/16/the-biggest-beneficiaries-of-the-government-safety-net-working-class-whites/?utm_term=.7c5c61b835ad

Jimenez, J. (2015). Politics to support income. In *Social policy and social change: Toward the creation of social and economic justice* (p. 272). Thousand Oaks, CA: Sage.

Johnson, P. (2005). *A glossary of political economy terms*. Retrieved from http://www.auburn.edu/~johnspm/gloss/entitlement_program

Kelly, A. (2015, April 4). The neglected majority: What Americans without a college degree think about higher education. *Forbes*. Retrieved from https://www.forbes.com/sites/akelly/2015/04/28/the-neglected-majority-what-americans-without-a-college-degree-think-about-higher-education-part-1/#6c49602b72cf

Levin, J. (2013, December 20). The truth behind the lies of the original 'welfare queen' [Television series episode]. Interview by M. Block. In All Things Considered. NPR.

Mack, J. (2012, September 9). *Are social security and medicare 'entitlement' programs?* Retrieved from http://www.mlive.com/opinion/kalamazoo/index.ssf/2012/09/ are_social_security_and_medica.html

Moorhead, M. (2012, September 18). *Mitt Romney says 47 percent of Americans pay no income tax*. Retrieved February 16, 2017, from http://www.politifact.com/truth-o-meter/statements/2012/sep/18/mitt-romney/romney-says-47-percent-americans-pay-no-income-tax/

O'Neill, J. (2001). *Gaining ground? Measuring the impact of welfare reform and work* (17). Retrieved from Manhattan Institute, Center for Civic Innovation website: https://www.manhattan-institute.org/html/gaining-ground-measuring-impact-welfare-reform-welfare-and-work-5795.html

Pfeiffer, B. (2017). *Federal safety net.* Retrieved from http://federalsafetynet.com/index.html

Piven, F. F., & Cloward, R. A. (1979). *Poor people's movements: Why they succeed, how they fail.* New York, NY: Vintage books.

Policy Basics. (2015). *Policy basics: Where do our federal tax dollars go?* Retrieved from Center on Budget and Policy Priorities website: http://www.cbpp.org/research/federal-budget/policy-basics-where-do-our-federal-tax-dollars-go

Prager, D. (2017, March). *The most dangerous addiction of them all: Entitlements.* Retrieved from https://townhall.com/columnists/dennisprager/2017/03/21/the-most-dangerous-addiction-of-them-all-entitlements-n2301802

Rector, R. (2012, May 3). *Examining the means-tested welfare state: 79 programs and $927 billion in annual spending," testimony before the budget committee* [Testimony]. Retrieved from http://www.heritage.org/research/testimony/2012/05/examining-the-means-tested-welfare-state

Rector, R. E. (1999). *The determinants of welfare caseload decline* (99-04). Retrieved from Heritage Foundation website: http://www.heritage.org/welfare/report/the-determinants-welfare-caseload-decline

Soss, J. (2002). *Unwanted claims: The politics of participation in the U.S. welfare system.* Ann Arbor, MI: University of Michigan Press.

USA.gov. (2017, February 28). *Government benefits.* Retrieved from https://www.usa.gov/benefits

Williamson, K. (2017, February 16). *Do whites benefiting disproportionately from welfare?* Retrieved from http://www.nationalreview.com/corner/444986/washington-posts-welfare-stupidity-whites-benefiting-disproportionately

ENDNOTES

1 In 1976, former California Governor and Republican presidential candidate Ronald Reagan issued a wholesale condemnation of Black female welfare recipients as ruthless con artists robbing the federal government blind and undermining the moral fabric of U.S. society. The

so-called "welfare queen," as Reagan stated in his diatribe, "has eighty names, thirty addresses, twelve Social Security cards and is collecting veterans benefits on four non-existing deceased husbands. And she is collecting Social Security on her cards. She's got Medicaid, getting food stamps, and she is collecting welfare under each of her names. Her tax-free cash income is over $150,000."

2 January also brings with it HUD's annual Point-in-Time Count (PIT Count). Quick PIT Count 101: a PIT Count is a one-night, unduplicated count of every person experiencing homelessness in a community. HUD requires that communities count their sheltered homeless population every year. They require that communities count their unsheltered homeless population every other year, on odd numbered calendar years. Communities are to conduct their count during the last 10 days of January.

Chapter 5
What I Think I Heard You Say:
Learning How to Improve Challenging Social and Political Interactions

Lisa Sechrest-Ehrhardt
University of the District of Columbia, USA

ABSTRACT

The United States is a diverse country which includes a vast tapestry rich in cultures, ethnicities, languages, and religions. The robust diversity is what defines the nation, its character, its identity, and its strength. This rich tapestry of diversity also provides the nation with a unique status among all nations and is viewed as a nation of immigrants. One aspect of such diversity is the complicated nature of social interactions between and among people who have different perceptions about the world. Often one's perception effects behavior in social interactions having positive or negative results. Using two theories, Symbolic Interaction and Cognitive, this chapter guides the reader to understanding the complicated relationships that arise when one interacts with and among others who may not perceive the world in the same manner.

INTRODUCTION

The world is a challenge place at times. Political, economic, and social factors, singularly and collectively, contribute to the challenges we encounter as we interact and socialize with others. Currently, simple conversations and differences of opinions regarding the topics mentioned can turn into ugly, argumentative, and on the rare occasion, become a physical confrontation.

DOI: 10.4018/978-1-5225-3843-1.ch005

Social interactions with others can become stressful and touchy when we perceive that others "just don't get it". Using two theories, Symbolic Interaction and Cognitive, this chapter guides readers to understanding the complicated relationships that sometimes arise when one interacts with and among others who may not perceive the world in the same manner. Part of the complication is between oneself, one's perceptions, and the contentious social interactions with others. Using parables and case examples the chapter offers detailed suggestions regarding how self-awareness can provide an avenue to easing tension in challenging social interactions.

Social Interaction Theory

A theory is a set of building blocks that explains a phenomenon. There are explanatory theories and change theories. Symbolic Interaction Theory is an explanatory theory and explains how people deal with the world. In contrast, Cognitive Theory is a change theory and facilitates, predicts, or explains the outcome of how people respond to a given situation, or how we arrive at a decision.

Symbolic Interaction Theory posits that the self and identity develop by using shared symbols that emerge through daily interactions with others in a shared community or society and that individual's identities change based on the continual social interactions within society (Blumer, 1969; Mead, 1937). A major concept of this theory is that the self is viewed as a social being that experiences constant growth and change as it "the self" interacts within the environment (Sechrest-Ehrhardt, 2012). As we mature and start developing a sense of self we begin to figure out our role in society. Symbolic Interaction suggests that much of our learning about who we are and where we fit in the bigger scheme of things is a result of putting ourselves in "the role of the other" (Charon, 2004, p. 114). This suggestion is extremely important as it proposes that as we begin to learn about ourselves and at the same time taking on the role of "other" helps us to understand how that other person may perceives us. Charon (2004) suggests, "if we want to influence or teach others we need to understand "where they are at" so that what we do makes sense to them" (p. 114). When people take the role of the other they engage in an active process where they can understand and actively form their actions per their definitions of what they perceive others are thinking or doing.

At this point, I am guessing that you might be thinking, "This is a confusing concept" and asking, "How is it going to help me form better relationships so that I can better navigate social interactions in today's changing world?" Let me first state that there is no more important time than now to understand this concept. The idea of assuming the role of "the other" to better navigate social interactions is extremely crucial at this juncture in United States history. I believe that the United States is experiencing what those of us in the field of social science call a "paradigm shift" i.e., a change in thinking. Our society is currently experiencing a shift in basic assumptions about how we, the United States, view the world. This societal, and change in thinking makes it essential that each one of us develops the skill of consciously taking the role of "other" to gain a sense of how to interpret and understand how others may perceive us at any given time in any social interaction. The social interactions I am referring to can and often occur in one's family, neighborhood, community, academic environment, or place of employment. Social interactions occur every time we interact with others. Simply stated, if we desire to make sense of significant world changes, which appear to be happening at an alarming speed and feel like they are happening to us, then we had better grasp an understanding about how others perceive us so that we can are in a stronger position in social interactions. We appear to be trapped in a blame game in which many of the players, ourselves included, refuse to take responsibility for actions or roles in social interactions. We are talking at each other instead of to each other. We can only see one side of the equation without fully understanding how some of our actions may contribute negatively to the outcome in social interactions. Perhaps most challenging is the fact that many of us believe that it is the "other" who needs to change, become more introspective, and be open to seeing "our side of the equation". We may do this without ever considering that perhaps we may need to do the same.

How many times have you had an argument with someone, and then questioned that person's intelligence motives, or sanity? After several futile attempts to convince the other person that they are wrong, ignorant, vindictive, or "bat shit" crazy for adopting that perspective, you begin to feel frustrated. During this process, you quietly assure yourself that, "if that jerk could only understand where I am coming from" he or she would appreciate the situation and "clearly realize that I am correct." If you are truly being honest with yourself, I suspect that type of frustrating situation (i.e., social interaction) has happened more than a few times.

You might be thinking, "Why do I need to "get in the head of the other person" who has no clue of my perspective of the world?" or "Why should I consider how to figure out what this other person might think about me when I already know what they think by their actions and words, especially when they have no clue of what it means to be female, African-American, Gay, Lesbian, Jewish, Muslim, or poor? Perhaps, you are thinking that taking the role of the other is a pointless exercise that will only make you more frustrated about the current state of affairs. No matter what you say or do, another person's disparaging remarks and attitude aimed at you only provides fodder for you to retaliate in kind. Message received loud and clear! While some of your thoughts may be true, living in a constant state of being guarded and necessitating to retaliation is neither healthy nor conducive for the human soul. Harboring anger and mistrust of others hampers one's ability to meaningfully engage in positive social interactions. So, it might be worthwhile to step back and learn more about yourself and "others" so that you can be proactive instead of reactive in social interactions.

Before proceeding, I unequivocally state that under no circumstances am I condoning that one accepts or tolerate any form of sexist, racist, anti-Semite, anti-Muslimism, or elitist behavior. What I am suggesting is that we each provide ourselves the opportunity to step back, reflect on, and assess social interaction from a different vantage point. This requires that we begin to understand the social dynamics along with the social construction of the political and socioeconomic power structure of the United States. One chapter within a book cannot claim to provide a person with all the tools they will need to successfully navigate the social, political, and economic terrain of the United States. However, understanding the social dynamics between and within these factors and being cognitively aware of one's personal actions can affect social interactions related to these factors is a reasonable and logical place to start.

To learn and understand more about others, we first need to learn more about ourselves. We must become self-aware. Self-awareness is defined as "an awareness of one's own personality or individuality" (Merriam-Webster Dictionary, 2007, p. 1126). Becoming self-aware includes each of us tapping into our own identity. Identity is who we are, who we say we are, and sometimes what others say we are. It is a multidimensional concept. Beverly Tatum (2010), a prominent psychologist, describes identity as a complex concept that is shaped by an individual's characteristics, family dynamics, historical factors, and social political factors. Psychologist Erik Erikson (1968) suggested that identity develops in social, cultural, and historical contexts. He also emphasized that a major task of identity formation includes the internalizing of beliefs, values, and relationships to define the self within a cultural context.

This view of identity suggests that self-awareness embraces an understanding of self within social, cultural, political, and historical contexts.

As discussed above, Symbolic Interaction Theory posits that the self and identity develop by using shared symbols that emerge through daily interactions with others in a shared community or society and that all individuals experience an ever-changing identity based on continual social interactions within society (Blumer, 1969; Mead, 1937). For one to apply this theory to practice and learn how to act in social interactions, it is important to have a clear sense of Symbolic Interaction Theory. The following is an excerpt from my doctoral dissertation which will facilitate a better understanding of the concept.

There are five central tenets of symbolic interaction theory, 1) the role of social interaction, 2) the role of thinking, 3) the role of definition, 4) the role of the present, and 5) the role of the active human being (Blumer, 1969). The first tenet of Symbolic Interaction theory perceives communities of consisting of active participants who engage and interact with each other. By interacting with each other, individuals and communities are in a process of constant change and evolution. These interactions are dynamic, and as individuals interact back and forth, a more dynamic and active individual emerges rather than the same individual repeatedly interacting within the environment (Blumer, 1969; Charon, 2004).

The second tenet suggests that individuals' interactions are influenced by their thinking. The role of thinking is extremely important in Symbolic Interaction Theory. The internal process of thinking has a significant effect on people's actions. Individuals' actions are in accordance with how they are thinking in specific situations and are often influenced to some extent by interactions with others. However, the thinking that occurs within one's self is very important.

Third, as people interact within the environment, situations are not fully or immediately understood. However, as different situations unfold, people attempt to understand the circumstances of the situations. Subsequently, as people begin to understand situations, they attach meaning to and define the situations, and after a situation is defined and is given a meaning, an individual acts accordingly. The definitions that are formed and assigned to certain situations are a result of interactions with others and interactions within ourselves.

The fourth tenet of Symbolic Interaction Theory suggests that when a person takes action, they do so because of their present situation. Personal actions are contingent on how a situation is defined by the individual at that particular moment, what the individual thinks at that particular moment, and the interaction that is occurring at that particular moment. Predictably, an individuals' past or background may influence the situation if they think about it; however, it is redefined adapted in the present in order to deal with the current situation (Blumer, 1969; Charon, 2004).

The fifth tenet of Symbolic Interaction Theory is that people are active. Everything that is done is done with regards to interaction with the environment, interaction with the self, or interactions with others within the environment. Individuals become who they are by interacting, by thinking about the interacting, by defining the interacting, by applying past thoughts to current situations, and by making decisions in the present based on factors in the immediate situation (Charon, 2004).

The main concept one should understand about Symbolic Interaction Theory is that in addition to the distinct character of interaction between and among human beings, people interpret and define other's actions and, in turn, assigns meaning to one another's actions (Blumer, 1969). The personal meaning that is attached to the interactions contributes to a person's identity" (Sechrest-Ehrhardt, 2012).

The following narrative provides an example of this phenomena. As young children begin their development, they also begin to develop an identity. Their identity is initially shaped by social interactions with family members and subsequently by social interactions with extended family, playmates, and their surrounding community. As children mature their identity is further shaped and molded by social interactions in a broader spectrum of the community and by additional interactions with media, school, more friends and acquaintances, and neighbors. Children begin to define themselves as an object based on others definition of them as an object. Other people in society often label and define a person to himself or herself and through this process, the social interaction, a person becomes an "object" to himself or herself (Blumer, 1969). For example, a little boy who is described by his parents and other people in his community as "Buddy, the athlete" may begin to define himself as "Buddy, the athlete".

It is important to note that the development of self is an ongoing process. Self-identity develops over time and consists of people giving meaning to social interactions within the social, cultural, political, and economic context. "People tend to view themselves in relations to others and may find a sense of belonging and pride in identifying with others who share similar experiences (Phinney, Root & Tatum, as cited in Sechrest-Ehrhardt, 2012, p. 21). This example could be related to the previous example regarding Buddy, who used to be an athlete.

Meaning making is also a critical factor in social interactions between and among people. The meaning associated with a social interaction is different for people based on a variety of and a combination of meaning of symbols assigned to concepts in society. Symbolic Interaction Theory defines symbols as social objects used to represent whatever people in a society agree those symbols represent (Charron, 2004). For example, a cross may represent a sign for Christianity, a yellow flashing light on a road sign may indicate that one should slow down and be vigilant, a thumb extended upward while the other fingers on a hand are closed may symbolize a gesture or expression of assent or approval, "OK" or "all is good". Symbols are also used for communication between and among people in society. Per Symbolic Interaction Theorists, symbols are social, meaningful, and significant (Blumer, 1948, Charron, 2004). Subsequently, that means symbols are defined and gain meaning in social interactions.

The term meaning which is key to the concept of symbol in Social Interaction becomes somewhat tricky to understand, specifically because people often have different meanings attached to symbols used in society. Although a society has norms and shared symbols which members of that society use in social interactions with each other, the process of "meaning making", the associations attached to these symbols, can result in something different to members of a society based on that person's identity. Identity can include race, ethnicity, gender, and or ability. Although members of society may understand the societal meaning assigned to a specific symbol, they may have a different meaning or perception of that symbol depending on their societal status. This is particularly evident with issues regarding race and social interactions involving racism. It is imperative to separate racism from the other forms of discrimination in the United States because from my experience as a professional social worker, diversity consultant/trainer, and African-American woman, I believe that racism stands alone as the single most significant factor that extolls the greatest harmful effects on the people it aims to destroy, disregard, discount, or dismiss Black, Brown and other peoples of color. Dr. Michael Eric Dyson, noted scholar, author, and sociology professor at Georgetown University, Washington, DC, and expert on the deleterious effects of racism in the United States asserts, "Racism remains the central problem in our culture; its brutal persistence brings out the ugliest features of the national character" (Dyson, 2004, p. 35). Consequently, those who fail to acknowledge that racism is a central theme that affects most of our daily social interactions will continue to be reactive and ill-prepared in social interactions.

Racism is not an easy concept top define and has been conceptualized many ways throughout the history of the United States. Each perception appears to capture varying elements of racism, however, according to Miller and Garrin, (2017), trying to answer the question what is racism? "may never be answered completely, and will always be contested", adding that "it is not as if anyone who is studying or writing about this subject has a completely 'objective' vantage point, because in a racialized society and world, everyone is racially situated" (p. 15). One aspect of racism is that it is a system of advantage where some individuals benefit based on their race. It is a system where those who are "advantaged, Whites, often benefit from cultural messages, institutional policies and laws, beliefs, and actions of individuals, while those who are disadvantaged, people of color, are disadvantaged by those same cultural messages, institutional policies and laws, beliefs, and actions" (Tatum, in Rothenberg & Kelly, 2014, p.128). Along with advantages come privileges that Whites have simply because they have White skin. The benefits associated with White privilege are "both hidden and transparent". Jennifer Holloday, author of the article "On Racism and White Privilege" suggests that the United States has a preference for "whiteness" and that this preference "saturates" our society (Teaching Tolerance, 2017, www.tolerance.org/article/racism-and-white-privilege, retrieved 3/12/17). White privilege is a topic that is extremely difficult for individuals to discuss. It is a topic of social conversations in which individuals often become reactive or proactive given their meaning and understanding, or lack thereof, associated with Whiteness. In her seminal article "White Privilege: Unpacking the Invisible Knapsack," Peggy McIntosh, Ph.D., a White feminist, and anti-racism scholar, identified the social rewards and advantages she experienced and those that her fellow colleagues who are women of color did not. McIntosh initiated a journey of self-awareness after reading two essays by Black women scholars, who stated, "White women were oppressive to work with". Bothered by the Black scholars' firm stance, McIntosh began to question whether there was any truth to what the scholars described. She stated that she prayed about this issue and discovered that she, in fact, enjoyed many privileges in her life that she took for granted, and became aware that those same privileges were not afforded to her African-American colleagues. She is clear in stating that she did not ask for these advantages and oftentimes she was unaware of the advantages. She reiterated that she was awarded benefits just because she was White. Below is a list of some of the White privileges McIntosh lists;

White Privileges:

- If I should need to move, I can be pretty sure of renting or purchasing housing in an area which I can afford and in which I would want to live.
- I can be pretty sure that my neighbors in such a location will be neutral or pleasant to me.
- I can go shopping alone most of the time, pretty well assured that I will not be followed or harassed.
- I can turn on the television or open to the front page of the paper and see people of my race widely represented.
- Whether I use checks, credit cards or cash, I can count on my skin color not to work against the appearance of financial reliability.
- I can arrange to protect my children most of the time from people who might not like them.
- I do not have to educate my children to be aware of systemic racism for their own daily physical protection.
- I can be pretty sure that my children's teachers and employers will tolerate them if they fit school and workplace norms; my chief worries about them do not concern others' attitudes toward their race.
- I can talk with my mouth full and not have people put this down to my color.
- I can swear, or dress in second hand clothes, or not answer letters, without having people attribute these choices to the bad morals, the poverty or the illiteracy of my race.
- I can speak in public to a powerful male group without putting my race on trial.
- I can do well in a challenging situation without being called a credit to my race.
- I am never asked to speak for all the people of my racial group.

McIntosh's revelations are important to understanding the meaning connected with social interaction. One's status in society is based on their race, gender, sexual orientation, socio-economic status, religion as well as the meaning attached to social interactions. Let us examine at the situation of purchasing a home. If all things are equal, choosing what neighborhood one wishes to live in and purchasing a house should depend on circumstances related to personal finances, proximity to work, grocery stores, and parks, quality of schools, and perhaps whether you like the types of houses offered in a neighborhood. However, those purchasing decisions are not equally offered or distributed.

Historically, African-Americans and other people of color have never had the identical privileges afforded to them as afforded to Whites with regard to purchasing a home (Kuebler & Rugh, 2013; Williams, 2015). Purchasing a home in a desired neighborhood has almost never been the same experience for African-Americans and other people of color as it is for Whites. A person of color with a favorable credit rating and financial status to purchase a home in a certain neighborhood does not often receive the same considerations as White Americans. For example, research conducted by the U.S. Department of Housing and Urban Development (HUD, 2013) revealed that home buyers were treated differently by banking institution, lending institutions, real estate agents and others depending on who they were. Specifically, Black, Hispanic, Asian, and white home buyers contacted real estate brokers to arrange appointments to visit properties that were on the market. In this study, the home buyers were "testers" (i.e., people who tested the system for fairness and equal rights). All testers were the same gender, age, and all were equally well-qualified to rent or own the properties. HUD reported that nearly all the testers could arrange appointments with the real estate brokers. However, after the initial stage of the study, not everyone was treated the same. Each home buyer or renter (i.e., "tester") met with real estate brokers who told them about the properties and then toured the properties. Their findings revealed that the number of available properties depended on the race or ethnicity of the prospective home buyer or renter. "In nearly all cases, whether renting or buying, minorities were told about and shown fewer properties than white people. Blacks were told about and shown about 17% fewer homes than whites, while Asians were told about 15.5% fewer homes and shown nearly 19% fewer properties" (www.cbsnews.com/news/racism-alive-and-well-in-housing Retrieved, 3/12/17).

Using Symbolic Interaction Theory as a framework, the meaning associated with purchasing a home is different for African-Americans and another person of color than it is for whites. For whites, the meaning associated with purchasing a home can include pride, financial success, stability, and comfort. For African-Americans and people of color the meaning associated with purchasing a home include some of those same attributes, but they might also include rejection, denied being shown certain homes, and fear. Although people of color qualify financially, they may not receive a loan from the bank based on racial prejudice, or exclusion and are not accepted by neighbors after home is purchased. Given equal or similar circumstances, the meaning associated with purchasing a home is different for Whites compared to Blacks based, in part, on racism and, one of the spoils of racism, White Privilege.

Cognitive Theory

As discussed above, Symbolic Interaction Theory is an explanatory theory and explains how one arrives at a certain place (i.e., psychologically) in social interactions. There is another theory that complements the current discussion. Cognitive Theory is a psychological theory that defines human behavior as a product of the human thought process. The theory also asserts that people's conscious thinking is the foundation for "most behavior and emotional experience" (Walsh, 2006, p. 132). People act and behave in ways that make sense to us based on our perceptions about ourselves, others, and the world. The relationship between thoughts, events, and emotions, are demonstrated in the cognitive model below was developed by Beck.

Moreover, Cognitive Theory is a change theory and explains the outcome of the social interaction. Symbolic Interaction combined with Cognitive Theory provides an effective foundation to develop a sense of self-awareness, which can prepare us to understand the connection between self and others in current socio-political situations that are often fraught with tension and animosity.

Beck (1995) theorized that it is not only an event that causes a person to have a certain emotion, but also the manner a person interprets that event causes a

Figure 1. Cognitive Theory

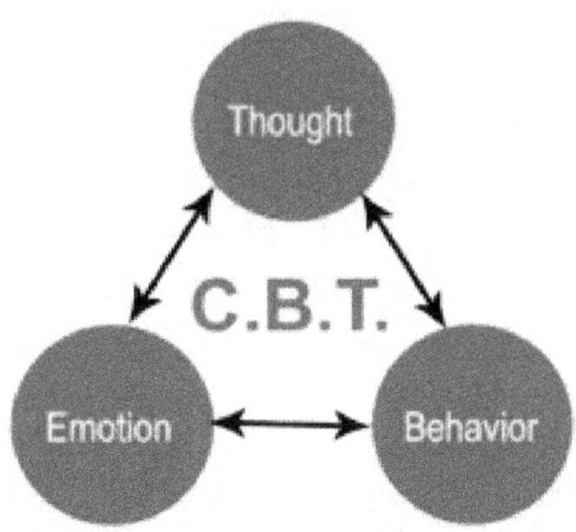

certain emotion. He simply stated, "The way people feel is associated with the way in which they interpret and think about a situation" (Beck, 1995, p. 14).

A person's beliefs about themselves, others, and the world begin to develop during their childhood. These beliefs are known as core beliefs. Core beliefs are "understandings that are so fundamental" and deeply stored within a person's brain, that they are "not even articulated to the person themselves" (Beck, 1995, p. 15).

Core beliefs are a primary form of belief and are thought to be global, unyielding, and overgeneralized (Beck, 1995). For example, a core belief of a young girl might be that "girls are not good at sports". Her core belief may not surface when she is demonstrating awesome skills in a sporting event; however, that core belief might surface when she is confronted by others that her skills threaten the boys with whom she is competing, or is told that young girls should not be interested in sports. Although she is an awesome athlete with competitive skills, she may focus on her core belief --"girls are not good at sports" -- and disregard the conflicting information. By trying to disregard the fact that she is good in sports, she maintains a belief even though it is inaccurate and in some cases dysfunctional". Consequently, when she stimulates her core belief "girls are not good at sports" she will interpret the situation and herself in a negative way.

People also have Intermediate Beliefs and Automatic Thoughts. Our Intermediate beliefs are triggered by core beliefs and include attitudes, rules, and assumptions about the world. Intermediate beliefs are usually not verbalized. Intermediate beliefs fit between core beliefs and Automatic Thoughts (see Figure 2 below). Automatic thoughts are the words and thoughts that go through a person's mind, are usually associated with a specific situation or a set of circumstances, and are considered a "superficial level" of thought (Beck, 1995, p. 15). Below is an example of an intermediate belief with the same young girl described above.

- **The Attitude:** "I can play sports if I like to",
- **The Rule or Expectation:** "I should play and be completive in sports",
- **The Assumption:** "If I like to play sports, and I am a completive athlete, I might earn a scholarship to college".

The intermediate beliefs that this young female athlete has about participating in sports influences her perception of the situation and sequentially how she thinks feels and behaves.

Cognitive Theory forwards that people attempt to make sense out of their world from the earliest stages of development. Each of us tries to organize our experiences in ways that make sense and help us adapt to our environment (Beck 1995). Together, our social interactions in the framework of Symbolic Interaction Theory discussed above with others lead to our understanding of how the world works and how we function in the world, and our thinking (cognitive processes) about our social interaction in the world helps us attach meaning (i.e., beliefs and thoughts) to situations in the world.

The current social, political, and economic situation in the United States has created an unsettling concern with many people. Social interactions with others are troubled with tension, anger, anxiety, and, in some circumstances, violence. Currently, a large minority in the United States experienced shock from the unpredicted, unlikely election of Donald Trump to President of the United States. Donald Trump is an unconventional politician who entered the political arena in the summer of 2015 announcing his candidacy for President. His brash, bombastic rhetoric was harshly ridiculed by everyone in the press, political circles, business world, sporting events, and kitchen tables across America. He became the brunt of jokes in some circles and on social media with people anxiously awaiting to read what friends had tweeted or posted on Facebook, making sure that they too posted or tweeted their own spoofs about Donald Trump "The Joker". The unconventional behavior and speech of then candidate Trump appeared to be just want some people wanted, while on the other hand this eccentric, bombastic, behavior and attitude concerned many who felt that the candidate was "not playing by the rules". The new uncertain "social interaction" made many people in the United States feel uncomfortable and ambiguous as to how to "make meaning" of the unprecedented demeanor of the presidential race. This uncertainty led to a social political atmosphere in the United States not experienced in decades. There appeared to be a hovering anxiety that swept the nation because there was no "norm". Although we are a diverse nation, individuals have different beliefs, assumptions, and thoughts about the world, and ones' place in the

Figure 2. Core beliefs

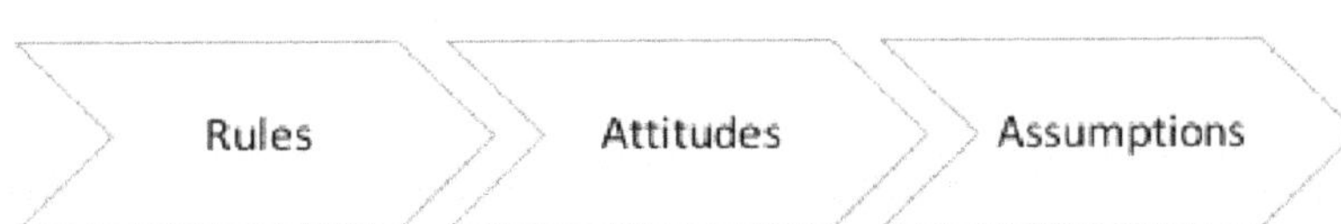

world, there are some common symbols and meanings held by most people in the United States and stability in those symbols and meanings appeared to be shifting at pace far too fast to comprehend.

Let us explore how a group of people can view a presidential candidate deliver a speech and have different perceptions (cognitive processes) associated with what was said. The following is an excerpt of President Trump's speech announcing his candidacy for President of the United States:

So, ladies and gentlemen, I am officially running for President of the United States and we are going to make our country great again. It can happen. Our country has tremendous potential. We have tremendous potential. We have people that aren't working. We have people that have no incentive to work. But they're going to have incentive to work. Because the greatest social program is a job. And they'll be proud, and they'll love it, and they'll make much more money than they would have ever made. And they'll be doing so well, and we're going to be thriving as a country. Thriving. It can happen.

I will be the greatest jobs president that god ever created, I tell you that. I'll bring back our jobs from China, from Mexico, from Japan, from so many places. I'll bring back our jobs, and I'll bring back our money. Right now, think of this - we owe China $1.3 trillion. We owe Japan more than that. So they come in, they take our jobs, they take our money and then they loan us back the money and we pay them interest. And then the dollar goes up, so their deal's even better. How stupid are our leaders? How stupid are these politicians to allow this to happen? How stupid are they?. (Daily News.com, retrieved 3/7/17)

For some people, these words were encouraging and promising. "I like Trump, he speaks the truth". For years, many people who felt left out of the American dream believed candidate Trump spoke to them and supported their ideas and beliefs about America and the way things are supposed to be. The trademark tag of his candidacy written across a trucker cap "Make America Great Again" resonated with the individuals and families who live in the Rust Belt and who witnessed first-hand jobs disappear by the thousands as factories closed or relocated to international locations. These are people who could always count on a job at the steal, automobile, or parts factory when they finished, and in some instances, did not finish, high school. These are the people who for generations always knew that America would take care of them. These are the same people who felt betrayed by the American Dream when the factories shut off the lights and closed the doors for good leaving them behind with very little hope for the future. Donald Trump spoke to them.

I will be the greatest jobs president that God ever created, I tell you that. I'll bring back our jobs from China, from Mexico, from Japan, from so many places. I'll bring back our jobs, and I'll bring back our money. (Donald J. Trump)

That's right – our jobs and our money. It sounds terrific, all the American jobs lost to foreigners will come back to America, and Americans will have those jobs, and our country will "Be Great Again". Some readers might identify with "these people" and for some readers "these people" represent friends, families, and the communities they grew up in. For others, "these people" are clueless individuals who have no idea of how America and the world work. How can they believe such crap?

For those who think, how could anyone believe anything candidate Trump says or said you need not look no further than the 2016 New York Times bestseller, "Hillbilly Elegy, A Memoir of a Family and a Culture in Crisis" by J. D. Vance. In the introduction to his book, Mr. Vance describes that his book is not about his doing something extraordinary but rather because he, "achieved something quite ordinary", which doesn't happen to most kids who grow up as did he (Vance, 2016, p. 1). Vance grew up in one of the steel towns that I mentioned and is driven and compelled for others to understand the lives of poor White working class people. He provides a window for others to get a glimpse of the suffering and psychological effects that growing up in the Rust Belt community has on individuals, families and communities where the hope of the American Dream has all but vanished. Vance's memoire forces the readership to take the role of "other" by agonizingly displaying many of the meanings associated with social interactions experienced by him, his family, and his extended family. Vance wants those who are not a member of his family or community to assume the role of the "other".

Vance and his clan, as he sometimes refers to his family, are of Scottish-Irish decent. This ethnic group of Americans has a long history in America believed to be the first group of White Americans to settle in the middle part of country or the Ohio River basin including Indiana, Ohio, Kentucky, Tennessee, West Virginia, and other parts of the country known as Appalachia. They are the people often referred to as rednecks, hillbillies, white trash, and crackers. Vance suggests that for these people "poverty is the family tradition" (p. 3).

While Vance explains the hardships experienced by the White working class of Steel Belt that changed into the Rust Belt as jobs disappeared. He also stresses the fact that many hardships experienced by this group were brought on by the meaning assigned to symbols and social interactions within the families and communities of the Rust Belt. He discussed the importance of loyalty, work, and religion. Family is of utmost important despite the dysfunction that is frequently exhibited by family members on a regular basis. However, Vance iterates that family can also be the factor that keeps kids like him from breaking away from the cycle of poverty and making it out. He believes that countless kids like him grow up lacking social capital. Social capital is "the network of social connections that exist between people, and their shared values and norms of behaviour, which enable and encourage mutually advantageous social cooperation" (Collins English Dictionary - Complete & Unabridged 10th Edition, Retrieved March 15, 2017). Vance reviewed the research that indicated many kids similar to him who grow up poor, working class, and White in communities, experienced a higher incidence of Adverse Childhood Experiences (ACE). ACEs can include, but are not limited to, having an abusive parent, watching parents fight on a regular basis, having an alcoholic parent, having a parent who is addicted to drugs, witnessing one parent abuse the other parent, being sexually abused, being neglected, not having enough food, lacking safe shelter, or attending a substandard school. Vance suggests that many of the ACEs he, his friends, and other children who grow up in families and communities like his experience contribute to an elevated sense of hopelessness, a "unique since of cynicism" (Ted Talk, 2017), and isolation. Subsequently, the meanings they attached to social symbols of success were something that would not be attained by them. Thus, it influences how they interact with others in social interactions.

Here is why it is crucial to understand Symbolic Interaction Theory and even more important to learn how to take the role of "other", or to understand how another person might perceive the same situation differently from you. Whether you are a person who can identify with the words and promises purported by Donald Trump or you are a person who disagrees with the candidate's words and promises, if you can assume the role of the other, "walk in his or her shoes", you might gain a better understanding of how and why that person believes and acts in their particular way. Imagine you are a person who grew up in a community like many of the people described in Vance's book. There would be no jobs, poor education, economically stressed, and with little hope of achieving prosperity for you and your family. And then you hear someone state, "I will be the greatest jobs president that God ever created, I tell you that. I'll bring back our jobs from China, from Mexico, from Japan, from so many places. I'll bring back our jobs, and I'll bring back our money" (Daily News.com, 2017). It is easy to jump on the band wagon. It makes sense to listen to the candidate who appears to be addressing exactly what you think and feel. You do not have a job, but all the Mexicans, Asians, and Blacks have jobs. Some of 'them' seem to be doing better than you and your family, who are hardworking Americans, and that just is not right. They took your jobs and you want them back. For this group, it is us against them, and them includes Mexicans, Asians, Blacks, foreigners, the "elites", and anyone not fitting in to their meaning of American.

If you allow yourself to assume the role of the other, in this case an underemployed or unemployed working class White Ethnic who lives in the Rust Belt, then you might begin to gain empathy to the hardships these people experience. Then, you can understand how to engage in social interaction in which you can discuss your differences with some level of civility and comprehension of that person's perspective. Perhaps, you can influence the "other" to see things as you do, the other may influence you to see things the way they do, or both of you can compromise and agree to disagree despite your differences.

Above I introduced the topic of self-awareness as a mechanism to better understanding one's self and in turn to then assume the role of the other. Remember that our place in society, race, gender, sexual orientation, socio-economic status, ethnicity, and religion affects the meaning attached to social interactions. Becoming self-aware requires us to self-explore. This means exploring our family's ethnic, racial, religious, and socio-economic origins. For example, if you are Irish-Catholic, then you need to determine the importance of Irish heritage and what it means to you and your family. If grand-parents or great grand-parents migrated to the United States during Ireland's 19th Century Potato Famine, then you need to understand the affect that hardship had on your family then and its current effects on you and your family. Add to that, an understanding discrimination against Irish immigrants and an understanding of the importance of the Catholic faith to Irish- American families like yours.

The same is true for comprehending one's beliefs regarding gender and socio-economic status. In the self-awareness process, people need to examine personal feelings and attitudes about gender and gender roles. We need to ask, "What are my feelings about being male, or female? What are my attitudes about members of the opposite gender? What was I taught in my family concerning the value of or treatment of someone of the opposite gender? What was I taught about how to be as a male or female? How do I feel to be a member of the financial upper-class? What are my attitudes towards those who are in a lower socio-economic status? What was I taught about people who are poor? These questions and many others support our understanding of the "meanings" associated to symbols with the origin of our family. It is the meanings attached or assigned to symbols in society that helps us understand the world and teach us how to behave in social situations. Consequently, understanding the meaning attached to symbols through the process of self-awareness, learning the meanings attached to beliefs about religion, race, ethnicity, socio-economic status, ability, and gender, helps us understand the biases we bring into social interactions with others. It helps us comprehend how we think about ourselves, others, and the world. Most importantly, self-awareness helps us understand our own imperfections. Thus, initially understanding our own imperfections allows us to assume the role of the other and to have an empathic understanding of others' meanings and perceptions of the world.

The connection between self, other, and the world is also supported by cognitive processes, our thinking, and thoughts, about the world and our perceptions regarding events that happen in the social environment (Bandura, 1997; Beck, 1995; Walsh, 2006). This is known as Cognitive Theory, and as mentioned above, "Cognitive theory postulates that we develop habits of thinking that form the basis for our screening and judgment about how to behave" (Walsh, 206, p. 132). We have thoughts about an event which triggers a belief or thought which in turn triggers and emotion or action. When psychotherapists use Cognitive theory to assist their clients the cognitive interventions used by the therapists are aimed at "enhancing the rationality of the clients' thinking pattern" (Walsh, 2006, p. 132). When we find ourselves in a social interaction and an "event" occurs we might be able to employ some of the skills of psychotherapists. Let me iterate that only trained, licensed psychotherapists have the clinical skills to assist people with cognitive interventions. However, when an event occurs which activates a thought or belief and then activates an emotion, if we use our self-awareness and take the role of the other we can get a better understanding of how that person perceives us, and then act in a manner to enhance positive social interactions and or diffuse negative social interactions. The following is a social interaction that occurred between and among several people on a Facebook thread. See if you can identify the cognitive processes in which the author of the post could assume the role of the other to gain an understanding of how that person perceived them.

The following is an excerpt from a Facebook thread following a video post of First Lady Michelle Obama's commencement speech to the 2015 graduating class at Tuskegee Institute. The original post provided admiration for then Fist Lady Michelle Obama, and while serval people made comments supporting the First Lady's speech one person had a different opinion about the First Lady, and a very different worldview from the person who posted the video and from others who commented on the post. This thread lasted the duration of four days. Although Facebook is public domain, the names of those who posted to this thread have been changed and non-salient posts were omitted.

Facebook Post:

Gerald: *Really? Her and her husband have both frittered away the perfect opportunity to raise up black culture and inspire MILLIONS, has done nothing but complain about EVERYTHING (all while traveling around the world on the taxpayers nickle) and blame EVERYBODY ELSE. Yeah, inspiring..... (smh)*

Leigh: *Do you really believe what you posted Gerald? And if yes, I totally disagree with you. They have inspired millions of people, not just African-Americans, but people of all races. Are they perfect? Absolutely not, is it their responsibility to "uplift" your words African-American culture, perhaps. I think they do. I do not understand what appears to be your anger at President and Mrs. Obama. Please share.*

Leigh: *Oh and by the way Gerald, I have experienced some of the same "insults" she mentioned in her speech. The reality is most of the time I, much like the First Lady, chose appropriate times to address the attacks. The assaults hurt and they always stay with you. She did an excellent job letting the audience know how she stays strong and keeps moving forward!*

Gerald: *Sorry, I don't believe they are quite the inspiration that you do. And it is sad that I have to put in the caveat that it has nothing to do with the color of their skin, because race is unimportant to me, personally. All I hear is whining, from the both of them, constantly...and yet look where they are. They lay blame for all their woes, never do you hear them take any responsibility themselves. Nobody is perfect, everybody has struggles in life - Lord knows I've had my own fair share of them, and yet I didn't blame anyone but myself.*

The INSPIRED millions, and the MAJORITY of those millions were common white folk too, because white people voted for them too. They could have said "YES WE DID....and you can too!", but instead all they do is point and scream (I see Donald Sutherland in "Invasion of the Body Snatchers", that part at the very end) and blame....everything/everyone...but....themselves.

Angry at them? No my friend, not in the least. I'm disappointed, because I see the country that I served and love falling apart before my eyes. And it ain't just them, it's both sides of the aisle.

Marsha: *Leigh, thank you so much for expressing my thoughts! White folks truly do not understand and it seems they don't want to understand, even if it comes from the POTUS and FLOTUS. As for race being unimportant Mr. O'Neill. You obviously don't know the history of African Americans and probably don't want to know. If the Republicans who conspired to destroy this presidency (and take the country with them) FROM DAY ONE had cooperated even half the time, our country would have new infrastructure for everyone and less tax breaks for the rich, not to mention all the laws designed to steal votes from those whose race you claim not to see... I guess you don't want ALL Americans to have healthcare either... Do the country a favor and stop watching FOX news, read any book by Tim Wise and educate yourself, please!*

Gerald: *With all due respect (and I mean that sincerely), you don't know me or anything about me. I don't know anything about "African Americans"? My beautiful 11year old daughter is Ethiopian, a no-kidding African American. And no, it wasn't "white guilt" And no, it wasn't "white guilt" that caused my wife and I to choose Ethiopia to adopt from, I hold no guilt because I've never owned a slave, nor has my family. As for history, I study history and am a voracious reader of history. The plight of blacks in this nation was a Southern White Democrat manifestation, as were Jim Crow laws and the KKK. Those evil Republicans were the ones that pushed civil rights laws, but because a Democrat president signed it you all place your gratitude on LBJ - the very same man who said "let's give the Negros just enough to get by, but not enough to make a difference, and I'll have them voting Democrat for the next 100 years." That's classy. The war on poverty has redistributed something like $37T (trillion) dollars to minorities, and what has changed? Nothing, because they (Dems) don't want it to change. But nothing I say will convince you of that. Ever hear the saying "give a man a fish and he'll each for a day, teach a man to fish and he'll never go hungry again"? If you* *understood ANYTHING about the "right", we believe that everybody can fish....*

How about Margaret Sanger, the founder of Planned Parenthood? She was all for the removal of what she considered "the inferior", which included the mentally/physically handicapped, and non-whites. How many young black children have been exterminated in the past 60 years? Try 50+ MILLION. But US terrible, racist Republicans only try to stop abortion, consider it the killing of the innocent (regardless of color).

Maybe you need to expand your horizons, ma'am. From where I sit, anyone with the letter (D) next to their name hasn't really done the black cause and culture much good. The facts speak for themselves.

I love the whole "infrastructure" rant these days. Blame the 1%, who - by the way - make up for 48% of the taxes collected in this country every year. Tell you what, out of the 42 million people that are on welfare, how about we put shovels in their hands, teach them how to use the heavy equipment, give them the training they need...the already are on the "government payroll". Even if only 1/2 are able bodied, that is still 21 MILLION people that could be put on this very important project! What is wrong with that idea? Imagine all the folks that would get that boost in their self-esteem every time they drove the highway or crossed the bridge they built or fixed. Nothing feels better than a job well done!

As for Fox News....that meme is getting old. I repeat, you don't know a damn thing about me, but I can tell by your post you think I'm a racist. Well, racism is not only a white thing, keep that in mind.

I repeat, color means nothing to me. Like MLK, I too believe strongly in the "content of character" vice the "color of skin". Maybe you should give it a shot. My apologies if I've offended anyone.

***Marsha:** Sorry, but MLK believed in the beauty of race - read Where Do We Go From Here: Chaos or Community? - and you will hear the POTUS and FLOTUS all over again as HE recounts the slights and insults as a result of race. As for Republicans and abortion... please... They care about a fetus but not about the child, hence cuts in everything that would benefit children, from insurance to healthcare to college, etc., etc. As for your Ethiopian child, I pray that child does not become a confused person of color. The 1% do not pay their fair share of taxes, period; why not mention corporate welfare in the form of oil subsidies, NFL non-profit status, etc., etc. No I don't know a* *damn thing about you, but then again, you have said more than you know about yourself and it doesn't make me want to know you. And yes, apology accepted.*

Marsha: *Let me also add that the plight of African Americans was done by a majority of whites, not just southerners either directly or passively, by not opposing injustice Northerners profited from the goods of the south who made their money from enslaved Africans. The term the "south up north" applies to the rest of the country... today as well as yesterday. Not sure what history books you are reading, but put "Lies My Teacher Told Me: Everything My High School History Textbook Got Wrong" by James W. Loewen, a white historian who studied a dozen of the most popularly used history texts and found that they ALL tell lies about American history. He writes that "American history is written to comfort the descendants of the oppressor." So unless you have gone out of your way to read another narrative, it is highly likely that what you think is true history is a lie. Hope you tell your African child that humanity began in Africa and Africans established the foundation of civilization. Didn't really mean to unload on you, but I so TIRE of people like yourself bashing OUR President and First Lady and claiming not to be racist. AND racism does not go both ways; one must have power to be racist. I'm done.*

Marsha: *Leigh pardon my rant... It's just getting very hard to take!!!*

Gerald: *Nothing more to say about this. I told you how I felt (and believe it or not, most people feel as I do about stuff)....but you spout what the party line is. Depressing actual, that you can't hear my heartfelt words....you dismiss them because I'm a white guy.*

Many would consider that "racist". I call it "disappointing". Best of luck to you and yours, and that is sincerely meant too. Good night.

Leigh: *Wow! I am thinking about how to respond. I will state this, when I teach my diversity class and lead diversity training I stress that one must be careful when using statements such as "all..." "every..." "those people". It is extremely important for one to understand "otherness" as well as his or her thoughts regarding "the other". Way too much information to put in a FB post.*

Leigh: *Gerald, As I thought about whether or not to respond to your post about the First Lady's commencement speech lots of things came to mind. However, what stuck out the most were thoughts that my parents shared with me and my siblings about their journey as ...See More*

Gerald: *Leigh....I seek only understanding. Your history of your family, and of what I know of you, has clearly been subject to its share of ignorance. You brought up something - and you may think I'm stirring the pot, but I assure you I am not. The "N" word...See More*

Sabrina: *Michelle Obama for president! Such a beautiful heartfelt speech from a woman with so much to share. Loved her as our FLOTUS, but I'd love the chance to vote for her.:)*

Gerald: *With all due respect, you'd think we could have these conversations (as educated people), because without discussion there can be no common ground attained. Thanks for calling me "uneducated", former classmate!*

Gerald: *Leigh...I will repeat. I am not angry, I am disappointed. Does racism exist? Absolutely. Is it an abomination? Absolutely. Is it getting better? Absolutely - and you can debate me all you want on that. All the really ignorant people that passed ...See More*

Joe: *I have known Leigh for over 30 years, I am grateful that she has made the effort to share something that she found meaningful. It gives me insight into who Leigh is and her world view. Thanks, Leigh.*

Joanne: *Leigh thanks for doing the heavy lifting on this one -- sheesh*

Gerald: *What gets me is that nobody believes that I'm on your "side"..... Because I lean Conservative, I get shouted down. No discussion, I'm just considered uneducated/racist/heretic/whatever...because you are all liberal and therefore "enlightened". No ro...See More*

Marsha: *Leigh, I am so proud of you and appreciate your response, recanting the family history. Our family has weathered the storm of racism in America and has made important contributions to the society- in the navy, education, engineering, music, etc. So we still rise!*

Leigh: *I appreciate the discussion on this issue. Gerald I did not unfriend you and I do not think I said that you were uneducated in my post. I will check, the post was written early I the am and has some typos. I felt the need to have you look at things from another perspective. I do disagree with many of your beliefs.*

Laurie: *Leigh, thank you for your heartfelt and thoughtful comments. Thank you for so eloquently expressing all that I know and understand to be the experiences my parents, my children and I have had.*

Rodger: *Gerald) you are NOT on my side but not because you (lean) conservative. Your solutions are simplistic and typical of someone who thinks everyone can learn to run a backhoe professionally in a day. I suggest that the ones that are better designing projects or being other workers be sent to school and you run the shovel. There IS no discussion because in your world you paint everyone with a different idea or solution then yours as a whiner or slacker. Your posts scream of paranoia and fear of educated people who have the training and experience to get the job done. Worst of all you think you are in the majority in this country while putting liberals in your box and declaring they are all enlightened when you believe YOU are the enlightened fisherman. Get on that shovel and do something productive instead of complaining about other people who need the help.*

Gerald : *Thanks for taking what I said, and spinning the living crap out of it. I suggest TRAINING for people, you tell me they can't learn to drive a backhoe in a day. YOU recommend that I grab a shovel and let other get the training.*

Shawn: *Apparently, neither we, nor the Obamas, nor our ancestors have suffered as much as some adopted children from the third world have and the gentleman wants to school us. Class dismissed.*

Gerald: *Are you done? For chrissakes, stop reading between the lines! I was talking about MY perspective, because I was "schooled" by Ms. Stapleton to "expand my horizons". I swear each and every one of you has a damn reading comprehension problem....*

Shawn: *Although you have repeatedly professed to be leaving the thread, here you are again. There are a vast number of reasons why your arguments* *have found little resonance here. It is difficult to "expand one's horizons" without empathy in the toolbox. Best wishes for your journey.*

Gerald: *You have me all figured out. You all do, and it cracks me up. If I don't clap my flippers like a trained seal to YOUR beliefs...oh hell, never mind.*

Chuck: *You Go, Michelle.......Gerald, Mrs. Obama was sharing her experiences as the first black first lady. If you don't think its been different for her from every first lady prior, then yes you are a very ignorant person. You may disagree with her husband, however, she makes no policies as first lady so you can't make say that you disagree with her policies. She is a black woman, so you really can't say that you have shared, felt, or know any of her experiences. As for me, I'd never pick an argument with any woman....it's a losing battle and they bare children.*

Laurie: *Imagine if everything they said was positive and uplifting..... Then they would be duplicitous and less than truthful... Oh wait! They would be your traditional political couple rather than someone who is fostering better, more open dialogue.*

Shawn: *In shiny, happy people-land, the GOP has no culpability whatsoever. Only the POTUS and FLOTUS.*

SOLUTIONS AND RECOMMENDATIONS

There is a lot of emotion involved in this thread. Different perspectives, different worldviews, and different levels of response in this social interaction are evident. Some individuals casually contributed to the on-line social interaction while others became totally engaged and strongly voiced their feelings and worldviews. What appeared to be a simple sharing of thoughts and beliefs ignited a verbal exchanged of perceptions about Mrs. Obama, race, oppression, class, and political view. To begin to apply self-awareness regarding this social interaction one might want to ask ones' self the following questions. Do I agree with the thoughts and expressions of any participants? If yes, what about their expressed thoughts made sense to me? How do my thoughts and worldview connect with any participant in this Face Book thread? Do I agree with any one person's or several peoples' political views? Do I object to anything that someone posted? If you answered yes to any of the questions, ask yourself why do I disagree with that? How do I connect with that person? Adding another dimension to your self-awareness, you can ask yourself the following questions, Do any of the post make me angry? or Do they make me think about regarding an issue in a different way? What do I think about the comments that discussed race and racism in the United States? These are just some of the questions that one needs to ask if they want to gain a better understanding of what role their "self" plays in social interactions. Furthermore, how their worldview affects social interaction with others.

Some of the participants in the Facebook social interaction appeared unable to take the role of other, some seemed to lack self-awareness, and some appeared to attack any statements that threatened their perceptions regarding race, equity, and social justice in the United States. These participants could not tolerate a worldview different than theirs and when feeling threatened, lashed out with verbal attacks at those who thought differently from them. There was some diversity in awareness among the participants. Conversely, some participants could recognize differences in worldviews and chose to interact in a different manner. They stated their view and encouraged others to consider other perceptions of the situation. This is noticeable in seeing how some participants were able disagree with others, but did not appear to have the need to attack those with whom they disagreed. Instead they suggested alternative viewpoints for others to consider and supported their posts with facts. The participants who showed self-awareness did not seem overly irritated or "outraged" by another person's point of view. In fact, if one re-reads the Facebook thread one can find several instances in which those who were more self-aware appeared to offer supportive suggestions to those who were "outrage" by differing perceptions.

The more self-aware one is, the more cognizant one is of the dynamics of social interactions, and being able to take the role of other will help one be better prepared to engage in conversations and social interactions without becoming ill-tempered, harboring rage, and wishing negativity to others who disagree with one's thoughts and beliefs. All of us need to prepare ourselves to engage in a manner that we can express our thoughts and beliefs regarding an event and come away a better person due to our ability to assess, maintain a proactive position, and learn in social interactions. Consider the 2016 Presidential race. The political environment in the United States during the summer of 2015 seemed like a roller coaster ride, with countless twists and turns, and highs and lows. There was abundant activity in both the Democratic and Republican parties. Democrats trying to choose a candidate between

Hillary Clinton and Bernie Sanders. And Republicans trying to choose a candidate from a crowded field of over 13+ candidates, with no clear front runner. Then, in the middle of all this activity a businessman from New York City announces that he will run for president. Stating:

I will be the greatest jobs president that god ever created, I tell you that. I'll bring back our jobs from China, from Mexico, from Japan, from so many places. I'll bring back our jobs, and I'll bring back our money. Right now, think of this - we owe China $1.3 trillion. We owe Japan more than that. So they come in, they take our jobs, they take our money and then they loan us back the money and we pay them interest. And then the dollar goes up, so their deal's even better. How stupid are our leaders? How stupid are these politicians to allow this to happen? How stupid are they? (Daily News.com, retrieved 3/7/17)

Continuing his speech by blaming "others", those who are different, for the problems experienced by some people in the United States:

When Mexico sends its people they're not sending the best. They're not sending you, they're sending people that have lots of problems and they're bringing those problems. They're bringing drugs, they're bringing crime. They're rapists and some, I assume, are good people, but I speak to border guards and they're telling us what we're getting. (Retrieved, March 7, 2017)

Candidate Donald Trump recognized how working class, rural, socio-economically challenged middle America were thinking and feeling, and he sharpened his political message. He targeted, immigrants, "the Mexicans, they're rapists", "Muslims", they are terrorists, poor people who live in urban areas "the Blacks", Women, "they are a problem for businesses", and global entities, "China", NAFTA, unfair trade deals, and NATO "Obsolete", as the source of their social, political, and economic problems. He used his message as a weapon to agitate disenfranchised voters and pointed at "Others" as the place to discharged their frustration and anger.

CONCLUSION

So, the next time you hear a presidential candidate discharge words of animosity towards "others", or you hear a co-worker, neighbor, or friend blame "others" for all the social ills, societal difficulties, and "what's wrong with the world", it might benefit you to pause for a moment. Give yourself time to assess the situation and you ask yourself, "How can anyone believe the sexist, homophobic, racists, ageist, anti-sematic, things this person is saying? You can step back, evaluate the situation, take the role of "other", (i.e., others who agreed with what the candidate stated), and attempt to understand how someone in certain circumstances, and with a similar worldview could agree with and support the candidate's statements and promises.

Donald Trump expertly used the tactical tool of blaming others for the social and economic issues currently experienced in the United States, and his tactic was successful, and potentially dangerous. It permitted people who are frustrated about the loss of their job, pessimistic about the future, and who felt cheated out of a prospect to "grab the golden ring", an opportunity to vilify and target "those people" who they assumed to be the cause of all our country's problems. By design, Donald Trump provided hope to those who grew up in similar circumstances like Vance's clan throughout the United States. You may not agree with the views of then candidate Trump, however, if you are self-aware and take the role of the other you may understand why others believed what they believed.

REFERENCES

Beck, J. S. (1995). *Cognitive therapy*. New York: Guilford Press.

Blumer, H. (1969). *Symbolic interactionism: Perspectives and method.* Englewood Cliffs, NJ: Prentice Hall.

Charon, J. M. (2004). *Symbolic interactionism: An introduction, an interpretation, an integration*. Pearson Prentice Hall.

Dyson, M. E. (2004). *The Michael Eric Dyson reader*. New York: Basic Civitas Books.

Erikson, E. (1968). *Identity youth and crisis*. New York: Norton.

Holloday, J. (2017). *Teaching Tolerance*. Retrieved from www.tolerance.org/article/racism-and-white-privilege

Kuebler, M., & Rugh, J. S. (2013). New evidence on racial and ethnic disparities in homeownership in the United States from 2001 to 2010. *Social Science Research*, *42*(5), 1357–1374. doi:10.1016/j.ssresearch.2013.06.004 PMID:23859736

McIntosh, P. (1990). White privilege: Unpacking the invisible knapsack. *Independent School*, *49*(2), 31.

Mead, G. H. (1934). *Mind, self, and society from the standpoint of a social behaviorist*. Chicago: University of Chicago Press.

Meriam-Webster Dictionary. (2007). *Merriam Webster Colligate dictionary* (11th ed.). Springfield, MA: Merriam-Webster, Inc.

Miller, J., & Garren, A. (2017). *Racism in the United States*. New York: Springer Publishing.

Sechrest-Ehrhardt, L. (2012). *Understanding the racial identity development of multiracial young adults through their family, social, and environment, experiences*. ProQuest UMI: 3508801.

Social Capital. (n.d.). Retrieved from Dictionary.com website: http://www.dictionary.com/browse/social-capital

Tatum, B. (2014). Defining Racism: Can We Talk? In *Race, class, and gender in the United States*. New York: Worth Publishers.

Tatum, B. D. (1997). *Why are all the Black kids sitting together in the cafeteria? And other conversations about race*. New York, NY: Basic Books.

U.S. Department of Housing and Urban Development. (2013). *Housing discrimination against racial and ethnic minorities 2012*. Retrieved from https://www.huduser.gov/portal/Publications/pdf/HUD-514_HDS2012_execsumm.pdf

Vance, J. D. (2016). *Hillbilly Elegy*. New York: HarperCollins.

Walsh, J. (2006). *Theories for direct social work practice*. Thomson, Brooks/Cole.

Williams, A. P. (2015). Lending discrimination, the foreclosure crisis and the perpetuation of racial and ethnic disparities in homeownership in the US. *Wm. &. Mary Bus. L. Rev., 6*, 601.

KEY TERMS AND DEFINITIONS

Cognitive Theory: a psychological theory that defines human behavior as a product of the human thought process.

Diversity: A range of differences between and among people

Identity: Embraces the characteristics, family, ethnicity, race, and or political affiliation by which an individual identifies him or herself.

Meaning-Making: The cues that individuals use to provide understanding to the values, norms, and roles established in social and environmental context.

Privilege: Having special rights or advantages only preserved for a certain group.

Racism: The belief that differences in race explain deficits of certain groups of people or a belief that differences among the various racial groups determine individual achievement.

Self-Awareness: A fluid process of acquiring knowledge about one's self to understand one's self in relation to others and the world.

Social Interaction: Interactions between and among individuals and or groups. Social interactions can include political, cultural, and economical.

ENDNOTES

1 Potato Famine- Beginning in 1845 and lasting for six years, the potato famine killed over a million men, women and children in Ireland and caused another million to flee the country (The History Place, retrieved 4/23/17).

Chapter 6
Decoding Difference:
How We Treat "Others" Examining the Effects of Marginalizing Those Viewed as Different

Lisa Sechrest-Ehrhardt
University of the District of Columbia, USA

ABSTRACT

Race, ethnicity, and gender issues have always been important matters in American politics. However, during the past two presidential elections these issues were the vanguard topics displayed on centerstage. The United Sates has a tainted history with respects to certain populations which it has discriminated against and marginalized throughout the country's history, and the tensions surrounding these issues erupted like a volcano. The United States became polarized as people began to align with different political and social ideologies depicting how those who are regarded as being different, "others", should be treated. This chapter provides a brief history of marginalized populations in the United States and uses Critical Race Theory and self-awareness as means to help the reader understand the impact on society when racism and inequality are woven into the fabric of the country.

INTRODUCTION

During my thirty years of facilitating diversity training workshops, I have accumulated numerous teachable moments that often served as case examples in subsequent training sessions and workshops. These moments occurred during

DOI: 10.4018/978-1-5225-3843-1.ch006

the workshop, but many occurred during the workshop breaks or after the workshop was complete. Due to the nature of the inquiries or "challenges", I think it is safe to say that much of what I facilitated and encouraged the group to discuss often strikes a nerve. I am always interested to engage with people who want to know more or who want me to "clear up" the information that I shared. However, I am more curious and intrigued as to how people find indirect ways to inform me that they are "not racist" yet they were troubled about what I stated regarding race. Some participants became angry with me while others appeared to be struggling with what I attribute, in part, to misdirected anger.

One of my diversity workshop goals is to create a safe haven where participants can engage in meaningful and purposive dialog to heighten their self-awareness regarding race, ethnicity, gender, socio-economic status, and ability dynamics. While workshops may be geared to address specific needs of an organization, group or community, several workshops and trainings address the broader issue of inequity and social injustice in our society. At the beginning of each workshop, I introduce myself, highlight my professional experience as a diversity trainer, and inform participants that my approach does not include "talking at" them, but instead help them engage in interactive discourse to support the initiation of their journey towards self-awareness and discovery, while simultaneously learning the nuances of diversity or more specifically, differences between and among people from different backgrounds. My perspective is that many of us are clueless of our own perspectives regarding "others". Depending on one's self-perceptions of privilege, one can venture through life not having to consider anything outside of their worldview. Having a dominant status by being born into a certain race, sex, social class, or ability provides those individuals with a protective bubble that affords them the luxury of not having to understand how "others" navigate life in the social context. The part of my workshops that often makes participants uncomfortable is when discussions and role playing regarding social privilege directly addresses the issues of race and racial inequality. Nonverbal behavior of participants clues me into an awareness that the topic of race is uncomfortable, unsettling for many. For example, rolling of eyes, fidgeting in one's seat, frowning, body tension, and looking around the room to see how others respond are some of the body language mannerisms exhibited during workshops. Occasionally, a workshop participant suggests that "we have come a long way" and that "race relations are much better than they use to be", additional suggestions indicated that race is "not as important" nor as "much a problem as it used to be". Some participants believed and advocated that we are moving towards a "post racial society" highlighting the fact that our nation, not once, but twice elected a President that was African-American. Other participants have even stated that they felt "uncomfortable talking about race" and believed that because they were "white" they were at a disadvantage in the workshop. Respectfully, I disagree with many of the participants' suggestions about race and racial inequality. I strongly believe that discussions regarding race and racial inequality can, and do, trigger strong emotions which many workshop participants as well as many in the larger society attempt to avoid at all costs.

Race, Racism, and Racial Inequality

Racism and racial inequity are alive and active in the United States. Unfortunately, racism is like a cancer which infiltrates virtually nearly every aspect of life in the United States. If an individual pays attention to the environment outside of their immediate surroundings, it is easy to identify the effects of racism and racial inequity. One need not look farther than the internet or the nightly news casts to catch a glimpse of an incidence where race was a significant factor. In his book, *Developing Cultural Humility Embracing Race, Privilege, and Power,* Miguel Gallardo states, "If we learned anything from the presidential elections of 2008 and 2012, it is that issues of race and racism are still very much a part of this nation's cultural fabric" (Gallardo, 2014, p. 8). Regrettably, some participants in my workshops lacked a basic understanding of racial issues in the United States because they lacked an awareness of greater societal issues that do not interfere with their daily living. If individuals live in a community where there is minimal socioeconomic, racial, or ethnic diversity and everything in their lives occurs smoothly without any conflict, drama or barrier, then those individuals may be able to go through the activities of daily living with diminutive awareness or recognition that others' lives are not as privileged as their own. They may not comprehend that "others" lives are not as easy, predictable or controlled as theirs. They might not understand why it is difficult for "others" to "pull themselves up by their bootstraps" like their ancestors were able to accomplish, because the "others" ancestors did not have the same opportunities or acceptance in American society as their ancestors. What is obvious for "others" regarding race and racial injustices in the United States is often oblivious to members of privileged groups in the United States. A privilege group might be members of the "top 1%" in the United States. The top 1% consists of families whose annual income is approximately $390,000. However, this number varies according to the state in which a person lives (Money.cnn.com/2015/12/29/news/economy/top-1-income/. Retrieved April 25, 2017). We have made significant progress as a nation, however, there is considerably more work to be done regarding race and racial injustice in the United-States.

Race, Ethnicity, and Social Discourse

As discussed above, I am committed to helping people engage in meaningful and purposive dialog to raise their self-awareness across the dynamics of race, ethnicity, gender, socio-economic status, and ability. This process involves becoming more aware of those dynamics particularly in the United States. Through discourse and dialog my goal is to build bridges that lead to common ground and in the process, breaks down barriers that perpetuate fear, mistrust, and isolation.

Recently, I conducted a series of workshops at a high school that wanted to improve discussions and dialog concerning diversity and inclusion in the high school. The surrounding community where the high school is located is racially, ethnically, and socio-economically diverse. A unique quality of the high school is that the student population speaks over 35 different languages. After a workshop, a father who had several children attending the high school, approached me and stated that he was very glad that I did not talk about race in my workshop. I was a bit surprised by his statement because although the focus of the discussion that evening was not primarily about race, the discussion incorporated social injustices and inequity based on being "different" or "not part of" mainstream America. The workshop topics included language, financial, gender, ethnic, and class differences; each at some point encompass the issue of race. When I asked him why he felt that way he said, "Talking about race wrecks everything". As I attempted to have him explain more about his thoughts and feelings, he revealed very little details about his family life, his immigration to United States, and the difficulties he and his family experienced upon arriving in the United States. What was interesting to me was that he did not acknowledge any connection between his ethnic minority status, which was non-White and how his ethnic and "perceived" racial status in America may have contributed to the difficulties he and his family experienced. That moment did not provide an opportune time to further explore the participant's awareness or comfort level regarding race, but I invited him to attend the next workshop believing that the topic and format might be beneficial to him. Unfortunately, he did not return for the next workshop. I wish him well as he genuinely appeared to be a father that was concerned and committed to his children receiving a quality education without any barriers based on their race and ethnicity.

To develop an awareness of diversity, one must begin to discuss race. I often think about the participants in my workshops and wonder how much, if any, of an effect the content of the workshop changes their worldview. Finding common ground on diversity issues is not an straightforward process. It requires preparation, research, dedication, consultation, and -- even for diversity trainers and consultants --- a constant commitment to improving one's self-awareness. Throughout my self-awareness journey, I have attempted to share as much of my knowledge about diversity, race, and ethnicity as I can. There are many experts, professionals, scholars and mentors who I owe a unlimited debt of gratitude for paving the way for me to impart knowledge regarding diversity issues and principally diversity issues related to race and ethnicity. A central theme regarded by several scholars who study diversity issues in the United States is the history race and discrimination towards marginalized populations in the nation. To truly comprehend the effects of racism, one must be familiar with the history of race in the United States. Subsequently, to begin decoding difference between and among people from varying backgrounds, individuals must have an understanding of culture, race, and ethnicity, the meaning associated with being different, and the effects of being a member of a marginalized population in the United States.

The Importance of Understanding Culture and Context

To acquire a better understanding of the dynamics of race and ethnicity it is important to have knowledge regarding the overarching concept of culture. Culture is not an easily defined concept, as it encompasses many aspects of people's lives. Merriam-Webster dictionary defines culture as, "the customary beliefs, social forms, and material traits of a racial, religious, or social group and the characteristics features of everyday existence shared by a people in a place or time" (Merriam-Webster, 2003, p. 304). Explained in another way, it is a broad concept that refers to the shared and learned attributes, values, beliefs, behavior, and traditions that are associated with and to one another which preserve a certain group (DHHS, 1999, Pinderhughes, 1989). According to Devore & Schlesinger (1998), culture embraces the ideas and values conveyed by a cultural group and that overtime these ideas and values can become characteristics of everyday life so that members of certain groups adopt behaviors that are subconscious.

Many social scientists are challenged to describe culture in simple terms because culture is a multi-faceted complex concept that varies significantly across different groups. Social workers, psychologists, and other social scientists often disagree on "how to best describe culture" because they have become "entangled in the intricacies of the systemic processes characterizing it" (Pinderhughes, 1989, p. 6). Pinderhughes suggests that one way to grasp a better understanding of culture is from an open systems approach. This approach stresses the importance of the interdependence of the various aspects of human functioning. Pinderhughes states (1998):

In order to understand individual behavior or emotion one must consider the relationships among the individual, the family, and the local system; the value orientations of the individual, family, subgroup, and social system; the geographical setting; and the interpenetration of all these systems and processes that operate in a reverberating and reciprocal manner. In addition, culture may be defined as the sum of total ways of living developed by a group of human beings to meet biological and psychosocial needs. (p. 6)

Ethnicity is a subset of culture and is generally regarded as a more tangible concept. It refers to a common connectedness among people based on concepts such as language, religion, sharing similar rituals, preference for music and food, traditional dress, spiritual practices, and social interaction (Devore & Schlesinger, 1989; Mindell, Habenstein & Wright, 1998; Pinderhughes, 1989; Schafer, 2007). According to McGoldrick, Pearce, and Giordano (1982), "ethnicity describes a sense of commonality transmitted over generations by the family and reinforced by the surrounding community. It involves conscious and unconscious processes that fulfill a deep psychological need for identity and historical continuity (p. 4). Examples include the connectedness different ethnic groups embrace with respect to language, dress, and food. Each time I meet with different groups for diversity workshops I invited participants to get in touch with their ethnic heritage. There is always a variety of answers regarding what makes a person feel connected to family, heritage, and ethnicity. Language is something that many Latino, Caribbean, Korean, and Japanese participants state makes them feel connected to others who share their same values. Some participants express that wearing the traditional dress of their country of origin makes them feel connected to their ethnic heritage, adding that it provides them with a sense of pride. Furthermore, almost every member of an ethnic minority group shares that traditional ethnic food makes them feel connected to family and can bring comfort when they are not near family and loved ones.

The group often defines individuals' ethnic identity or the ethnic heritage into which one is born. As a member of an ethnic group a person shares "a sense of cultural and historic uniqueness with other members of the same group" and to act as a member of an ethnic group a person "expresses feelings or calls attention to" the uniqueness of his or her ethnic group. (Mindell et al., 1998, p. 8). Having a connection to and with others can foster a sense of pride in one's ethnic heritage and can also strengthen one's values system (Phinney, 1992, Pinderhughes, 1989) "Ethnic values and practices foster the survival of the group and of the individuals within. They also contribute to the formation and cohesiveness of the group and to both the group and individual identity (Pinderhughes, 1989). According to Mindell and his colleagues, "the maintenance of ethnic identification and solidarity ultimately rests on the ability of the family to socialize its members into the ethnic culture and thus to channel and control, perhaps program, future behavior" (Mindell et al., p. 8). One of the primary means individuals can learn about their ethnic identity is through family interactions.

Ethnic groups are often categorized as minority groups. "A minority group is a subordinate group whose members have significantly less control or power over their own lives than do members of a dominant or majority group" (Schaefer, 2007, p. 7). Ethnic minority groups are differentiated from the dominant or majority group based on factors such as language, cultural differences, religious beliefs, and group values towards issues such as child rearing, dating, marriage (Mindell et al., 1998, Pinderhughes, 1989, Schaefer, 2007). Often the ethnic family is supported by the larger ethnic group and conversely the larger ethnic group supports the ethnic family, and as mentioned previously a person, or persons, can gain a sense of identity by belong to or associating with an ethnic group. Feeling that one is connected and having a sense of belonging and affiliation is extremely important to and for all people

American Pluralism

America's diverse population includes people from different racial and ethnic groups, who speak different languages, practice different religious, and celebrate many different traditions (McGoldrick et al., 1989, Mindell et al, 1998, Schaefer, 2007). Many Americans' ancestors came from different parts of the world and arrived in the United States in search of an improved life quality of life. And by most accounts, America is a nation of immigrants. "Here is not merely a nation, but a teeming nation of nations", was penned by Walt Whitman in a reference regarding the diversity of America. Even though America is commonly believed to be a nation of immigrants and a "melting pot" of cultures, many scholars (Aguirre, 2003; Dinnerstein, 2003; Gossett, 1974; Schaefer, 2007) think that the popular idea of America being a nation of immigrants does not fully embrace nor include the populations of people from Africa, Asia, and Latin America who also make up this nation of immigrants. Curiously, Native Americans (or First Americans) are also excluded from the "melting pot" theory. In most instances, the immigrants being referred to as "the nation of immigrants" are generally referring to European immigrants (Aguirre, 2003) who entered America via the east coast. According to Aguirre (2003),

"Even though American Indians, Asians, enslaved blacks and Mexicans were part of the founding of the United States, they are excluded from the 'founding immigrant myth' of the United States because they were not considered as part of the Anglo-Saxon core (Aguirre, 2003). In a sense, European settlers regarded them as "others", not part of the "we" they perceived themselves as being. As a result, the other populations were marginalized and were regarded by the European settlers as people and communities to be colonized and exploited for labor" (p. 12).

The populations identified by Aguirre are both racially and ethnically different from White European immigrants. Each of the groups listed above have experienced severe discrimination and exclusion from the American Dream (Adams, 1931). Although many of the immigrants from Europe experienced ethnic and religious discrimination upon arrival to the United States, several groups such as the Irish, Italians, Polish, Jews and Eastern Europeans were still able to "melt" into the nation of immigrants due to racial similarities to the English, Scottish, German, and Dutch settlers (Aguirre, 2003; Dinnerstein et al., 2003; Schaefer, 2007). The "others" who were racially different from the "Anglo-Saxon core" (Aguirre, (2003), could not "melt in" nor "blend in" so readily, and became and often remained throughout the history of the United States, marginalized populations.

Native Americans

Native Americans were the first people to inhabit North America (Aguirre, 2003; Gossett, 1974; Schaefer, 2007). The magnitude of the cultural diversity of Native Americans is so pronounced and complex that it is beyond the scope of this chapter. However, it is a population that is historically rich with a diversity marked "by an overriding characteristic, reflected by a high degree of linguistic and cultural variation" (Mindell et al., 1998, p. 382).

When the first European settlers arrived in America they quickly realized that they were the "minority" in a new land inhabited by a "large and diverse American Indian population" (Aguirre, 2003, p. 1). It is estimated that over 5 million Native Americans lived in North America and their population consisted of vast differences in culture, language, and lifestyles among the various tribes. Today most peoples' understanding of tribes does not include the rich history and complexity of the various Native American tribes. Although several Native American groups shared some social and cultural traits (Aguirre, 2003, Mindell et al., 1998) each group "built a specific relationship with the land they inhabited" (Aguirre, 2003, p. 1). For example, Native Americans living in the Eastern sections of North America "developed a complex set of social and economic activities based on hunting, farming, and fishing" while Native Americans in the Southwestern part of North American "developed societies based on hunting, agriculture, and sheepherding" (Aguirre, 2003, p.1). Contrary to what many Americans, and foreigners, were taught about the European explorers and settlers being greeted by "wild savages", the truth is, European settlers were greeted by "an American Indian population rich in its own linguistic, cultural, and social diversity" (Aguirre, 2003, p. 1).

The manner in which the Europeans viewed the Native Americans and other peoples who were different from them appears to have contributed to the ethnic and racial conflicts that are currently present in American society. In his book titled, Race: The History of an Idea in America, Gossett (1974) describes how the English settlers first encountered the race "problem" with the Native Americans and again a few years later when they imported Africans to serve as slaves. English settlers considered enslaved Native Americans and Africans as evil savages. By establishing the cruel and inhumane process of slavery, English settlers subjugated and ascribed subordinate status to Native Americans and Africans and instituted a discriminatory practice so fierce that the psychological impact still affects society today.

Native Americans have suffered land seizure, subjugation, discrimination, forced assimilation, and "imprisonment" by being forced to live on reservations (Schaefer, 2007). When the first Europeans arrived on the shores of America they brought with them a host of diseases that killed a significant number of Native Americans in the Western Hemisphere. Europeans exposed Native American to diseases such as smallpox, diphtheria, cholera, measles, typhoid and scarlet fever (Aguirre, 2003; Dinnerstein, Nichols & Reimers, 2003; Schaefer, 2007). The magnitude of the impact of the English settlers was perhaps more devastating than the Native Americans could have imagined. Dinnerstein et al, (2003) wrote:

In 1607, the Indians were politically independent, economically self-sufficient, and superior to whites in terms of using the natural environment. However, continuing relations with the English brought a downward spiral of major population loss, the erosion of tribal autonomy, and economic collapse, which left the tribes heavily dependent on the invading whites. (p. 8)

As the English and Native Americans continued to interact their cross-cultural relationship deteriorated precipitously. And as the "new colony grew" there were frequent and destructive campaigns waged against the different tribes. Some of these campaigns were waged in the name of Christianity, where missionaries intended to convert Native Americans. Other campaigns included wars, where battles were waged against the tribes resulting in mass mortality (Dinnerstein et al., 2003; Gossett, 1974; Schafer, 2007). From colonial times to as late as the 19th century, the United States formulated several treaties that were supposedly intended as peace negotiations with Native Americans. On the contrary, the treaties, in fact, were one-sided and discriminatory against Native Americans. Most treaties authorized the United State government to seize land inhabited by the different tribes and forced them to relocate to locations that were unfamiliar and uninhabitable. According to Schaefer (2003), "the 19th century was devastating to every Native American tribe in the areas claimed by the United States, and no tribe was the same after federal policy touched it" (p. 170). Native Americans today are affected by the racial discrimination and unfair government policies experienced by their ancestors.

African-Americans

Although a significant part of the ethnic diversity and history of America, Africans were the first "immigrants" albeit involuntary to arrive on American soil. Africans were kidnapped and transported to America to serve as slave labor. The main interest focused on economic interests of European settlers (Dinnerstein et al., 2003; Gossett, 1974: Mindell et al., 1998; Schaefer, 2007). According to Aguirre (2003), enslaved Africans "were treated like animals, subjected to harsh punishments, and used as commodities in barters or trades. Black slave women were used by white owners as mistresses, were mated with black males in order to increase an owner's slaveholdings, and were separated from their own children" (Aguirre, 2003, p. 14). Moreover, enslaved Africans were not perceived as persons, but instead as property (Aguirre, 2003; Gossett, 1974). Although some Africans were "freed" by their owners, it is estimated that approximately 90 percent of Africans brought to the Americas were sold into slavery (Aguirre, 2003, Dinnerstein et al., 2003).

There are an estimated 39 million African-Americans/Blacks living in the United States today (U.S. Census Bureau, 2010). Due to the power dynamics in the United States, and until the Presidential election of Barack Obama in 2008, and 2012 respectively, African- Americans have had "almost no major role in national and political decisions and have been allowed only a peripheral role in many of the crucial decisions that have influenced their own destiny" (Schaefer, 2007, p. 200). According to Schafer (2007):

The history of African-Americans is, to a significant degree, the history of the United States. Black people accompanied the first explorers, and a Black man was among the first to die in the American Revolution. The enslavement of Africans was responsible for the South's wealth in the nineteenth century and led to the country's most domestic strife. After Blacks were freed from slavery, their continued subordination led to sporadic outbreaks of violence in the rural South and throughout urban America. (p. 200)

Although slavery is no longer part of current American culture, the remnants of the devastation caused by slavery continue to influence race relations in modern society. The separation of families, slavery, and the marginalization African-Americans, particularly black males, has significantly impacted African-Americans and African-American families. "African-Americans have always been faced with the devaluation of their institutions, persons, values, and artifacts that are related to their cultures. This devaluation is based upon the historically ingrained concept of white superiority" (McAdoo, 1998, p. 363).

The European concept that whites are superior to blacks and other peoples of color has been handed down for generations (Dinnerstein et al., 2003; Gossett, 1974; McAdoo, 1998). The effects of white supremacy have often forced African-Americans into environments that are inferior to those experienced and enjoyed by White Americans. Some of these examples include, housing, healthcare, and educational and economic institutions, which according to McAdoo (in Mindel et al., 1998), "are socioeconomic elements that allow individuals and families access into the mainstream of American life" (p. 364).

Like many other racial and ethnic groups, there is much diversity within the African-American population. This diversity includes educational achievement, socioeconomic status, family composition, and religious and ethnic ties. It is important to acknowledge that despite slavery's attempt to dismantle black families, and the apparent societal devaluation of African-American families; many African-American families have continued with and preserved African family traditions. Many African-American families live in multigenerational households where there exists combinations of ascribed leadership roles, both male and female. "The African commitment to 'blood" kin has been the basis for established relationships for a significant number of household and family types, formed around the core of several consanguineal relatives" (McAdoo, 1998, p. 368). This African family tradition should perhaps be valued by all American families because it has helped African-American families thrive and survive over the generations (MaAdoo, 1998).

Asian Americans

This segment will briefly discuss the experiences of Chinese and Japanese Americans. Chinese and Japanese people began migrating to the United States in the early 1800s. Today, Asian-Americans are viewed as the so-called model minority; however, this has not always been the case. Asian-Americans, like Native-Americans and African Americans, have experienced a significant amount of racial discrimination. The Asian-American population consists of several distinct and diverse peoples - Chinese, Japanese, Koreans, Pacific Islanders, and others.

It is estimated the Asian population within the United States tripled between the mid-1800s and 1900. (Aguirre, 2003). This increase occurred at the time when gold was discovered in California mines. Chinese immigrants started arriving in the United States at this time and arrived "as sojourners" planning to return to China within three to five years. Their goal was to earn riches and return home (Aguirre, 2003; Schafer, 2007). Most Chinese immigrants became indentured servants upon arrival to the west coast of the United States. "Chinese laborers became a primary source of labor for gold mining, for building the transcontinental railroad, and for domestic chores. The general treatment of immigrants from China was not much different from that of [enslaved Africans] in the South" (Aguirre, 2003, p. 14). Chinese immigrants were exploited for labor and regulated to occupations that were outside of the mainstream of White American workers (Aguirre, 2003, Dinnerstein et al., 2003, Schafer, 2007). Chinese immigrants did work that many whites considered "menial and beneath their dignity" (Dinnerstein et al., 2003 p. 149). The Chinese worked as launderers, washing and ironing clothes, and cooked and prepared meals.

According to Schaefer (2007), America has had conflicting ideas about Chinese immigration from the beginning. On one side Americans welcomed Chinese immigrants because they provided a much needed, "hardworking" labor force. On the other side the predominantly European culture of the United States were fearful of the different culture of the Chinese and they were unwilling to accept or tolerate the difference.

"Many European Americans sensed economic competition from the Chinese labor force and this led to an anti-Chinese atmosphere in the Western United States" (Schafer, 2007, p. 353). And as economic difficulties increased for white men in California, Chinese immigrants begin to experience an increase in racial discrimination (Dinnerstein et al., 2003; Schafer, 2007) and unsubstantiated hatred. For example, the 1882 Chinese Exclusion Act was a response to militant white workers responding to high unemployment and low wages due to post-Civil War depression (Schein, 2006). Schein states, "The Exclusion Act was the centerpiece of a series of racist legislation designed to prohibit the entry of Chinese laborers into the country for ten years and to deny citizenship rights to all Chinese already in the United States" (Schein, 2006, p. 102). This act was not repealed until 1943 (Schafer, 2007).

The exclusion and marginalization of Chinese immigrants can be seen today in the contemporary Chinese American labor force. Most of the Chinese labor force resides in the Chinatown sections of major metropolitan cities. This is due largely to the fact that for generations Chinese immigrants and Chinese Americans were banned from working almost anywhere else (Schaefer, 2007).

Japanese Americans

Japanese emigration to the United States began in the mid to late 1800s. By 1890 it is estimated that nearly 12,000 Japanese had settled in Hawaii and another 3,000 on the mainland, a majority in California (Feagin, 1989; Mindel et al., 1998). An interesting fact regarding the Japanese immigration to the United States is that the exodus from Japan was due in part to the attempt by Emperor Meiji to increase Japan's trade and political power with the Western world. Unlike many other immigrant groups who came to the United States to improve their lives and their families' lives, the Japanese ruling class "perceived immigration as part of their imperial and colonial policies. Japanese rulers believed they, along with the white race, had an aptitude for colonization, and they sought every opportunity to expand their interests abroad" (Dinnerstein et al., 2003, p. 163). Emperor Meiji believed that workers who left Japan would spread Japanese culture to the Western world, and they might also boost "the nations coffers by returning part of their foreign earnings to relatives in Japan" (Dinnerstein et al., 2003, p. 163).

Like Chinese immigrants, Japanese immigrants took menial jobs and labored in industries that white workers considered were beneath them. Many Japanese immigrants worked on the sugar plantations in Hawaii and in canning plants and agricultural fields on the mainland. Their wages were low and the working conditions were often abhorrent. The industriousness of the Japanese workers make them extremely popular with employers but unpopular with labor unions and other employees (Dinnerstein et al., 2003; Schaefer, 2007).

After Hawaii was annexed in 1898, over 60,000 Japanese moved from Hawaii to mainland United States and effectively increased their presence in the work force. As Japanese presence increased, resentment towards Japanese workers increased. According to Schafer (2007), "the same Whites who disliked the Chinese made the same charges against the Japanese" (p. 359). The discrimination and animosity aimed at the Japanese immigrants limited their ability to earn a living. Laws were passed that prohibited anyone who was ineligible for citizenship to own land, and if a person was fortunate enough to own land, leases were limited to three years. Schafer states (2007),

"The anti-Japanese laws permanently influenced the form that Japanese American Business enterprise was to take. The land laws forced the Japanese into the cities, where government and union restrictions prevented a significant number from obtaining jobs" Often the only available option left was self-employment. Japanese immigrants, more than any other groups, ran hotels, grocery stores, and other medium-sized businesses (Schaefer, 2007, p. 359).

Japan's attack on Pearl Harbor on December 7, 1941 is one of the most memorable events in United States history and perhaps the most devastating for Japanese-Americans. At the time of the attack many Japanese had acquired United States citizenship or were born in the United States to parents who were American citizens. Although many Japanese were loyal citizens "the long history of anti-Japanese prejudice had conditioned the public to believe that this tiny minority was actually a threat to the United States" (Mindel et al., 1998, p. 316). Fear and racism lead many to believe that the Japanese in Pearl Harbor actually aided the Japanese pilots who attacked the United States.

Shortly after the United States entered into World War II, President Roosevelt signed Executive Order 9066 that designated certain areas in the country as restricted areas and authorized the building of relocation camps (Feagin, 1989; Mindel et al., 1998; Schaefer, 2007). Any person on the West coast having one-eighth or more Japanese ancestry was identified, detained and transported to evacuation camps. The executive order affected approximately 90 percent of the 126,000 Japanese living on the mainland. "Of those evacuated, two thirds were citizens, and three fourths were under age 25" (Schaefer, 2007, p. 361). The Japanese were only permitted to take personal items with them. No arrangements were made to have any household items or other possessions protected or stored. The government did very little to protect the belongings that were left behind and many "Japanese evacuees assumed all risks and liability and agreed to turn over their property for an indeterminate amount of time" (Schaefer, 2007, p. 361). Regrettably, most Japanese lost all of their personal and family assets. Specifically, "homes and possessions were abandoned or stolen; personal treasures were sold for a fracture of their value; farms and gardens were ruined; and families disintegrated" (Mindel et al., 1998, p. 316).

Negative sentiments towards the Japanese were rampant throughout and after the war and stereotypes and stereotypic caricatures of Japanese could be found almost everywhere. Many scholars (Dinnerstein, 2003; Ellison &

Martin, 1999; Feagin, 1989; Mindel et al., 1998; Schaefer, 2007) agreed that racism played a major part in the way Japanese Americans were What has been noted is that while the Japanese were place in internment camps, German Americans and Italian Americans were largely ignored. America was at war against the Japanese, Germans, and Italians however there was no apparent threat to America from German and Italian immigrants (Schaefer, 2007). One cannot ignore the significance that race played during this particular time in American history. Additionally, the significance of race in the treatment of Native-Americans, African-Americans, and Chinese Americans, who are not part of the dominant Anglo-Saxon core of America. For political, economic, and social reasons they have been marginalized throughout the history of the United States.

Critical Theory and Race

It is important to examine race, ethnicity, and social injustice from a theoretical perspective. Theory is a key component in the comprehension of increased self-awareness and understanding of the dynamics of racism, ethnic discrimination, and social injustice in the United States. A theory is "an interrelated set of concepts that are based on observations". As noted in the previous chapter, a theory is also defined as a set of building blocks that explains a phenomenon. The relationship between the different concepts of the theory is expressed using hypotheses, and the hypotheses of a theory can be tested to explain or predict a certain phenomenon (Robbins, Chattergie, & Canda, 1997).

Critical Theory is a theory which originated from the Frankfurt School in Germany and evolved from the scholarship of Karl Marx. Critical Theory focuses on "how economics, capital, and the market drive social process and processes". Critical Theory "critiques and questions the class-based society that currently exists in any human predicament (Denzin & Lincoln, 2003; Guba, 1990; Tyson, 2006). There is not just one critical theory but many critical theories (Denzin & Lincoln, 2003; Guba, 1990) and although many different critical theories exist certain characteristics underlie each aspect of each theory.

The Stanford Encyclopedia cites Horkheimer's definition of a critical theory as being relevant and "adequate only if it meets three criteria: it must be explanatory, practical, and normative, all at the same time. That is, it must explain what is wrong with current social reality, identify the actors to change it, and provide both clear norms for criticism and achievable practical goals for social transformation (Stanford Encyclopedia, 2005, p.1, (https://plato.stanford.edu/entries/critical-theory retrieved April 27, 2017). For these reasons, I believe that critical theory is an excellent theory to leverage when examining cross-race and ethnic relations because the theory's ontology, epistemology, and methodology provides the professional social worker, researcher, or workshop participant with a tangible understanding of the underpinnings of racism, ethnic discrimination, and social injustice.

The ontology of critical theory, the nature of what is known, is historical realism. Critical theory posits that what is known, that which is reality for a person, is shaped by "social political, cultural, economic, ethnic, and gender values that are crystallized over time" (Denzin & Lincoln, 2003, p. 258). The epistemology of critical theory, the nature of the relationship between the knower and the reality of what is known, is transactional and subjectivist. Reality is transactional in that the relationship between the knower and what is known is a reciprocal process. Reality is subjectivist in that the relationship between the knower and what is known is amalgamated, and the reality is a product of the interactions between the knower and what is known. The methodology of critical theory is dialogic and dialectic. Knowledge is acquired, or uncovered in discussions and reasoning in dialog between and among participants (Denzin & Lincoln, 2003; Guba, 1990).

A hallmark of the critical theory paradigm is that it aims to free people from injustices and discrimination which "enslave" them. According to many scholars, (Aguirre, 2003; Denzin & Lincoln, 2003; Dinnerstein et al., 2003; Ellison & Martin, 1999; Gossett, 1974; Pinderhughes, 1989; Schafer, 2007) there are many social injustices affecting many groups of people throughout the world. Because there are extensive injustices and "because such theories aim to explain and transform all the circumstances that enslave human beings, many 'critical theories' in the broader sense have developed" (Stanford Encyclopedia of Philosophy, 2005, p.1).

The critical theory paradigm is different from traditional theories because it challenges the status quo of social, political, and economic "truths" (Denzin & Lincoln, 2003). According to Guba (1990), with the critical paradigm "the objective or disinterested inquirers and inquiry does not exist, and the main aim of the critical theory is to reunite that which has been divided in modern era---knowledge and practical/moral concerns" (p. 181). Guba further notes that scholars and social researchers involved in critical theory are committed to "the study of society and schooling and must be joined to a commitment to produce the social conditions necessary for emancipation and empowerment" (Guba, 1990, p. 181). Therefore, the social worker, psychologist, or social science researcher must also be committed taking their knowledge and utilizing it in order to transform social injustices.

For the reasons mentioned above, I believe that Critical Race Theory, which is part of the Critical Theory paradigm, can be a powerful means to understanding the dynamics of race and racism within the United States. Additionally, used in conjunction with racial, ethnic, and social injustice awareness training, Critical Race Theory can be used transform peoples' beliefs and perceptions about people from different racial and ethnic backgrounds. Subsequently, that awareness can be transferred to a better understanding regarding differences and meanings associated with social, economic, political, gender, religious, and ability issues.

Critical Race Theory emerged in the mid-1970s from the work conducted by legal scholars who "were deeply concerned over the slow pace of racial reform in the United States" (Denzin & Lincoln, 2003, p. 408). The first Critical Race theorists posited that the manner in which people challenged the system was itself ineffective, and instituted a new method of examining, understanding, explaining, and eventually changing the way race and ethnicity were handled within the legal, political, economic and social systems (Denzin & Lincoln, 2003).

Critical Race Theory incorporates an ethnic and racial epistemology, arguing and supporting that "the ways of knowing and being are shaped by the individual's standpoint or position in the world" (Denzin & Lincoln, 2003, p. 408). The subjectivist's epistemology contracts "the knower" of the knowledge to share their viewpoint of the situation with others. There is not just one truth, but many truths and experiences that contribute to the knowledge base regarding race. In other words, there is not just the "dominant position- mainstream America" of racism, and its effects on racial populations that have been discriminated against, but there is also the position of the "other-marginalized racial groups" whose experience offers a totally different perspective of racism.

Critical Race Theory, like critical theory, embraces a "critical version of hermeneutics that seeks to uncover the causes of distorted communication and understanding" (Guba, 1990, p. 181). Through interactive dialog people uncover truths about race and racism by gaining knowledge in an environment which places importance on the historical conditions which have contributed and impacted race in American society. According to Blecher, (as cited in Guba 1990), "the idea is to render individual and social processes 'transparent to the actors involved, enabling them to pursue their further development with the consciousness and will- rather than remaining the end-product of a casual chain operative behind their backs'" (Guba, 1990, p. 181). Through a transactional process individuals involved in a particular situation, for example institutional racism in the United States, racial or ethnic discrimination in a school, in the work place, or in a diversity workshop, can become more aware of their own personal struggles and began to understand how they are part of a larger system which encompasses distorted perceptions about race and ethnicity, and because they are inextricably part of this system their perceptions regarding "others" is also distorted.

There are four major tenets of Critical Race Theory. The first tenet is, that racism is a norm of American society that is interwoven throughout every aspect of American life and because of this, racism "appears both normal and natural to people in this society" (Denzin & Lincoln, 2003, p. 410). A goal for critical race theorist and for those who fight for racial social justice is to expose all forms of racism, as well as any residual aspect of racism. As mentioned previously, like many critical theories, critical race theory embraces the "critical version of hermeneutics that seeks to uncover the causes of distorted communications and understanding" (Guba, 1990, p. 181). Guba draws attention to the fact that many of the communications and understandings that people have are often, "historically formed distortions that operate behind the seemingly normal, unquestioned interactions of our daily lives" (Guba, 1990, p. 181). From the critical perspective, it appears that opinions and ideologies that Americans have regarding people from different racial and ethnic backgrounds fit into the category of "historically formed distortions". People tend to believe what they are taught about people who are different from themselves without having any factual basis for the information they believe to be true. Oftentimes stereotypes about a certain racial or ethnic group have a long history, become over exaggerated, and develop into negative generalizations about an entire group (Schafer, 2007). A major task of critical race theory is to illuminate social, political, and economic racism that exists and to formulate strategies for educating and transforming society's opinions and behaviors regarding race. I believe that this task can best be achieved hermeneutically, in situations where individuals feel free to express personal ideas and beliefs about race and racism. This is the reason why it is crucial to create and maintain a safe environment within my workshops to the extent that participants feel that they can express their thoughts and innermost feelings as they become self-aware of their personal attitudes and beliefs about race, ethnicity, and social injustice.

The second tenet of Critical Race Theory incorporates storytelling to "analyze the myths, presuppositions, and received wisdoms that make up the common culture about race and that invariably render blacks and other minorities one-down" (Denzin & Lincoln, 2003, p. 410). Storytelling provides narratives of everyday experiences from different perspectives or viewpoints. Stories – both fiction and non-fiction -- provide the unwritten account of history and personal circumstances. "Critical race theorists have built on everyday experiences with the perspective, viewpoint, and power of stories and persuasion to come to a better understanding of how Americans see race" (Delgado & Stefancic, 2001, p. 38).

According to Delgado (1995), the experience of oppression is very important to the collective development the critical race perspective, and a person's story is critical to a person's perspective of the world. In order to understand the impact of racial and ethnic discrimination, a person's story must be told and heard in the first person so that others can understand the effects of the injustices the "storyteller" has experienced. "The hope is that well told stories describing the reality of black and brown lives can help readers bridge the gap between their worlds and those of others. Engaging stories can help us understand what life is like for others, and invite the reader, into a new and unfamiliar world" (Delgado & Stefancic, 2001, p. 40).

When people are afforded the opportunity to listen to and hear others' stories they can begin to develop a better comprehension of the power dynamics associated with race. Depending on who may be telling the story the story, the listener is provided with a worldview of race that often views race as "other", or a world view of race "same" or similar". For those who are members of the majority group, usually whites, this means that "like the dominant culture in most countries, they only think of race when talking about others. Whiteness is not seen as their race" (Williams, 2004, p. 165). Williams, an educator who teaches a wide range of students from different racial backgrounds, describes how he is "not sure there is any other subject that makes students more uncomfortable than race". The topic of race appears to "shut down genuine conversation among students of any color" (p. 164). Williams supports the tenet of Critical Race Theory that narratives or stories allow people to analyze the myths and presuppositions associated with race in this country. He believes that educators are often influenced by the dominant cultural narratives that makes race visible when educators "see it in the Other" (Williams, 2004, p. 164). He also recognizes that educators often revert to code words like, basic writer, ESL, or, model minority as markers for race and oftentimes not truly understanding that they are perpetuating the dominant narrative of the other.

Delgado and Stefancic (2001) posit that stories are extremely powerful for people in minority communities. They state that, "Many victims of racial discrimination suffer in silence, or blame themselves for their predicament. Stories can give them a voice and reveal that others have similar experiences" (Delgado & Stefancic, 2001, p. 43). Personal narratives can contribute to the process of change by calling attention to "neglected evidence and reminding people of our common humanity" (Delgado & Stefancic, 2001, p. 43). The power of "storytelling" is perhaps best understood in a reference provided by Williams (2004). "If we listen to the narratives outside the dominant culture, not only for what they tell us about individuals but also for how they help us understand different conceptions of our culture and its institutions, they can help us develop an understanding of race that reaches beyond individual morality" (p. 167).

The third tenet of Critical Race Theory posits that it is necessary to be persistent with the critique of liberalism. The original critical race scholars theorized that the traditional methods of liberal, legal, and civil rights practices did not venture far enough to actually change the effects of societal racism (Denzin & Lincoln, 2003). They argued "that racism requires sweeping changes, but liberalism has no mechanism for such change. Instead, liberal, legal practices support the painstakingly slow process of arguing legal procedures to gain citizen rights for people of color" (Denzin & Lincoln, 2003, p. 410). The social activism aspect of critical race theory requires the scholar, professional, and any other inquirer of knowledge regarding the abuse of power or racial injustices, to take action in order to decrease domination and oppression, and increase freedom and empowerment for all who are oppressed (Denzin & Lincoln, 2003; Guba, 1990; Ladson-Billings, 2003).

The fourth and final tenet of critical race theory posits that Whites have been the primary beneficiaries of the civil rights legislation. An example of this is the current policy regarding Affirmative Action. Denzin and Lincoln (2003) argue:

Although the policy of affirmative action is under attack throughout the nation, it is a policy that has also benefited Whites. A close look at the numbers reveals that the major beneficiaries of affirmative action hiring policies have been white women. The logic of this argument is that many of these women earn incomes that support household in which other Whites live--- men, women, and children. Thus, White women's ability to secure employment ultimately benefits Whites in general. (p. 410)

By highlighting the racial inequities in American society, critical race theory and critical race theorist examine the power dynamics within and among people from different racial groups. And because racism in the United States is believed to be institutionally inculcated (Denzin & Lincoln, 2003, Dinnerstein et al., 2003; Ellison & Martin, 1999; Gossett, 1974; Pinderhughes, 1989; Schafer, 2007; West, 2001), critical race theory and theorists aim to explain what is wrong with the current power structure, identifying those who profit and those who lose.

Throughout history social science researchers have studied people of color and minorities (Delgado & Stefancic, 2001). Researchers have compared notes and hypothesized about the "history, culture, problems and prospects of various racial and ethnic minority groups". Although much of the information has provided insight into these groups the "facts" and inferences that have been provided are often based on outsider information (Delgado & Stefancic, 2001, Denzin & Lincoln, 2003). Other scholars believe that a more authentic representation of ethnic and racial groups can be provided when a member of a particular group conducts the research (Asante, 1987, Bell, 1980, Delgado, 2001, Stefanic, 2001,Williams, 1991). To present the total picture of racial groups in America it has also been suggested that scholars should consider researching whiteness and what it means to be "White in America" (Delgado & Stefancic, 2001; Schaefer, 2007). Recently scholars have begun investigating and examining the "construction of the white race" (Delgado & Stefancic, 2001, p. 75). So much of the country's history is associated along racial lines particularly white-black lines, or white non-white lines, that some researchers exploring issues of "whiteness" attempt to gain a better understanding of the power dynamics between the races by examining the establishment of the "we" and the "other" social structure of the United States (Delgado & Stefancic, 2001; Schaefer, 2007).

People who are considered White are part of the dominant group and have benefited from many of the privileges associated with whiteness. Non-whites have often been excluded from the same privileges enjoyed by whites. Many scholars recognize that race is a socially constructed concept, but also recognize that there many aspects of our social structure that suggest that whites do benefit from being white. Schafer (2003) suggests that there are two aspects of White as a race which are important for Americans to consider. First, "is an examination of the historical creation of whiteness" and second, "how contemporary White people reflect on their racial identity" (Schaefer, 2007, p. 125).

In American culture, whiteness is associated with things that are good. White often symbolizes innocence, purity, virginity, and hope (Delgado & Stefancic, 2001, Dinnerstein et al., 2003; Gossett, 1974). However, "in contrast, darkness and blackness often carry connotations of evil and menace" (Delgado & Stefancic, 2001, p. 75). Black is used to describe things sinister such as villains, being blackballed or blacklisted, or having a black cloud over one's head. American literature and media is believed to reinforce white superiority and privilege (Delgado & Stefancic, 2001). "Whiteness is also normative something that sets the standard. Other groups such as Indians, Latinos, Asian-Americans, and African-Americans, are described as non-white. That is, they are defined in terms of opposition to whiteness-that which they are not" (Delgado & Stefancic, 2001, p. 77).

Although many white Americans pay little attention and thought to being white, simply by being white, a person benefits from being associated with the dominant group (Delgado & Stefancic, 2001; Dinnerstein et al., 2003; McIntosh, 1988; Schaefer, 2007). "Whiteness carries with it a sense of identity of being white as opposed to being, for example, Asian or African" (Schaefer, 2007, p. 127). According to McIntosh (2007):

The other side of racial oppression is the privilege enjoyed by dominant groups. "Being White or being successful in establishing a white identity carries with it distinct advantages, some of these include; being considered financially reliable when using checks, credit cards, or cash; Taking a job without having coworker suspect it came about because of your race; never having to speak for all the people of your race; and watching television or reading a newspaper and seeing people of your own race widely represented. (p. 127)

It may be difficult for some Whites to acknowledge that they are benefactors of the power dynamics and social racial injustices that discriminate against racial and ethnic minorities, particularly when they believe that they have not consciously participated in racist ideology or discriminatory practices. Despite these beliefs, Whites, according to McIntosh (1981), benefit from a system of favors, exchanges, and courtesies from which outsiders of color are frequently excluded, and many whites often believe that programs such as Affirmative Action discriminate against them, and that more qualified whites are passed over for less qualified minorities (Schaefer, 2007).

CONCLUSION

The information presented in this chapter raises extremely important issues and questions regarding the study of race, racism, ethnic discrimination, and social injustice in the American culture. How do we as a nation continue to address and change the power dynamics of race and ethnicity in a system where the effects of racism are so ingrained in societal institutions that they are part of the human psyche? How can professionals, who work with diverse populations, began to get people to share their feelings about race and racism when some are not cognizant of the impacts of racism in their personal lives? What part, if any, can diversity trainers, scholars, and other professionals have in leading changes in the social systems that effect not only persons from diverse racial and ethnic minority groups, but that also effect White Americans?

Horkheimer, one of the founding members of the Frankfurt School, stated that "any truly critical theory of society has as its objects human beings as producers of their own historical form of life" (Horkheimer in Stanford Encyclopedia, 2005, p.1). With respect to this view, one might postulate that the explanatory goal of the critical theory, in this case critical race theory, is to acknowledge, understand, and overcome the circumstances that oppressed groups of people experience by participating in "interdisciplinary research that includes psychological, cultural, and social dimensions, as well as institutional forms of domination" (Stanford Encyclopedia, 2005, p. 2).

By participating in racial and ethnic awareness workshops scholars, professionals, and workshop participants can explore the history of race in America, and can begin to develop an enhanced understanding of institutional racism, racial and ethnic discrimination, social injustices, and the power dynamics established due to the meaning associated with "difference" and "Other" in the United States.

Racial and ethnic awareness training that applies critical race theory as a means to inform, educate, and change people's attitudes and beliefs about people from different racial backgrounds may prove to be an extremely effective method of transforming American society. As mentioned previously, critical theory challenges the status quo of the current knowledge base and offers alternative ways of knowing. Critical race theory builds upon the foundations of critical theory and offers professional social workers and psychologists a view of the world from a nontraditional perspective. By incorporating the critical paradigm in racial and ethnic awareness training, and by providing an environment where participants of every race -- African-American, Asian-American, Latin-American, Native-American, and European-American -- feels safe to openly discuss and share their beliefs and perceptions about race, people can begin their journey of self-awareness and subsequently, I believe when people become self-aware they can begin to transform their perspectives regarding race.

REFERENCES

Adams, J. T. (1931). The epic of America. Reference & Research Book News, 27(5).

Aguirre, A. (2003). *Racial and ethnic diversity in America*. Santa Barbara, CA: ABC-Clio, Inc.

Delgado, R., & Stefancic, J. (2001). *Critical race theory an introduction*. New York, NY: New York University Press.

Denzin, N., & Lincoln, Y. (2003). *The landscape of qualitative research theories and issues*. Thousand Oaks, CA: Sage Publications.

Devore, W., & Schlesinger, E. (1989). *Ethnic-sensitive social work practice*. Maryland Heights, MO: Mosby Company.

Dinnerstein, L., Nichols, R., & Reimers, D. (2003). *Natives and strangers a multicultural history of Americans*. New York, NY: Oxford University Press.

Ellison, C., & Martin, W. (1999). *Race and ethnic relations in the United States, readings for the 21st century*. Los Angeles, CA: Roxbury Publishing Company.

Feagin, J. (1989). *Racial & ethnic relations*. Englewood Cliffs, NJ: Prentice-Hall, Inc.

Gossett, T. (1974). *Race: The history of an idea in America*. New York, NY: Schocken Books.

Guba, E. (1990). *The paradigm dialog*. Thousand Oaks, CA: Sage Publications.

Ladson-Billings, G. (2004). Racialized discourses and ethnic epistemologies. In *The Sage handbook of qualitative research*. Thousand Oaks, CA: Sage.

McGoldrick, M., Pearce, J., & Giordano, J. (1989). *Ethnicity and family therapy*. New York, NY: The Guilford Press.

Mindel, C., Haberstein, R., & Wright, R. (1998). *Ethnic families in America patterns and variations* (4th ed.). Englewood Cliffs, NJ: Prentice Hall.

National Association of Social Workers. (2001). *NASW standards for cultural competence in social work practice*. Washington, DC: NASW Press.

Parker, L., & Stovall, D. (2004). Actions following words: Critical race theory connects to critical pedagogy. *Educational Philosophy and Theory*, *36*(2), 167–182. doi:10.1111/j.1469-5812.2004.00059.x

Pinderhughes, E. (1989). *Understanding race, ethnicity, and power the key to efficacy in clinical practice*. New York, NY: The Free Press.

Powell, J. F. (2005). *The first Americans: race, evolution and the origin of native Americans*. Cambridge University Press. doi:10.1017/CBO9780511525667

Schaefer, R. (2007). *Race and ethnicity in the United States* (4th ed.). Englewood Cliffs, NJ: Pearson-Prentice-Hall.

Schaefer, R. (2007). *Racial and ethnic groups* (11th ed.). Englewood Cliffs, NJ: Pearson- Prentice-Hall.

Schein, R. (2006). *Landscape and race in the United States*. New York, NY: Routledge.

Stanford Encyclopedia of Philosophy. (2005). *Critical theory*. Retrieved from http://plato.stanford.edu/ entries/critical-theory

Tyson, L. (2006). *Critical theory today a user-friendly guide* (2nd ed.). New York, NY: Routledge.

U. S. Census. (2010). Retrieved from https://www.census.gov/2010census/

U.S. Department of Health and Human Services. (2001). *Mental health: culture, race, and ethnicity a supplement to mental health: A report of the surgeon general*. Rockville, MD: USDHH.

Williams, B. (2004). The truth in the tale: Race and counter storytelling in the classroom. *Journal of Adolescent & Adult Literacy*, *48*(2), 164–169. doi:10.1598/JAAL.48.2.7

KEY TERMS AND DEFINITIONS

Culture: The customary beliefs, social forms, and material traits of racial, religious, or social group and the characteristics features that define the group.

Critical Race Theory: A theory used by social scientists to examine social and cultural aspects of society within the context of race, power and law.

Ethnic Group: Is the connectedness among people based language, religion, rituals, music, food, dress, traditional dress, spiritual practices, and social interaction.

Immigrant: A person who migrates to another country with the idea of becoming a permanent resident.

Racism: The belief that differences in race explain deficits of certain groups of people or a belief that differences among the various racial groups determine individual achievement and or deficit.

Social Injustice: Social practices and judgements targeting specific groups. These practices are considered unjust.

Tenet: A main belief or principle of a philosophy.

ENDNOTES

The term "Frankfurt School" arose informally to describe the thinkers affiliated or merely associated with the Frankfurt Institute for Social Research; it is not the title of any specific position or institution per se, and few of these theorists used the term themselves.

The Frankfurt School is a concept of social theory and philosophy associated with the Institute for Social Research at the Goethe University Frankfurt, Germany. Founded during the interwar period, the School consisted of thought leaders who were critical of existent capitalist, fascist, nor communist systems that had formed at the time. Many of these theorists believed that traditional theories could not fully explain the turbulent and unexpected development of capitalist societies in the 20th century. Critical of both capitalism and Soviet socialism, their writings pointed to the possibility of an alternative path to social development.

Related Readings

To continue IGI Global's long-standing tradition of advancing innovation through emerging research, please find below a compiled list of recommended IGI Global book chapters and journal articles in the areas of political science, racism, and socio-economics. These related readings will provide additional information and guidance to further enrich your knowledge and assist you with your own research.

Abubakar, I. R., & Dano, U. L. (2018). Socioeconomic Challenges and Opportunities of Urbanization in Nigeria. In U. Benna & I. Benna (Eds.), *Urbanization and Its Impact on Socio-Economic Growth in Developing Regions* (pp. 219–240). Hershey, PA: IGI Global. doi:10.4018/978-1-5225-2659-9.ch011

Adams, S., & Klobodu, E. K. (2018). Urbanization, Financial Development, and Sustainable Development in West Africa. In U. Benna & I. Benna (Eds.), *Urbanization and Its Impact on Socio-Economic Growth in Developing Regions* (pp. 155–177). Hershey, PA: IGI Global. doi:10.4018/978-1-5225-2659-9.ch008

Agarwal, R., & Agarwal, P. (2015). Business, Government, and Society Synergy for Sustainable Livelihood: A Case Study of Sabars from Jharkhand. In S. Kalia, B. Bhalla, L. Das, & N. Awasthy (Eds.), *Promoting Socio-Economic Development through Business Integration* (pp. 252–262). Hershey, PA: IGI Global. doi:10.4018/978-1-4666-8259-7.ch018

Agarwal, S. (2015). An Empirical Investigation into the Key Characteristics of Socio-Technical Societies: Social Identity, Social Exchange, and Social Vicinity. In S. Kalia, B. Bhalla, L. Das, & N. Awasthy (Eds.), *Promoting Socio-Economic Development through Business Integration* (pp. 263–274). Hershey, PA: IGI Global. doi:10.4018/978-1-4666-8259-7.ch019

Aggarwal, P., & Anand, R. (2015). NGO Sudhaar: Empowering the Livestock Dependents. In S. Kalia, B. Bhalla, L. Das, & N. Awasthy (Eds.), *Promoting Socio-Economic Development through Business Integration* (pp. 192–204). Hershey, PA: IGI Global. doi:10.4018/978-1-4666-8259-7.ch014

Agrawal, A. V., Sharma, C., Joshi, N., Jindal, S., Raghavendra, V., & Kango, V. (2015). Organic Farming: Growth and Issues. In S. Kalia, B. Bhalla, L. Das, & N. Awasthy (Eds.), *Promoting Socio-Economic Development through Business Integration* (pp. 292–309). Hershey, PA: IGI Global. doi:10.4018/978-1-4666-8259-7.ch021

Ak, R., & Bingül, B. A. (2018). Kuwait. In S. Ozdemir, S. Erdogan, & A. Gedikli (Eds.), *Handbook of Research on Sociopolitical Factors Impacting Economic Growth in Islamic Nations* (pp. 276–292). Hershey, PA: IGI Global. doi:10.4018/978-1-5225-2939-2.ch014

Banerjee, A. K. (2017). "Why Can't I Have the Vote?": Women's Poetry, Politics, and the First World War. In Ö. Çakırtaş (Ed.), *Ideological Messaging and the Role of Political Literature* (pp. 117–144). Hershey, PA: IGI Global. doi:10.4018/978-1-5225-2391-8.ch007

Benna, U., & Benna, I. (2018). Revisiting Urban Theories: Their Impacts on the Developing World's Urbanization. In U. Benna & I. Benna (Eds.), *Urbanization and Its Impact on Socio-Economic Growth in Developing Regions* (pp. 1–22). Hershey, PA: IGI Global. doi:10.4018/978-1-5225-2659-9.ch001

Bhandari, J., Rahul, M., & Tiwari, S. R. (2015). Regional Economic Imbalances: Business and Foreign Direct Investment in India. In S. Kalia, B. Bhalla, L. Das, & N. Awasthy (Eds.), *Promoting Socio-Economic Development through Business Integration* (pp. 1–16). Hershey, PA: IGI Global. doi:10.4018/978-1-4666-8259-7.ch001

Bolgherini, S., & Lippi, A. (2016). Italy: Remapping Local Government from Re-Allocation and Re-Shaping to Re-Scaling. In U. Sadioglu & K. Dede (Eds.), *Theoretical Foundations and Discussions on the Reformation Process in Local Governments* (pp. 265–287). Hershey, PA: IGI Global. doi:10.4018/978-1-5225-0317-0.ch011

Bonifaz, G. X. (2016). Between Legitimation and Decentralisation: Explaining the Rise of a Plurinational State with Autonomies in 21st Century Bolivia. In U. Sadioglu & K. Dede (Eds.), *Theoretical Foundations and Discussions on the Reformation Process in Local Governments* (pp. 400–440). Hershey, PA: IGI Global. doi:10.4018/978-1-5225-0317-0.ch017

Bozkurt, İ. M., & Koç, M. (2018). Islamic Republic of Iran. In S. Ozdemir, S. Erdogan, & A. Gedikli (Eds.), *Handbook of Research on Sociopolitical Factors Impacting Economic Growth in Islamic Nations* (pp. 122–146). Hershey, PA: IGI Global. doi:10.4018/978-1-5225-2939-2.ch007

Bristow, D. C. (2017). What Danger Can There Be in Being the Shadow of a Gunman in Dublin, at Easter, in 1916?: Political Hauntologies in Joyce, O'Casey, and Yeats. In Ö. Çakırtaş (Ed.), *Ideological Messaging and the Role of Political Literature* (pp. 1–24). Hershey, PA: IGI Global. doi:10.4018/978-1-5225-2391-8.ch001

Brookfield, S. (2014). Racializing the Discourse of Adult Education. *International Journal of Adult Vocational Education and Technology*, *5*(4), 20–41. doi:10.4018/ijavet.2014100102

Çakırtaş, Ö. (2017). Mustapha and Greville: Constructing Anglo-Ottoman Diplomacy and Machiavellian Identities in Early Modern English Drama. In Ö. Çakırtaş (Ed.), *Ideological Messaging and the Role of Political Literature* (pp. 145–158). Hershey, PA: IGI Global. doi:10.4018/978-1-5225-2391-8.ch008

Callanan, M. (2016). Institutionalizing the Politics-Administration Dichotomy in Local Government: Reforming the Council-Manager System in Ireland. In U. Sadioglu & K. Dede (Eds.), *Theoretical Foundations and Discussions on the Reformation Process in Local Governments* (pp. 153–178). Hershey, PA: IGI Global. doi:10.4018/978-1-5225-0317-0.ch007

Campbell, A. (2016). "Imperialism" and "Federalism": The Ambiguity of State and City in Russia. In U. Sadioglu & K. Dede (Eds.), *Theoretical Foundations and Discussions on the Reformation Process in Local Governments* (pp. 353–372). Hershey, PA: IGI Global. doi:10.4018/978-1-5225-0317-0.ch015

Campos, E. Jr. (2017). "Power Is Only a Word": Language, Control, and the Orwellian Philosophy of Nineteen Eighty-Four. In Ö. Çakırtaş (Ed.), *Ideological Messaging and the Role of Political Literature* (pp. 25–42). Hershey, PA: IGI Global. doi:10.4018/978-1-5225-2391-8.ch002

Cannavale, C. (2017). Post-Bureaucratic Firms' Internationalization: A Cross-Cultural Perspective. In P. Malizia, C. Cannavale, & F. Maimone (Eds.), *Evolution of the Post-Bureaucratic Organization* (pp. 126–151). Hershey, PA: IGI Global. doi:10.4018/978-1-5225-1983-6.ch007

Cappelli, M. L. (2017). The Digital Politics of Pain: Exploring Female Voices in Afghanistan. In Ö. Çakırtaş (Ed.), *Ideological Messaging and the Role of Political Literature* (pp. 160–176). Hershey, PA: IGI Global. doi:10.4018/978-1-5225-2391-8.ch009

Cengiz, V. (2018). Afghanistan. In S. Ozdemir, S. Erdogan, & A. Gedikli (Eds.), *Handbook of Research on Sociopolitical Factors Impacting Economic Growth in Islamic Nations* (pp. 314–331). Hershey, PA: IGI Global. doi:10.4018/978-1-5225-2939-2.ch016

Chachra, K., Seelam, G., Singh, H., Sarkar, M., Jain, A., & Jain, A. (2015). The Impact of Kisan Call Centers on the Farming Sector. In S. Kalia, B. Bhalla, L. Das, & N. Awasthy (Eds.), *Promoting Socio-Economic Development through Business Integration* (pp. 76–88). Hershey, PA: IGI Global. doi:10.4018/978-1-4666-8259-7.ch006

Chakraberty, S. (2015). Capacity Building through Knowledge Management: How Vedic Concepts Can Interpret the Occurrences at Maruti Suzuki India, Manesar. In S. Kalia, B. Bhalla, L. Das, & N. Awasthy (Eds.), *Promoting Socio-Economic Development through Business Integration* (pp. 355–377). Hershey, PA: IGI Global. doi:10.4018/978-1-4666-8259-7.ch025

Chandiramani, J., & Airy, A. (2018). Urbanization and Socio-Economic Growth in South Asia Region. In U. Benna & I. Benna (Eds.), *Urbanization and Its Impact on Socio-Economic Growth in Developing Regions* (pp. 130–154). Hershey, PA: IGI Global. doi:10.4018/978-1-5225-2659-9.ch007

Chirisa, I., Matamanda, A. R., & Mukarwi, L. (2018). Desired and Achieved Urbanisation in Africa: In Search of Appropriate Tooling for a Sustainable Transformation. In U. Benna & I. Benna (Eds.), *Urbanization and Its Impact on Socio-Economic Growth in Developing Regions* (pp. 88–106). Hershey, PA: IGI Global. doi:10.4018/978-1-5225-2659-9.ch005

Chirisa, I., Mukarwi, L., & Matamanda, A. R. (2018). Social Costs and Benefits of the Transformation of the Traditional Families in an African Urban Society. In U. Benna & I. Benna (Eds.), *Urbanization and Its Impact on Socio-Economic Growth in Developing Regions* (pp. 179–197). Hershey, PA: IGI Global. doi:10.4018/978-1-5225-2659-9.ch009

Chitranshi, J. (2015). Talent Management. In S. Kalia, B. Bhalla, L. Das, & N. Awasthy (Eds.), *Promoting Socio-Economic Development through Business Integration* (pp. 124–134). Hershey, PA: IGI Global. doi:10.4018/978-1-4666-8259-7.ch009

Claes, M., & Jacquemin, T. (2017). Cognitive Biases in Decision Making in Post-Bureaucratic Organizations. In P. Malizia, C. Cannavale, & F. Maimone (Eds.), *Evolution of the Post-Bureaucratic Organization* (pp. 358–382). Hershey, PA: IGI Global. doi:10.4018/978-1-5225-1983-6.ch017

Cobbinah, P. B., & Adams, E. A. (2018). Urbanization and Electric Power Crisis in Ghana: Trends, Policies, and Socio-Economic Implications. In U. Benna & I. Benna (Eds.), *Urbanization and Its Impact on Socio-Economic Growth in Developing Regions* (pp. 262–284). Hershey, PA: IGI Global. doi:10.4018/978-1-5225-2659-9.ch013

Dama, N. (2018). Iraq. In S. Ozdemir, S. Erdogan, & A. Gedikli (Eds.), *Handbook of Research on Sociopolitical Factors Impacting Economic Growth in Islamic Nations* (pp. 147–160). Hershey, PA: IGI Global. doi:10.4018/978-1-5225-2939-2.ch008

De Ceuninck, K., Steyvers, K., & Valcke, T. (2016). As You Like It or Much Ado about Nothing?: Structural Reform in Local Government in Belgium. In U. Sadioglu & K. Dede (Eds.), *Theoretical Foundations and Discussions on the Reformation Process in Local Governments* (pp. 237–264). Hershey, PA: IGI Global. doi:10.4018/978-1-5225-0317-0.ch010

Debnath, R. M., Singh, S., & Gupta, A. (2015). Tale of Two Entrepreneurs. In S. Kalia, B. Bhalla, L. Das, & N. Awasthy (Eds.), *Promoting Socio-Economic Development through Business Integration* (pp. 89–111). Hershey, PA: IGI Global. doi:10.4018/978-1-4666-8259-7.ch007

Demirhan, K. (2017). Participation, Civil Society and the Facebook Use of NGOs in Turkey. In K. Demirhan & D. Çakır-Demirhan (Eds.), *Political Scandal, Corruption, and Legitimacy in the Age of Social Media* (pp. 223–246). Hershey, PA: IGI Global. doi:10.4018/978-1-5225-2019-1.ch010

Demirhan, K. (2017). Scandal Politics and Political Scandals in the Era of Digital Interactive Media. In K. Demirhan & D. Çakır-Demirhan (Eds.), *Political Scandal, Corruption, and Legitimacy in the Age of Social Media* (pp. 25–50). Hershey, PA: IGI Global. doi:10.4018/978-1-5225-2019-1.ch002

Di Martino, M. L. (2017). The "Development" Dilemma in the Literary Production of the 19th, 20th, and 21st Centuries: Rethinking Ideologies Across Literature. In Ö. Çakırtaş (Ed.), *Ideological Messaging and the Role of Political Literature* (pp. 60–82). Hershey, PA: IGI Global. doi:10.4018/978-1-5225-2391-8.ch004

Dollery, B., Kortt, M., & Drew, J. (2016). Australian Local Government Perspectives on Contemporary Structural Reform. In U. Sadioglu & K. Dede (Eds.), *Theoretical Foundations and Discussions on the Reformation Process in Local Governments* (pp. 179–204). Hershey, PA: IGI Global. doi:10.4018/978-1-5225-0317-0.ch008

Durgun, Ö. (2018). United Arab Emirates. In S. Ozdemir, S. Erdogan, & A. Gedikli (Eds.), *Handbook of Research on Sociopolitical Factors Impacting Economic Growth in Islamic Nations* (pp. 253–275). Hershey, PA: IGI Global. doi:10.4018/978-1-5225-2939-2.ch013

Erdoğan, S., & Gedikli, A. (2018). The State of Qatar. In S. Ozdemir, S. Erdogan, & A. Gedikli (Eds.), *Handbook of Research on Sociopolitical Factors Impacting Economic Growth in Islamic Nations* (pp. 212–252). Hershey, PA: IGI Global. doi:10.4018/978-1-5225-2939-2.ch012

Erikha, F., Putra, I. E., & Sarwono, S. W. (2016). ISIS Discourse in Radical Islamic Online News Media in Indonesia: Supporter or Opponent. In M. Khader, L. Neo, G. Ong, E. Mingyi, & J. Chin (Eds.), *Combating Violent Extremism and Radicalization in the Digital Era* (pp. 70–90). Hershey, PA: IGI Global. doi:10.4018/978-1-5225-0156-5.ch004

Erkekoğlu, L. C., & Madi, İ. (2018). The Hashemite Kingdom of Jordan. In S. Ozdemir, S. Erdogan, & A. Gedikli (Eds.), *Handbook of Research on Sociopolitical Factors Impacting Economic Growth in Islamic Nations* (pp. 95–121). Hershey, PA: IGI Global. doi:10.4018/978-1-5225-2939-2.ch006

Ermağan, İ., & İpek, V. (2018). Morocco. In S. Ozdemir, S. Erdogan, & A. Gedikli (Eds.), *Handbook of Research on Sociopolitical Factors Impacting Economic Growth in Islamic Nations* (pp. 51–67). Hershey, PA: IGI Global. doi:10.4018/978-1-5225-2939-2.ch004

Eroğlu, B., & Gedikli, Z. (2018). Niger. In S. Ozdemir, S. Erdogan, & A. Gedikli (Eds.), *Handbook of Research on Sociopolitical Factors Impacting Economic Growth in Islamic Nations* (pp. 41–50). Hershey, PA: IGI Global. doi:10.4018/978-1-5225-2939-2.ch003

Esen, Ö., & Aydın, C. (2018). Tunisia. In S. Ozdemir, S. Erdogan, & A. Gedikli (Eds.), *Handbook of Research on Sociopolitical Factors Impacting Economic Growth in Islamic Nations* (pp. 68–94). Hershey, PA: IGI Global. doi:10.4018/978-1-5225-2939-2.ch005

Essien, E. D. (2017). Navigating the Nexus between Social Media, Political Scandal, and Good Governance in Nigeria: Its Ethical Implications. In K. Demirhan & D. Çakır-Demirhan (Eds.), *Political Scandal, Corruption, and Legitimacy in the Age of Social Media* (pp. 157–184). Hershey, PA: IGI Global. doi:10.4018/978-1-5225-2019-1.ch007

Fabiano, A., & Hornstein, H. (2017). Building an Ethical Culture in the Post-Bureaucratic Era: Empowerment, Dialogue, and Virtue. In P. Malizia, C. Cannavale, & F. Maimone (Eds.), *Evolution of the Post-Bureaucratic Organization* (pp. 206–232). Hershey, PA: IGI Global. doi:10.4018/978-1-5225-1983-6.ch010

Fanaian, T. (2017). The Theocratic Deception Trap: Khomeini's Persuasion Techniques and Communication Patterns in His Books, Guardianship of the Jurist 1979 and Testament 1989. In E. Lewin, E. Bick, & D. Naor (Eds.), *Comparative Perspectives on Civil Religion, Nationalism, and Political Influence* (pp. 62–105). Hershey, PA: IGI Global. doi:10.4018/978-1-5225-0516-7.ch003

Fink, G. (2017). Power Systems: How Power Works in Different Systems. In P. Malizia, C. Cannavale, & F. Maimone (Eds.), *Evolution of the Post-Bureaucratic Organization* (pp. 41–60). Hershey, PA: IGI Global. doi:10.4018/978-1-5225-1983-6.ch003

Gabrielli, G., & Zaccaro, F. (2017). Human Resource Management in Post-Bureaucratic Organizations: New Challenges and Concerns. In P. Malizia, C. Cannavale, & F. Maimone (Eds.), *Evolution of the Post-Bureaucratic Organization* (pp. 252–273). Hershey, PA: IGI Global. doi:10.4018/978-1-5225-1983-6.ch012

Garcia, B. C. (2018). From Network Builders to Knowledge Clusters: A Value-Based Transborder-Region. In U. Benna & I. Benna (Eds.), *Urbanization and Its Impact on Socio-Economic Growth in Developing Regions* (pp. 44–65). Hershey, PA: IGI Global. doi:10.4018/978-1-5225-2659-9.ch003

García, M. J., & Sancino, A. (2016). Directly Elected Mayors vs. Council Appointed Mayors – Which Effects on Local Government Systems?: A Comparison between Italy and Spain. In U. Sadioglu & K. Dede (Eds.), *Theoretical Foundations and Discussions on the Reformation Process in Local Governments* (pp. 288–303). Hershey, PA: IGI Global. doi:10.4018/978-1-5225-0317-0.ch012

George, R. A., Vijayshree, M., Charak, P. D., Rana, K. S., Agarwal, S., & Dhiraj, A. V. (2015). Tackling Energy Issues in Rural India. In S. Kalia, B. Bhalla, L. Das, & N. Awasthy (Eds.), *Promoting Socio-Economic Development through Business Integration* (pp. 324–337). Hershey, PA: IGI Global. doi:10.4018/978-1-4666-8259-7.ch023

Gillath, N. (2017). Avoiding Conscription in Israel: Were Women Pawns in the Political Game? In E. Lewin, E. Bick, & D. Naor (Eds.), *Comparative Perspectives on Civil Religion, Nationalism, and Political Influence* (pp. 226–256). Hershey, PA: IGI Global. doi:10.4018/978-1-5225-0516-7.ch009

Grønning, T. (2017). Co-Existence of Bureaucracy and Post-Bureaucracy: The Case of a Contract Research Organization. In P. Malizia, C. Cannavale, & F. Maimone (Eds.), *Evolution of the Post-Bureaucratic Organization* (pp. 105–125). Hershey, PA: IGI Global. doi:10.4018/978-1-5225-1983-6.ch006

Gupta, P. A., Sharma, V., & Gade, M. K. (2015). Rice Husk Power Systems: Exploring Alternate Source of Energy. In S. Kalia, B. Bhalla, L. Das, & N. Awasthy (Eds.), *Promoting Socio-Economic Development through Business Integration* (pp. 112–123). Hershey, PA: IGI Global. doi:10.4018/978-1-4666-8259-7.ch008

Gupta, S., Yadav, G., Choudhary, A., & Kaur, A. (2015). Emergent Trends in Sustainable Technologies in Thailand: Developing OTOP-Based Manufacturing Capabilities in Rural India. In S. Kalia, B. Bhalla, L. Das, & N. Awasthy (Eds.), *Promoting Socio-Economic Development through Business Integration* (pp. 48–59). Hershey, PA: IGI Global. doi:10.4018/978-1-4666-8259-7.ch004

Halder, S., Chandrashekhar, P., Asthana, A., Kumar, K., Choudhary, G., & Reshma, A. (2015). Rural Outreach for Banks: Challenges and Possible Solutions. In S. Kalia, B. Bhalla, L. Das, & N. Awasthy (Eds.), *Promoting Socio-Economic Development through Business Integration* (pp. 135–148). Hershey, PA: IGI Global. doi:10.4018/978-1-4666-8259-7.ch010

Haq, F., & Medhekar, A. (2018). The Economic Effects of Spiritual Tourism in India and Pakistan. In U. Benna & I. Benna (Eds.), *Urbanization and Its Impact on Socio-Economic Growth in Developing Regions* (pp. 66–86). Hershey, PA: IGI Global. doi:10.4018/978-1-5225-2659-9.ch004

Haşlak, İ., & Bilen, M. (2018). Bangladesh. In S. Ozdemir, S. Erdogan, & A. Gedikli (Eds.), *Handbook of Research on Sociopolitical Factors Impacting Economic Growth in Islamic Nations* (pp. 380–403). Hershey, PA: IGI Global. doi:10.4018/978-1-5225-2939-2.ch019

Herkman, J., & Matikainen, J. (2017). Neo-Populist Scandal and Social Media: The Finnish Olli Immonen Affair. In K. Demirhan & D. Çakır-Demirhan (Eds.), *Political Scandal, Corruption, and Legitimacy in the Age of Social Media* (pp. 1–24). Hershey, PA: IGI Global. doi:10.4018/978-1-5225-2019-1.ch001

Hu, W. (2016). Psychological Effects of the Threat of ISIS: A Preliminary Inquiry of Singapore Case Studies. In M. Khader, L. Neo, G. Ong, E. Mingyi, & J. Chin (Eds.), *Combating Violent Extremism and Radicalization in the Digital Era* (pp. 168–173). Hershey, PA: IGI Global. doi:10.4018/978-1-5225-0156-5.ch009

Ifedi, R. (2017). African-Born Female Academics in the U.S.: Experiences of Inclusion, Exclusion, and Access - Building Careers on Marginalized Identities. *International Journal of Bias, Identity and Diversities in Education*, *2*(1), 1–12. doi:10.4018/IJBIDE.2017010101

İncekara, A. (2018). Lebanon. In S. Ozdemir, S. Erdogan, & A. Gedikli (Eds.), *Handbook of Research on Sociopolitical Factors Impacting Economic Growth in Islamic Nations* (pp. 161–181). Hershey, PA: IGI Global. doi:10.4018/978-1-5225-2939-2.ch009

Innocenti, L., Sammarra, A., & Profili, S. (2017). From Control to Commitment Work Systems: The Role of HRM in the Post-Bureaucratic Transition. In P. Malizia, C. Cannavale, & F. Maimone (Eds.), *Evolution of the Post-Bureaucratic Organization* (pp. 274–296). Hershey, PA: IGI Global. doi:10.4018/978-1-5225-1983-6.ch013

J. C. S. (2018). The Impact of Urbanization Induced Foreign Direct Investment in Emerging India. In U. Benna, & I. Benna (Eds.), Urbanization and Its Impact on Socio-Economic Growth in Developing Regions (pp. 309-326). Hershey, PA: IGI Global. doi:10.4018/978-1-5225-2659-9.ch015

Jacob, J. (2015). Revitalizing ICDS: India's Flagship Child Care Program. In S. Kalia, B. Bhalla, L. Das, & N. Awasthy (Eds.), *Promoting Socio-Economic Development through Business Integration* (pp. 217–235). Hershey, PA: IGI Global. doi:10.4018/978-1-4666-8259-7.ch016

Jain, M., & Knieling, J. (2018). Growth of Census Towns in Capital Region of India: Informal Urbanization as a Symptom of Counter-Urbanization? In U. Benna & I. Benna (Eds.), *Urbanization and Its Impact on Socio-Economic Growth in Developing Regions* (pp. 23–43). Hershey, PA: IGI Global. doi:10.4018/978-1-5225-2659-9.ch002

Jha, C. K. (2017). Information Control, Transparency, and Social Media: Implications for Corruption. In K. Demirhan & D. Çakır-Demirhan (Eds.), *Political Scandal, Corruption, and Legitimacy in the Age of Social Media* (pp. 51–75). Hershey, PA: IGI Global. doi:10.4018/978-1-5225-2019-1.ch003

Kabullah, M. I., & Wahab, S. (2016). The Curbing of Corruption by Formal and Informal Accountability at the Indonesian Local Governments: Learning from Yogyakarta City. In U. Sadioglu & K. Dede (Eds.), *Theoretical Foundations and Discussions on the Reformation Process in Local Governments* (pp. 441–461). Hershey, PA: IGI Global. doi:10.4018/978-1-5225-0317-0.ch018

Kalagy, T. (2017). Values, Constraints, and Maneuvers: Processes of Academization among Ultra-Orthodox Women and Beduin Women in Israel. In E. Lewin, E. Bick, & D. Naor (Eds.), *Comparative Perspectives on Civil Religion, Nationalism, and Political Influence* (pp. 257–284). Hershey, PA: IGI Global. doi:10.4018/978-1-5225-0516-7.ch010

Kalia, S., Puri, N., & Chakraverty, I. (2015). Technological Innovations in Management Education. In S. Kalia, B. Bhalla, L. Das, & N. Awasthy (Eds.), *Promoting Socio-Economic Development through Business Integration* (pp. 30–47). Hershey, PA: IGI Global. doi:10.4018/978-1-4666-8259-7.ch003

Kandemir, O., & Gümüş, N. (2018). Libya. In S. Ozdemir, S. Erdogan, & A. Gedikli (Eds.), *Handbook of Research on Sociopolitical Factors Impacting Economic Growth in Islamic Nations* (pp. 22–40). Hershey, PA: IGI Global. doi:10.4018/978-1-5225-2939-2.ch002

Karagöl, E. T. (2018). Azerbaijan. In S. Ozdemir, S. Erdogan, & A. Gedikli (Eds.), *Handbook of Research on Sociopolitical Factors Impacting Economic Growth in Islamic Nations* (pp. 182–194). Hershey, PA: IGI Global. doi:10.4018/978-1-5225-2939-2.ch010

Kaya, O. (2017). Travel Politics Mirroring Anatolia, Asia Minor, and the Greek Islands. In Ö. Çakırtaş (Ed.), *Ideological Messaging and the Role of Political Literature* (pp. 235–287). Hershey, PA: IGI Global. doi:10.4018/978-1-5225-2391-8.ch013

Kaynak, S. (2018). Pakistan. In S. Ozdemir, S. Erdogan, & A. Gedikli (Eds.), *Handbook of Research on Sociopolitical Factors Impacting Economic Growth in Islamic Nations* (pp. 293–313). Hershey, PA: IGI Global. doi:10.4018/978-1-5225-2939-2.ch015

Keles, R. (2016). The Normative Base of Local Government: Progress in Local Democracy and the Reformation Process. In U. Sadioglu & K. Dede (Eds.), *Theoretical Foundations and Discussions on the Reformation Process in Local Governments* (pp. 24–41). Hershey, PA: IGI Global. doi:10.4018/978-1-5225-0317-0.ch002

Kerbizi, M. (2017). Communist Ideology and Its Impact on Albanian Literature. In Ö. Çakırtaş (Ed.), *Ideological Messaging and the Role of Political Literature* (pp. 200–221). Hershey, PA: IGI Global. doi:10.4018/978-1-5225-2391-8.ch011

Khalil, D., & Kier, M. (2017). Critical Race Design: An Emerging Methodological Approach to Anti-Racist Design and Implementation Research. *International Journal of Adult Vocational Education and Technology, 8*(2), 54–71. doi:10.4018/IJAVET.2017040105

Kihiko, M. K. (2018). Industrial Parks as a Solution to Expanding Urbanization: A Case of Sub-Saharan Africa. In U. Benna & I. Benna (Eds.), *Urbanization and Its Impact on Socio-Economic Growth in Developing Regions* (pp. 327–345). Hershey, PA: IGI Global. doi:10.4018/978-1-5225-2659-9.ch016

Klimczuk, A., & Klimczuk-Kochańska, M. (2016). Changes in the Local Government System and Regional Policy in Poland: The Impact of Membership in the European Union. In U. Sadioglu & K. Dede (Eds.), *Theoretical Foundations and Discussions on the Reformation Process in Local Governments* (pp. 328–352). Hershey, PA: IGI Global. doi:10.4018/978-1-5225-0317-0.ch014

Korstanje, M. E. (2017). The Allegory of Holocaust: The Rise of Thana Capitalism. In Ö. Çakırtaş (Ed.), *Ideological Messaging and the Role of Political Literature* (pp. 177–199). Hershey, PA: IGI Global. doi:10.4018/978-1-5225-2391-8.ch010

Korstanje, M. E. (2017). The Roots of Evilness and Biblical Literature: The Revolt of Lucifer. In Ö. Çakırtaş (Ed.), *Ideological Messaging and the Role of Political Literature* (pp. 83–97). Hershey, PA: IGI Global. doi:10.4018/978-1-5225-2391-8.ch005

Kucukali, U. F., & Kuşak, L. (2018). Environmental, Social, and Economic Indicators of Urban Land Use Conflicts: Evidence from Istanbul Metropolitan Area. In U. Benna & I. Benna (Eds.), *Urbanization and Its Impact on Socio-Economic Growth in Developing Regions* (pp. 285–308). Hershey, PA: IGI Global. doi:10.4018/978-1-5225-2659-9.ch014

Kumar, R. (2015). Waste Management Initiatives in Rural India. In S. Kalia, B. Bhalla, L. Das, & N. Awasthy (Eds.), *Promoting Socio-Economic Development through Business Integration* (pp. 338–354). Hershey, PA: IGI Global. doi:10.4018/978-1-4666-8259-7.ch024

Kumar, S., Rawat, M., Mahanta, P., Bhadauria, A., Subramanian, M., & Awasthi, S. (2015). Feasibility Study for Setting up a Community Radio. In S. Kalia, B. Bhalla, L. Das, & N. Awasthy (Eds.), *Promoting Socio-Economic Development through Business Integration* (pp. 60–75). Hershey, PA: IGI Global. doi:10.4018/978-1-4666-8259-7.ch005

Kyari, A. K. (2018). Managing Urbanisation Through Planned Government Expenditure Evidence from Nigeria. In U. Benna & I. Benna (Eds.), *Urbanization and Its Impact on Socio-Economic Growth in Developing Regions* (pp. 107–129). Hershey, PA: IGI Global. doi:10.4018/978-1-5225-2659-9.ch006

Leon, N. (2017). The Haredi Scholar-Society and the Military Draft in Israel: Counter-Nationalism and the Imagined Military Symbiosis. In E. Lewin, E. Bick, & D. Naor (Eds.), *Comparative Perspectives on Civil Religion, Nationalism, and Political Influence* (pp. 210–225). Hershey, PA: IGI Global. doi:10.4018/978-1-5225-0516-7.ch008

Lewin, E., & Bick, E. (2017). Introduction: Civil Religion and Nationalism on a Godly-Civil Continuum. In E. Lewin, E. Bick, & D. Naor (Eds.), *Comparative Perspectives on Civil Religion, Nationalism, and Political Influence* (pp. 1–31). Hershey, PA: IGI Global. doi:10.4018/978-1-5225-0516-7.ch001

Lisney, T., & Kiefer, A. (2016). Cooperation between Local Authorities in Europe as a Force for Strengthening Local Democracy. In U. Sadioglu & K. Dede (Eds.), *Theoretical Foundations and Discussions on the Reformation Process in Local Governments* (pp. 85–109). Hershey, PA: IGI Global. doi:10.4018/978-1-5225-0317-0.ch004

London, T. (2017). Creating Values-Based Accountability Systems for the Turbulence of Post-Bureaucratic Organizations. In P. Malizia, C. Cannavale, & F. Maimone (Eds.), *Evolution of the Post-Bureaucratic Organization* (pp. 233–251). Hershey, PA: IGI Global. doi:10.4018/978-1-5225-1983-6.ch011

Ma, L. (2017). Government Website, Social Media, and Citizens' Perceptions of Corruption: Evidence from Chinese Cities. In K. Demirhan & D. Çakır-Demirhan (Eds.), *Political Scandal, Corruption, and Legitimacy in the Age of Social Media* (pp. 185–204). Hershey, PA: IGI Global. doi:10.4018/978-1-5225-2019-1.ch008

Magala, S., & Zawadzki, M. (2017). Performing Academics: Return to Meritocracy? In P. Malizia, C. Cannavale, & F. Maimone (Eds.), *Evolution of the Post-Bureaucratic Organization* (pp. 88–104). Hershey, PA: IGI Global. doi:10.4018/978-1-5225-1983-6.ch005

Maggu, A., & Garg, J. (2015). Feasibility of Implementation of Solar Bottle Bulb in Urban Slums of India. In S. Kalia, B. Bhalla, L. Das, & N. Awasthy (Eds.), *Promoting Socio-Economic Development through Business Integration* (pp. 236–251). Hershey, PA: IGI Global. doi:10.4018/978-1-4666-8259-7.ch017

Maimone, F. (2017). Post-Bureaucratic Organizations as Complex Systems: Toward a Co-Evolutionary and Multiparadigmatic Perspective. In P. Malizia, C. Cannavale, & F. Maimone (Eds.), *Evolution of the Post-Bureaucratic Organization* (pp. 152–179). Hershey, PA: IGI Global. doi:10.4018/978-1-5225-1983-6.ch008

Malizia, P. (2017). Watercolour: Toward a Socio-Cultural and Post-Modern Approach to the Study of Post-Bureaucratic Organizations. In P. Malizia, C. Cannavale, & F. Maimone (Eds.), *Evolution of the Post-Bureaucratic Organization* (pp. 1–18). Hershey, PA: IGI Global. doi:10.4018/978-1-5225-1983-6.ch001

Manrique, C. G., & Manrique, G. G. (2017). Social Media's Role in Alleviating Political Corruption and Scandals: The Philippines during and after the Marcos Regime. In K. Demirhan & D. Çakır-Demirhan (Eds.), *Political Scandal, Corruption, and Legitimacy in the Age of Social Media* (pp. 205–222). Hershey, PA: IGI Global. doi:10.4018/978-1-5225-2019-1.ch009

McSweeney, B. (2017). A Post-Bureaucratic Age?: Caricatures, Claims, and Counter-Evidence. In P. Malizia, C. Cannavale, & F. Maimone (Eds.), *Evolution of the Post-Bureaucratic Organization* (pp. 19–40). Hershey, PA: IGI Global. doi:10.4018/978-1-5225-1983-6.ch002

Medhekar, A., & Haq, F. (2018). Urbanization and New Jobs Creation in Healthcare Services in India: Challenges and Opportunities. In U. Benna & I. Benna (Eds.), *Urbanization and Its Impact on Socio-Economic Growth in Developing Regions* (pp. 198–218). Hershey, PA: IGI Global. doi:10.4018/978-1-5225-2659-9.ch010

Mendiratta, K., Bhattacharyya, S., & Abhinav, G. V. (2015). Study of Carbon Footprint in Organizations. In S. Kalia, B. Bhalla, L. Das, & N. Awasthy (Eds.), *Promoting Socio-Economic Development through Business Integration* (pp. 176–191). Hershey, PA: IGI Global. doi:10.4018/978-1-4666-8259-7.ch013

Merviö, M. M. (2017). *Interpretation of Visual Arts Across Societies and Political Culture: Emerging Research and Opportunities* (pp. 1–110). Hershey, PA: IGI Global. doi:10.4018/978-1-5225-2554-7

Möltner, H., Morner, M., & Nevries, P. (2017). Self-Control Beyond Clans and Culture: A Behavioral Perspective on Internalizing Control. In P. Malizia, C. Cannavale, & F. Maimone (Eds.), *Evolution of the Post-Bureaucratic Organization* (pp. 181–205). Hershey, PA: IGI Global. doi:10.4018/978-1-5225-1983-6.ch009

Moretti, G. (2017). Social Organization, Social Tools: Social Media and Organizations in the Context of a Hybrid Culture. In P. Malizia, C. Cannavale, & F. Maimone (Eds.), *Evolution of the Post-Bureaucratic Organization* (pp. 342–356). Hershey, PA: IGI Global. doi:10.4018/978-1-5225-1983-6.ch016

Mormino, S. (2017). Learning in Post-Bureaucratic Organizations: The Role and Contribution of Social Media. In P. Malizia, C. Cannavale, & F. Maimone (Eds.), *Evolution of the Post-Bureaucratic Organization* (pp. 321–341). Hershey, PA: IGI Global. doi:10.4018/978-1-5225-1983-6.ch015

Naikal, A., & Bapna, M. (2015). Role of Knowledge Workers in Business Process and Innovation. In S. Kalia, B. Bhalla, L. Das, & N. Awasthy (Eds.), *Promoting Socio-Economic Development through Business Integration* (pp. 17–29). Hershey, PA: IGI Global. doi:10.4018/978-1-4666-8259-7.ch002

Nath, N., Chaudhuri, S., Sarkar, P., Saha, S., Singh, B., & Bhardwaj, N. (2015). Jugaad Inc: Evolution of Frugal Entrepreneurship and Lean Start Ups. In S. Kalia, B. Bhalla, L. Das, & N. Awasthy (Eds.), *Promoting Socio-Economic Development through Business Integration* (pp. 310–323). Hershey, PA: IGI Global. doi:10.4018/978-1-4666-8259-7.ch022

Nava, M. R. (2017). The Development of Intercultural Competences in Post-Bureaucratic Organizations. In P. Malizia, C. Cannavale, & F. Maimone (Eds.), *Evolution of the Post-Bureaucratic Organization* (pp. 401–421). Hershey, PA: IGI Global. doi:10.4018/978-1-5225-1983-6.ch019

Neo, L. S. (2016). An Internet-Mediated Pathway for Online Radicalisation: RECRO. In M. Khader, L. Neo, G. Ong, E. Mingyi, & J. Chin (Eds.), *Combating Violent Extremism and Radicalization in the Digital Era* (pp. 197–224). Hershey, PA: IGI Global. doi:10.4018/978-1-5225-0156-5.ch011

Neo, L. S., Dillon, L., Shi, P., Tan, J., Wang, Y., & Gomes, D. (2016). Understanding the Psychology of Persuasive Violent Extremist Online Platforms. In M. Khader, L. Neo, G. Ong, E. Mingyi, & J. Chin (Eds.), *Combating Violent Extremism and Radicalization in the Digital Era* (pp. 1–15). Hershey, PA: IGI Global. doi:10.4018/978-1-5225-0156-5.ch001

Neo, L. S., Shi, P., Dillon, L., Tan, J., Wang, Y., & Gomes, D. (2016). Why Is ISIS so Psychologically Attractive? In M. Khader, L. Neo, G. Ong, E. Mingyi, & J. Chin (Eds.), *Combating Violent Extremism and Radicalization in the Digital Era* (pp. 149–167). Hershey, PA: IGI Global. doi:10.4018/978-1-5225-0156-5.ch008

Neugröschel, M. (2017). Anti-Semitism as a Civil Religion: Progressive Paradigms in the Anti-Semitic Construction of German National Identity. In E. Lewin, E. Bick, & D. Naor (Eds.), *Comparative Perspectives on Civil Religion, Nationalism, and Political Influence* (pp. 106–124). Hershey, PA: IGI Global. doi:10.4018/978-1-5225-0516-7.ch004

Nişancı, E., Yıldırım, D. Ç., Çevik, N. K., & Sırım, V. (2018). Indonesia. In S. Ozdemir, S. Erdogan, & A. Gedikli (Eds.), *Handbook of Research on Sociopolitical Factors Impacting Economic Growth in Islamic Nations* (pp. 332–357). Hershey, PA: IGI Global. doi:10.4018/978-1-5225-2939-2.ch017

Ohsugi, S. (2016). Changing Local Government System in Japan: "Unfinished" Decentralization Reform and Local Revitalization. In U. Sadioglu & K. Dede (Eds.), *Theoretical Foundations and Discussions on the Reformation Process in Local Governments* (pp. 373–399). Hershey, PA: IGI Global. doi:10.4018/978-1-5225-0317-0.ch016

Panara, C. (2016). Concept and Role of Local Self-Government in the Contemporary State. In U. Sadioglu & K. Dede (Eds.), *Theoretical Foundations and Discussions on the Reformation Process in Local Governments* (pp. 42–84). Hershey, PA: IGI Global. doi:10.4018/978-1-5225-0317-0.ch003

Pang, J. S. (2016). Understanding Personality and Person-Specific Predictors of Cyber-Based Insider Threat. In M. Khader, L. Neo, G. Ong, E. Mingyi, & J. Chin (Eds.), *Combating Violent Extremism and Radicalization in the Digital Era* (pp. 107–128). Hershey, PA: IGI Global. doi:10.4018/978-1-5225-0156-5.ch006

Pleschberger, W. (2016). Democratic Preferences of the Indirectly-Elected Mayor, Open or Locked-In: A Contribution to the "Difference Hypothesis". In U. Sadioglu & K. Dede (Eds.), *Theoretical Foundations and Discussions on the Reformation Process in Local Governments* (pp. 110–139). Hershey, PA: IGI Global. doi:10.4018/978-1-5225-0317-0.ch005

Pohl, G. M. (2017). The Role of Social Media in Enforcing Environmental Justice around the World. In K. Demirhan & D. Çakır-Demirhan (Eds.), *Political Scandal, Corruption, and Legitimacy in the Age of Social Media* (pp. 123–156). Hershey, PA: IGI Global. doi:10.4018/978-1-5225-2019-1.ch006

Raja, S., & Sehgal, S. (2015). Role of Dairy Farming in Rural Development. In S. Kalia, B. Bhalla, L. Das, & N. Awasthy (Eds.), *Promoting Socio-Economic Development through Business Integration* (pp. 149–163). Hershey, PA: IGI Global. doi:10.4018/978-1-4666-8259-7.ch011

Rao, R. (2015). Rural Innovations: Text and Cases. In S. Kalia, B. Bhalla, L. Das, & N. Awasthy (Eds.), *Promoting Socio-Economic Development through Business Integration* (pp. 275–291). Hershey, PA: IGI Global. doi:10.4018/978-1-4666-8259-7.ch020

Ravazzani, S. (2017). Communication in Post-Bureaucratic Organizations: Confronting Diversity and Crisis. In P. Malizia, C. Cannavale, & F. Maimone (Eds.), *Evolution of the Post-Bureaucratic Organization* (pp. 297–320). Hershey, PA: IGI Global. doi:10.4018/978-1-5225-1983-6.ch014

Reid, M. (2016). Contemporary Local Government Reform in New Zealand: Efficiency or Democracy. In U. Sadioglu & K. Dede (Eds.), *Theoretical Foundations and Discussions on the Reformation Process in Local Governments* (pp. 205–236). Hershey, PA: IGI Global. doi:10.4018/978-1-5225-0317-0.ch009

Romyn, D., & Kebbell, M. (2016). Using the Internet to Plan for Terrorist Attack. In M. Khader, L. Neo, G. Ong, E. Mingyi, & J. Chin (Eds.), *Combating Violent Extremism and Radicalization in the Digital Era* (pp. 91–105). Hershey, PA: IGI Global. doi:10.4018/978-1-5225-0156-5.ch005

Rudge, L. T. (2017). Different Experiences and Perceptions of Campus Climate Among Minority Students at a Predominantly White Institution. *International Journal of Bias, Identity and Diversities in Education*, *2*(1), 40–56. doi:10.4018/IJBIDE.2017010104

Rzayev, H., & Hasanova, A. (2017). Aziz Nesin's "An Ass the Prime Vezier" as a Mirror of Inequality. In Ö. Çakırtaş (Ed.), *Ideological Messaging and the Role of Political Literature* (pp. 43–59). Hershey, PA: IGI Global. doi:10.4018/978-1-5225-2391-8.ch003

Sadioglu, U., & Dede, K. (2016). Current Discussions on the Question: Remarks of Local Government's Reform through Comparative Perspective. In U. Sadioglu & K. Dede (Eds.), *Theoretical Foundations and Discussions on the Reformation Process in Local Governments* (pp. 1–23). Hershey, PA: IGI Global. doi:10.4018/978-1-5225-0317-0.ch001

Saifudeen, O. A. (2016). Getting out of the Armchair: Potential Tipping Points for Online Radicalisation. In M. Khader, L. Neo, G. Ong, E. Mingyi, & J. Chin (Eds.), *Combating Violent Extremism and Radicalization in the Digital Era* (pp. 129–148). Hershey, PA: IGI Global. doi:10.4018/978-1-5225-0156-5.ch007

Saltman, E. M. (2016). Western Female Migrants to ISIS: Propaganda, Radicalisation, and Recruitment. In M. Khader, L. Neo, G. Ong, E. Mingyi, & J. Chin (Eds.), *Combating Violent Extremism and Radicalization in the Digital Era* (pp. 174–196). Hershey, PA: IGI Global. doi:10.4018/978-1-5225-0156-5.ch010

Samarjeet, S. (2017). Hashtag Ideology: Practice and Politics of Alternative Ideology. In K. Demirhan & D. Çakır-Demirhan (Eds.), *Political Scandal, Corruption, and Legitimacy in the Age of Social Media* (pp. 101–122). Hershey, PA: IGI Global. doi:10.4018/978-1-5225-2019-1.ch005

Sasson, K. (2017). Religion and Politics: A Troubled Relationship in a Volatile World. In E. Lewin, E. Bick, & D. Naor (Eds.), *Comparative Perspectives on Civil Religion, Nationalism, and Political Influence* (pp. 32–61). Hershey, PA: IGI Global. doi:10.4018/978-1-5225-0516-7.ch002

Senaratne, M. (2017). Testimony and Trauma in Sri Lanka's War Narratives. In Ö. Çakırtaş (Ed.), *Ideological Messaging and the Role of Political Literature* (pp. 222–234). Hershey, PA: IGI Global. doi:10.4018/978-1-5225-2391-8.ch012

Sheiner, D. Z. (2017). National-Liberty Reflections of the Exodus Myth in Palestine-Israel Print Media Advertisements, 1923-1958. In E. Lewin, E. Bick, & D. Naor (Eds.), *Comparative Perspectives on Civil Religion, Nationalism, and Political Influence* (pp. 190–209). Hershey, PA: IGI Global. doi:10.4018/978-1-5225-0516-7.ch007

Sinclair, M. (2017). Intuitive Knowledge Generation in Post-Bureaucratic Organizations. In P. Malizia, C. Cannavale, & F. Maimone (Eds.), *Evolution of the Post-Bureaucratic Organization* (pp. 383–400). Hershey, PA: IGI Global. doi:10.4018/978-1-5225-1983-6.ch018

Singh, R., Sharma, A., Kaur, A., Gupta, M., & TS, K. (2015). Solar Micro Grids: Impact and Future in Rural Uttar Pradesh – Case Study on MGP. In S. Kalia, B. Bhalla, L. Das, & N. Awasthy (Eds.), *Promoting Socio-Economic Development through Business Integration* (pp. 164-175). Hershey, PA: IGI Global. doi:10.4018/978-1-4666-8259-7.ch012

Slough, H., & Anderson, D. (2017). The Public Veil: Two Millennia of Strong Women in Politics. In Ö. Çakırtaş (Ed.), *Ideological Messaging and the Role of Political Literature* (pp. 99–116). Hershey, PA: IGI Global. doi:10.4018/978-1-5225-2391-8.ch006

Steinfatt, T., & Janbek, D. (2016). Persuasion and Propaganda in War and Terrorism. In M. Khader, L. Neo, G. Ong, E. Mingyi, & J. Chin (Eds.), *Combating Violent Extremism and Radicalization in the Digital Era* (pp. 16–38). Hershey, PA: IGI Global. doi:10.4018/978-1-5225-0156-5.ch002

Teles, F., & Kettunen, P. (2016). Why Municipal Cooperation Matters: Diversity and Research Agendas. In U. Sadioglu & K. Dede (Eds.), *Theoretical Foundations and Discussions on the Reformation Process in Local Governments* (pp. 140–152). Hershey, PA: IGI Global. doi:10.4018/978-1-5225-0317-0.ch006

Teper, Y. (2017). How Civic is Russia's New Civil Religion and How Religious is the Church? In E. Lewin, E. Bick, & D. Naor (Eds.), *Comparative Perspectives on Civil Religion, Nationalism, and Political Influence* (pp. 125–155). Hershey, PA: IGI Global. doi:10.4018/978-1-5225-0516-7.ch005

Tolu, H. (2017). Communication Between Real-World and Cyber-World: Conceptual Thinking on Cyber-Racism! *International Journal of Information Communication Technologies and Human Development, 9*(3), 38–54. doi:10.4018/IJICTHD.2017070104

Torok, R. (2016). Social Media and the Use of Discursive Markers of Online Extremism and Recruitment. In M. Khader, L. Neo, G. Ong, E. Mingyi, & J. Chin (Eds.), *Combating Violent Extremism and Radicalization in the Digital Era* (pp. 39–69). Hershey, PA: IGI Global. doi:10.4018/978-1-5225-0156-5.ch003

Tynes, B. M., Rose, C. A., Hiss, S., Umaña-Taylor, A. J., Mitchell, K., & Williams, D. (2014). Virtual Environments, Online Racial Discrimination, and Adjustment among a Diverse, School-Based Sample of Adolescents. *International Journal of Gaming and Computer-Mediated Simulations, 6*(3), 1–16. doi:10.4018/ijgcms.2014070101 PMID:27134698

Uysal, D. (2018). Syria. In S. Ozdemir, S. Erdogan, & A. Gedikli (Eds.), *Handbook of Research on Sociopolitical Factors Impacting Economic Growth in Islamic Nations* (pp. 195–211). Hershey, PA: IGI Global. doi:10.4018/978-1-5225-2939-2.ch011

Vakkala, H., & Leinonen, J. (2016). Current Features and Developments of Local Governance in Finland: The Changing Roles of Citizens and Municipalities. In U. Sadioglu & K. Dede (Eds.), *Theoretical Foundations and Discussions on the Reformation Process in Local Governments* (pp. 304–327). Hershey, PA: IGI Global. doi:10.4018/978-1-5225-0317-0.ch013

Vashisth, A. Aparajita, Gupta, P., Patil, P., & Agarwal, R. (2015). Mapping the Rural Retail of India. In S. Kalia, B. Bhalla, L. Das, & N. Awasthy (Eds.), Promoting Socio-Economic Development through Business Integration (pp. 205-216). Hershey, PA: IGI Global. doi:10.4018/978-1-4666-8259-7.ch015

Vergil, H., & Sekmen, F. (2018). Egypt. In S. Ozdemir, S. Erdogan, & A. Gedikli (Eds.), *Handbook of Research on Sociopolitical Factors Impacting Economic Growth in Islamic Nations* (pp. 1–21). Hershey, PA: IGI Global. doi:10.4018/978-1-5225-2939-2.ch001

Waller, L. G. (2017). There Is an App for That Too: Citizen-Centric Approach to Combating Corruption in the Digital Age through the Use of ICTs. In K. Demirhan & D. Çakır-Demirhan (Eds.), *Political Scandal, Corruption, and Legitimacy in the Age of Social Media* (pp. 76–100). Hershey, PA: IGI Global. doi:10.4018/978-1-5225-2019-1.ch004

Willoughby, C. R. (2018). The Challenge of Achieving Sustainable Mobility in the Cities of South Asia. In U. Benna & I. Benna (Eds.), *Urbanization and Its Impact on Socio-Economic Growth in Developing Regions* (pp. 241–260). Hershey, PA: IGI Global. doi:10.4018/978-1-5225-2659-9.ch012

Yefet, B. (2017). The Clash of Civil Religions in Post-Revolutionary Egypt. In E. Lewin, E. Bick, & D. Naor (Eds.), *Comparative Perspectives on Civil Religion, Nationalism, and Political Influence* (pp. 156–189). Hershey, PA: IGI Global. doi:10.4018/978-1-5225-0516-7.ch006

Yildiz, M., & Demirhan, K. (2016). Analysis and Comparison of the Role of Local Governments with Other Policy Actors in Disaster Relief via Social Media: The Case of Turkey. In U. Sadioglu & K. Dede (Eds.), *Theoretical Foundations and Discussions on the Reformation Process in Local Governments* (pp. 462–483). Hershey, PA: IGI Global. doi:10.4018/978-1-5225-0317-0.ch019

Yılmaz, S., & İçellioğlu, C. S. (2018). Malaysia. In S. Ozdemir, S. Erdogan, & A. Gedikli (Eds.), *Handbook of Research on Sociopolitical Factors Impacting Economic Growth in Islamic Nations* (pp. 358–379). Hershey, PA: IGI Global. doi:10.4018/978-1-5225-2939-2.ch018

Yolles, M. I. (2017). Understanding Bureaucracy. In P. Malizia, C. Cannavale, & F. Maimone (Eds.), *Evolution of the Post-Bureaucratic Organization* (pp. 61–87). Hershey, PA: IGI Global. doi:10.4018/978-1-5225-1983-6.ch004

Yüce, M. (2018). Kyrgyzstan. In S. Ozdemir, S. Erdogan, & A. Gedikli (Eds.), *Handbook of Research on Sociopolitical Factors Impacting Economic Growth in Islamic Nations* (pp. 404–426). Hershey, PA: IGI Global. doi:10.4018/978-1-5225-2939-2.ch020

About the Authors

Pamela Hampton-Garland is an Assistant Professor in the Adult Education, in the College of Arts and Sciences in the School of Education at the University of the District of Columbia. Dr. Hampton-Garland earned her doctoral degree in Curriculum and Teaching with a concentration in Cultural Studies from the University of North Carolina at Greensboro, her Master's degree in Adult Education and her Bachelor's degree in Psychology from North Carolina Agricultural and Technical State University. Dr. Hampton-Garland's research interests were developed through personal experiences with the pursuit of higher education and were theoretically identified during the proposal phase of her dissertation. Pierre Bourdieu's (1978) Cultural Capital is the theoretical platform that under-girds her research. The three areas of cultural capital include embodied, objectified and institutionalized capital. Dr. Hampton-Garland's research focuses on the transformations of adults as they strive to shift from generational poverty to sustainability. This area of research undergirds her interest in the development of this book.

Lisa Sechrest-Ehrhardt received a BA in Psychology from the University of Virginia (1982), an MSW from Boston College Graduate School of Social Work (1984) and a PhD from the National Catholic School of Social Service at The Catholic University of America (2012). Her career has focused on cultural diversity with an emphasis on race and ethnicity. As such her employment choices have included professional opportunities which have provided her with a vast array of experiences working with people of different cultural and ethnic backgrounds. As an independent diversity consultant she provides workshops to community organizations, schools, businesses, and religious groups. Her professional interest is driven by an enthusiasm to learn about and from diverse people. Her research interests are in the area of multiracial identity development. She is currently employed as an assistant professor in the social work program at the University of the District of Columbia and is an Independent Diversity Trainer/Consultant.

Benson G. Cooke received his B.A. degree from Morehouse College, and his M.S. and Ed.D. Degrees from The University of Massachusetts, Amherst. He currently serves as a Professor of Counseling and Psychology, and formerly served as the (2011-2014) Chair of the Department of Psychology, Counseling and Human Development at The University of the District of Columbia in Washington, DC. Prior to his employment with UDC in 2006, Dr. Cooke has served in teaching and leadership positions at George Mason University, Xavier University of Louisiana, and The University of Massachusetts, Amherst. Additionally, he has held administrative and clinical positions within mental health treatment agencies since completing his graduate education. From 2009-2011 Dr. Cooke served as the National President for The Association of Black Psychologists (ABPsi). During his tenure in positions as national treasurer and later as national president, he effected improvement of the association's fiscal growth by strengthening the accounting systems, and the executive and organizational management, thereby enhancing and sustaining ABPsi's operational infrastructure. Dr. Cooke is the recipient of numerous national community-service, educational/faculty excellence, scholarship and professional service awards. Among these honors, Dr. Cooke received the 2016 ABPsi Distinguished Psychologist Award for his career contributions to the discipline, literature and practice of psychology that has supported culturally salient mental health treatment for the African American community. Dr. Cooke is also a Fellow and Diplomate in African Centered/Black Psychology from The Association of Black Psychologists. Dr. Cooke has been invited to present at professional presentations in conventions, conferences, symposiums, workshops, professional institutes, colleges and universities. He has also been interviewed on local; regional and national radio and T.V. programs across the U.S. He is the author of two books titled: Personal Empowerment for People of Color: Keys to Success in Higher Education, published in June 2001 by Kendall/Hunt Publishing Company and All About Depression published in August of 2013 also by Kendall/Hunt Publishing Company. He is also the co-author of book chapters, journal articles, magazine articles and on-line educational material. Following Hurricane Katrina in 2005, Dr. Cooke spearheaded with the support of fellow ABPsi colleagues the first ever national guidelines to provide culturally competent therapeutic interventions for first responders taking action in response to disaster relief for citizens residing in New Orleans, Louisiana and the Gulf Region. He was invited to present these therapeutic intervention strategies to American Psychological Association and the American Red Cross. Dr. Cooke's current research focuses on the development of generational treatment for depression and anxiety disorders across the lifespan in African Americans by incorporating practice-based cultural treatment approaches linked with evidence based epigenomic considerations. Dr. Cooke also continues to consult nationally on psychological issues impacting the African American community.

Index

A

African American 2, 9, 21, 29, 33-34, 43, 47-48, 78, 87, 128
American workers 57, 61, 68, 75, 151

C

Cognitive Theory 110, 119, 121, 126, 138
Critical Race Theory 139, 156-160, 162-163, 165
critical theory 154-156, 162-163
cultural conditioning 1, 5, 10-12, 15, 17, 21
culture 3, 7, 9, 16, 18-19, 35, 48, 66, 115, 123, 127, 129, 143-145, 147, 149, 151-152, 158-162, 165

D

diversity 7, 11, 51, 109, 115, 130, 134, 138-144, 146-147, 149-150, 157, 162

E

education 16, 33, 43, 61, 64, 75-78, 80, 90, 93, 97, 99, 102, 124, 131, 143
ethnic group 100, 123, 145, 157, 165
ethnicity 3-4, 11-12, 18-19, 21, 66, 115, 118, 125-126, 138-140, 142-144, 154, 156-158, 162

F

Facebook 67-70, 86-87, 90, 100, 103, 121, 126-127, 134
forgotten Americans 58-59, 62, 79

H

homegrown terrorism 29-31, 35-37, 42-43

I

identity 15, 17, 19, 34, 40, 43, 50, 109-110, 112-115, 138, 144-145, 161
immigrant 146, 152, 165

J

Japanese American 153

M

manifestation 29, 128

N

NAFTA 57-58, 61, 64, 135
Native American 31, 147-148

P

Political Interactions 109

R

race 1-3, 5, 8-9, 11-14, 16-19, 21, 29, 31, 34-36, 38, 40, 42-43, 47, 66, 75, 79, 87, 90, 101, 115-118, 121, 125-129, 133-134, 138-143, 147, 149, 152, 154, 156-163, 165
race riots 29, 35, 42-43
racial hate 29, 37, 42, 46
racism 1-3, 11, 17-19, 21, 30-35, 37, 47, 115-116, 119, 129-131, 134, 138-139, 141, 143, 153-157, 159-160, 162, 165

S

self-awareness 50, 110, 112-113, 116, 119, 125-126, 133-134, 138-140, 142-143, 154, 163
social dynamics 112
social injustice 140, 154-156, 158, 162, 165
social interaction 110-115, 117, 119, 121, 125-126, 133-134, 138, 144, 165
stereotype 1, 4-5, 21, 35
stigma 3-4, 7, 14
Symbolic Interaction Theory 110, 113-115, 118-119, 121, 124

T

trade 4, 31, 57-65, 75, 135, 152
Twitter 16, 68-69

www.ingramcontent.com/pod-product-compliance
Lightning Source LLC
LaVergne TN
LVHW062124200926
848484LV00007B/1755